# Yale French Studies

NUMBER 73

## Everyday Life

| | | |
|---|---|---|
| ALICE KAPLAN AND KRISTIN ROSS | 1 | Introduction |

**I.** *Lefebvre and the Situationists*

| | | |
|---|---|---|
| HENRI LEFEBVRE | 7 | The Everyday and Everydayness |
| MAURICE BLANCHOT | 12 | Everyday Speech |
| EDWARD BALL | 21 | The Great Sideshow of the Situationist International |
| GREGORY L. ULMER | 38 | "A Night at the Text": Roland Barthes's Marx Brothers |

**II.** *Social Space*

| | | |
|---|---|---|
| WOLFGANG SCHIVELBUSCH | 61 | The Policing of Street Lighting |
| PIERRE BOURDIEU | 75 | The Invention of the Artist's Life |
| KRISTIN ROSS | 104 | Rimbaud and the Transformation of Social Space |
| ADRIAN RIFKIN | 121 | Musical Moments |
| ALICE YAEGER KAPLAN | 156 | Taste Wars: American Professions of French Culture |

**III.** *Signifying Practices*

| | | |
|---|---|---|
| JOAN DEJEAN | 175 | No Man's Land: The Novel's First Geography |
| LINDA ORR | 190 | The Blind Spot of History: Logography |
| TOM CONLEY | 215 | Le Quotidien météorologique |
| MOLLY NESBIT | 229 | What Was an Author? |

# Yale French Studies

Alice Kaplan and Kristin Ross, *Special editors for this issue*
Liliane Greene, *Managing editor*
*Editorial board:* Peter Brooks (Chairman), Ora Avni, Ellen Burt, Mary Lou Ennis, Shoshana Felman, Richard Goodkin, Christopher Miller, Margaret Miner, Charles Porter, Christopher Rivers, Allan Stoekl
*Staff:* Peggy McCracken, Lauren Doyle-McCombs
*Editorial office:* 315 William L. Harkness Hall
*Mailing address:* 2504A Yale Station, New Haven, Connecticut 06520
*Sales and subscription office:*
Yale University Press, 92A Yale Station
New Haven, Connecticut 06520
Published twice annually by Yale University Press

Copyright © 1987 by Yale University
All rights reserved.
This book may not be reproduced, in whole or in part, including illustrations, in any form (beyond that copying permitted by Sections 107 and 108 of the U.S. Copyright Law and except by reviewers for the public press), without written permission from the publisher.

Designed by James J. Johnson and set in Trump Medieval Roman by The Composing Room of Michigan, Inc. Printed in the United States of America by The Vail-Ballou Press, Binghamton, N.Y.
ISSN 0044–0078
ISBN for this issue 0–300–04047–4

ALICE KAPLAN AND KRISTIN ROSS

# Introduction

To advance a theory of everyday life is to elevate lived experience to the status of a critical concept—not merely in order to describe lived experience, but in order to change it. One of the purposes of this issue is to bring to the attention of an American readership new work informed by such a transformative project: a critique of everyday life elaborated in France in the '50s and '60s which remains underacknowledged and little translated in this country.

The strain of French thought produced in the '50s and '60s which *did* come to be known in American universities with enormous speed and authority was, of course, structuralism and its various derivatives. One of the reasons for the eventual institutional success of structuralism in America was undoubtedly its pedagogical efficiency: techniques of textual analysis could be smoothly transmitted to students who had grown up isolated from French cultural or historical referents. In France the dazzling technical innovations of structuralism were produced during the same decades that saw an intense intellectual and political critique—both inside and outside academic institutions—of consumer society. This questioning was to culminate in the events surrounding May '68.

Thought so intimately tied up with lived experience and political struggle would obviously not find the same American audience as structuralist discourse, which viewed its arena as textual. Postwar American academics still preoccupied with questions of lived experience and ideological debate tended to formulate those questions within dated existentialist categories involving authenticity and inauthenticity, good faith or bad faith. The critique of everyday life was to concern itself rather with extramoral perceptions; it was to find a small audience in the United States, as in England, Italy and West Germany, primarily among student activists and anarchist groups.

The critique of everyday life in France achieved notoriety with the activities of a fringe group called the Situationists. In the mid-1950s the Situationists formed themselves out of the shards of a number of avant-garde groups, including the dada-inspired International Lettrists, the antifunctionalist Society for an Imaginist Bauhaus, and the Scandinavian COBRA movement. They proclaimed their own era to be "The Society of the Spectacle"—the historical moment in which the logic of commodities had successfully seized and colonized all social and cultural relations, the totality of everyday life. They took their concept of everyday life from the one first substantially developed in the first volume of Henri Lefebvre's *Critique de la vie quotidienne*, published in 1947 (two more volumes would follow in subsequent decades). Everyday life, defined elliptically as "whatever remains after one has eliminated all specialized activities," is, Lefebvre argues, a limited historical phenomenon. It is inextricably tied to two parallel developments: first, to the rise of a middle class and the demise of the great "styles" formerly imposed in western societies by Church and Monarch; second, to the vast migration of those middle classes to urban centers, spaces where their everyday activities would become increasingly organized—hence perceptible.

Cultural interventionists rather than academics, the Situationists interpreted Lefebvre's concept of everyday life in an essentially spatial way. They initiated a series of empirico-utopian experiments under the general rubric *psychogeography*: the active study of mental states and spatial ambiances produced by the material organization of the urban terrain. They proposed a division of the city into affective zones or microclimates; in more or less organized and only carelessly documented traipses through Paris, they surveyed the city for what might be salvaged and used in a utopian reconstruction of social space. To link them to a French utopian/spatial tradition, we might mention several ghost intellectual figures hovering about Situationist activities: the Fourier of a *Nouveau Monde amoureux*; the Lafargue of a *Droit à la paresse*; the *Reclus* of a radical anticolonialist geography.

Perhaps the best way to appreciate the force of situationist activities is to compare them to traditional Marxist blueprints for action. We can outline two interrelated areas of difference. In their attempts to disrupt the dominant organization of social space, that is, in their essentially synchronic sensibility, the Situationists mark a significant departure from the diachronically oriented Marxism of the nineteenth century. Staying within a specifically Marxist vocabulary, we might say that the Situationists shifted their attention from the relations of production within the factory to that basic yet undertheorized problem of *social reproduction*—the myriad activities and conditions for existence that must be satisfied in order for relations of production to take place at all. Social reproduction—what we are calling here everyday life—has, of course, become in our own time the urgent issue on a host of political and cultural agendas, most significantly on that of feminism. For everyday life has always weighed heavily on the shoulders of women.

*Quotidie:* how many times a day? How many days? The quotidian is on the one hand the realm of routine, repetition, reiteration: the space/time where constraints and boredom are produced. Far from being an escape from this realm, segmented leisure time such as the weekend is rather a final cog permitting the smooth functioning of the routine. Even at its most degraded, however, the everyday harbors the possibility of its own transformation; it gives rise, in other words, to desires which cannot be satisifed within a weekly cycle of production/consumption. The Political, like the purloined letter, is hidden in the everyday, exactly where it is most obvious: in the contradictions of lived experience, in the most banal and repetitive gestures of everyday life—the commute, the errand, the appointment. It is in the midst of the utterly ordinary, in the space where the dominant relations of production are tirelessly and relentlessly reproduced, that we must look for utopian and political aspirations to crystallize.

At this point it should be clear how our conception of everyday life differs from that great accumulation and inventory of detail undertaken by the Annales School of historiography. Like that of the Annales School, the critique of everyday life we represent here veers away from canonical events and personages. But while the discourse of permanence produced by the Annales School would recenter history in an immutable village life or in climatic durée, we would insist on the mutable, and specifically on the power of the city both to constrain and to alter consciousness. For this reason, the articles we have included here bear little resemblance to the mimetic effort of cataloguing or describing "daily living" that has come to be associated with a title like ours.

What does it mean to approach cultural production from the vantage point of everyday life? It means attempting to grasp the everyday without relegating it either to institutional codes and systems or to the private perceptions of a monadic subject. Between, for example, the traffic court and the angry driver who has received a moving violation, we would need to evoke a complex realm of social practice and to map out not merely a network of streets, but a conjunction of habit, desire, and accident.

When it is successful, everyday life analysis offers a new alternative to a subject/object opposition so basic to postwar continental thinking as to correspond to its two major intellectual movements: phenomenology and structuralism. By this we mean that everyday life is situated somewhere in the rift opened up between the subjective, phenomenological, sensory apparatus of the individual and reified institutions. Its starting point is neither the intentional subject dear to humanistic thinking nor the determining paradigms that bracket lived experience. Institutions, codes, and paradigms are not abstract constructs confronting us in some official "out there." Nor do we come to institutions alone. We live them in historically specific ways, and we live them—we must insist on this now, when it has become all the more difficult to do so—as collective or as virtually collective subjects.

To read everyday life, what Hegel called "the prose of the world," is therefore to become engaged in an act of *poesis*. This means, for instance, that the everyday should not be assumed to be some quality inherent only in the great realist or mimetic narratives of the nineteenth and early twentieth centuries. Nor, as we suggested earlier, should it be located only in those specifically mimetic moments in a given text. It means, more importantly, that we understand *poesis* in the sense of a transformative or creative act. Everyday life harbors the texture of social change; to perceive it at all is to recognize the necessity of its conscious transformation.

Our thanks go first to Liliane Greene for her good-humored assistance in the production of this issue. Michèle Noël contributed her expertise as a translator in an early stage. During the summer of 1983, Greil Marcus was a valuable source of information. Gil Wolman and Henri Lefebvre generously shared with us their memories of Lettrist and Situationist activities.

We would also like to thank the American Philosophical Society, the University of California at Santa Cruz, and Duke University for their support. Finally, we are both happy to acknowledge the part played by the London Committee for Psychogeographical Research in the realization of this issue.

# I. Lefebvre and the Situationists

# HENRI LEFEBVRE

# The Everyday and Everydayness*

Before the series of revolutions which ushered in what is called the modern era, housing, modes of dress, eating and drinking—in short, living—presented a prodigious diversity. Not subordinate to any one system, living varied according to region and country, levels and classes of the population, available natural resources, season, climate, profession, age, and sex. This diversity has never been well acknowledged or recognized as such; it has resisted a rational kind of interpretation which has only come about in our own time by interfering with and destroying that diversity. Today we see a worldwide tendency to uniformity. Rationality dominates, accompanied but not diversified by irrationality; signs, rational in their way, are attached to things in order to convey the prestige of their possessors and their place in the hierarchy.

## FORMS, FUNCTIONS AND STRUCTURES

What has happened? There were, and there always have been forms, functions and structures. Things as well as institutions, "objects" as well as "subjects" offered up to the senses accessible and recognizable forms. People, whether individually or in groups, performed various functions, some of them physiological (eating, drinking, sleeping), others social (working, travelling). Structures, some of them natural and others constructed, allowed for the public or private performance of these functions, but with a radical—a root—difference: those forms, functions and structures were not known as such, not named. At once connected and distinct, they were part of an undifferentiated whole. Post-Cartesian analytic thought has often challenged these concrete "totalities": every analysis of objective or social reality has come up with some residue resisting

* Translation of Henri Lefebvre, "Quotidien et Quotidienneté," *Encyclopaedia Universalis,* and reprinted with their kind permission.

analysis, and the sum of such realities as seemed irreducible by human thought became a matter for infinite analysis, a reserve of divine thought. Every complex "whole," from the smallest tool to the greatest works of art and learning, therefore possessed a symbolic value linking them to meaning at its most vast: to divinity and humanity, power and wisdom, good and evil, happiness and misery, the perennial and the ephemeral. These immense values were themselves mutable according to historical circumstance, to social classes, to rulers and mentors. Each object (an armchair just as much as a piece of clothing, a kitchen utensil as much as a house) was thus linked to some "style" and therefore, as a work, contained while masking the larger functions and structures which were integral parts of its form.

What happened to change the situation? The functional element was itself disengaged, rationalized, then industrially produced, and finally imposed by constraint and persuasion: that is to say, by means of advertising and by powerful economic and political lobbies. The relationship of form to function to structure has not disappeared. On the contrary, it has become a declared relationship, produced *as such*, more and more visible and readable, announced and displayed in a transparency of the three terms. A modern object clearly states what it is, its role and its place. This does not prevent its overstating or reproducing the signs of its meaningfulness: signs of satisfaction, of happiness, of quality, of wealth. From the modern armchair or coffee grinder to the automobile, the form-function-structure triumvirate is at once evident and legible.

Within these parameters, there come to be constructed multiple systems or subsystems, each establishing in its own way a more or less coherent set of more or less durable objects. For example, in the domain of architecture, a variety of local, regional, and national architectural styles has given way to "architectural urbanism," a universalizing system of structures and functions in supposedly rational geometric forms. The same thing is true of industrially produced food: a system groups products around various functionally specific household appliances such as the refrigerator, freezer, electric oven, etc. And of course the totalizing system that has been constructed around the automobile seems ready to sacrifice all of society to its dominion. It so happens that these systems and subsystems tend to deteriorate or blow out. Are even the days of car travel numbered?

Whatever the case may be, housing, fashion and food have tended and still tend to constitute autonomous subsystems, closed off from one another. Each of them appears to present as great a diversity as the old modes of living of the premodern era. This diversity is only apparent. It is only arranged. Once the dominant forces making it possible for these elements to combine with one another is understood, the artificial mechanism of their grouping is recognized and the fatuousness of their diversity becomes intolerable. The system breaks down.

All such systems have in common a general law of functionalism. The everyday can therefore be defined as a set of functions which connect and join together systems that might appear to be distinct. Thus defined, the everyday is a *product*, the most general of products in an era where production engenders consumption, and where consumption is manipulated by producers: not by "workers," but by the managers and owners of the means of production (intellectual, instrumental, scientific). The everyday is therefore the most universal and the most unique condition, the most social and the most individuated, the most obvious and the best hidden. A condition stipulated for the legibility of forms, ordained by means of functions, inscribed within structures, the everyday constitutes the platform upon which the bureaucratic society of controlled consumerism is erected.

## A COMMON DENOMINATOR

The everyday is therefore a concept. In order for it to have ever been engaged as a concept, the reality it designated had to have become dominant, and the old obsessions about shortages—"Give us this day our daily bread . . ."—had to disappear. Until recently, things, furniture and buildings were built one by one, and each existed in relation to accepted moral and social references, to symbols. From the twentieth century onward, all these references collapse, including the greatest and oldest figure of them all, that of the Father (eternal or temporal, divine or human). How can we grasp this extraordinary and still so poorly understood configuration of facts? The collapse of the referent in morality, history, nature, religion, cities, space; the collapse even of perspective in its classical spatial sense or the collapse of tonality in music. . . . Abundance—a rational, programmed abundance and planned obsolescence—replacing shortage in the first world; destructive colonization of the third world and finally of nature itself. . . . The prevalence of signs; omnipresent war and violence; revolutions which follow one after another only to be cut short or to turn back against themselves . . . .

The everyday, established and consolidated, remains a sole surviving common sense referent and point of reference. "Intellectuals," on the other hand, seek their systems of reference elsewhere: in language and discourse, or sometimes in a political party. The proposition here is to decode the modern world, that bloody riddle, according to the everyday.

The concept of everydayness does not therefore designate a system, but rather a denominator common to existing systems including judicial, contractual, pedagogical, fiscal, and police systems. Banality? Why should the study of the banal itself be banal? Are not the surreal, the extraordinary, the surprising, even the magical, also part of the real? Why wouldn't the concept of everydayness reveal the extraordinary in the ordinary?

## REPETITION AND CHANGE

Thus formulated, the concept of the everyday illuminates the past. Everyday life has always existed, even if in ways vastly different from our own. The character of the everyday has always been repetitive and veiled by obsession and fear. In the study of the everyday we discover the great problem of repetition, one of the most difficult problems facing us. The everyday is situated at the intersection of two modes of repetition: the cyclical, which dominates in nature, and the linear, which dominates in processes known as "rational." The everyday implies on the one hand cycles, nights and days, seasons and harvests, activity and rest, hunger and satisfaction, desire and its fulfillment, life and death, and it implies on the other hand the repetitive gestures of work and consumption.

In modern life, the repetitive gestures tend to mask and to crush the cycles. The everyday imposes its monotony. It is the invariable constant of the variations it envelops. The days follow one after another and resemble one another, and yet—here lies the contradiction at the heart of everydayness—everything changes. But the change is programmed: obsolescence is planned. Production anticipates reproduction; production produces change in such a way as to superimpose the impression of speed onto that of monotony. Some people cry out against the acceleration of time, others cry out against stagnation. They're both right.

## GENERAL AND DIVERSIFIED PASSIVITY

Common denominator of activities, locus and milieu of human functions, the everyday can also be analysed as the uniform aspect of the major sectors of social life: work, family, private life, leisure. These sectors, though distinct as forms, are imposed upon in their practice by a structure allowing us to discover what they share: organized passivity. This means, in leisure activities, the passivity of the spectator faced with images and landscapes; in the workplace, it means passivity when faced with decisions in which the worker takes no part; in private life, it means the imposition of consumption, since the available choices are directed and the needs of the consumer created by advertising and market studies. This generalized passivity is moreover distributed unequally. It weighs more heavily on women, who are sentenced to everyday life, on the working class, on employees who are not technocrats, on youth—in short on the majority of people—yet never in the same way, at the same time, never all at once.

## MODERNITY

The everyday is covered by a surface: that of modernity. News stories and the turbulent affectations of art, fashion and event veil without ever eradicating the everyday blahs. Images, the cinema and television divert the everyday by at times offering up to it its own spectacle, or sometimes the spectacle of the distinctly noneveryday; violence, death, catastrophe, the lives of kings and stars—those who we are led to believe defy everydayness. Modernity and everydayness constitute a deep structure that a critical analysis can work to uncover.

Such a critical analysis of the everyday has itself been articulated in several conflicting ways. Some treat the everyday with impatience; they want to "change life" and do it quickly; they want it all and they want it now! Others believe that lived experience is neither important nor interesting, and that instead of trying to understand it, it should be minimized, bracketed, to make way for science, technology, economic growth, etc.

To the former, we might reply that transforming the everyday requires certain conditions. A break with the everyday by means of festival—violent or peaceful—cannot endure. In order to change life, society, space, architecture, even the city must change. To the latter, we might reply that it is monstrous to reduce "lived experience," that a recognition of the inadequacy of pious humanism does not authorize the assimilation of people to insects. Given the colossal technical means at our disposal and the terrifying dangers which lie in wait for us, we would risk, in that case, abandoning humanism only to enter into "superhumanism."

Translated by Christine Levich<br>with the Editors

MAURICE BLANCHOT

# Everyday Speech[1]

The Everyday: What is Most Difficult to Discover

In a first approximation, the everyday is what we are first of all, and most often: at work, at leisure, awake, asleep, in the street, in private existence. The everyday, then, is ourselves, ordinarily. In this first stage, let us consider the everyday as without a truth proper to itself: our move then will be to seek to make it participate in the diverse figures of the True, in the great historical transformations, in the becoming of what occurs either below (economic and technical change) or above (philosophy, poetry, politics). Accordingly, it will be a question of opening the everyday onto history, or even, of reducing its privileged sector: private life. This is what happens in moments of effervescence—those we call revolution—when existence is public through and through. Commenting upon the law regarding suspects during the French Revolution, Hegel showed that each time the universal is affirmed in its brutal abstract exigency, every particular will, every separate thought falls under suspicion. It is no longer enough to act well. Every individual carries in himself a set of reflections, of intentions, that is to say reticences, that commit him to an oblique existence. To be suspect is more serious than to be guilty (hence the seeking of confession). The guilty party relates to the law to the extent that he manifestly does everything he must in order to be judged, that is, in order to be suppressed, brought back to the void of the empty point his self conceals. The suspect is that fleeting presence that does not allow recognition, and, through the part always held back that he figures forth, tends not only to interfere with, but to bring into accusation, the workings of the State. From such a perspective, each

1. Translated from Maurice Blanchot, "La Parole quotidienne," in *L'Entretien infini* (Paris: Gallimard, 1959), 355–66.

governed is suspect, but each suspect accuses the one who governs and prepares him to be at fault, since he who governs must one day recognize that he does not represent the whole, but a still particular will that only usurps the appearance of the universal. Hence the everyday must be thought as the suspect (and the oblique) that always escapes the clear decision of the law, even when the law seeks, by suspicion, to track down every indeterminate manner of being: everyday indifference. (The suspect: any and everyone, guilty of not being able to be guilty.)

But, in a new step, the critique (in the sense that Henri Lefebvre, by establishing "the critique of everyday life," has used this principle of reflection[2]) is no longer content with wanting to change day-to-day life by opening it onto history and political life: it would prepare a radical transformation of *Alltäglichkeit*. A remarkable change in point of view. The everyday is no longer the average, statistically established existence of a given society at a given moment; it is a category, a utopia and an Idea, without which one would not know how to get at either the hidden present, or the discoverable future of manifest beings. Man (the individual of today, of our modern societies) is at the same time engulfed within and deprived of, the everyday. And—a third definition—the everyday is also the ambiguity of these two movements, the one and the other hardly discernible.

From here, one can better understand the diverse directions in which the study of the everyday might be oriented (bearing now upon sociology, now upon ontology, at another moment upon psychoanalysis, politics, linguistics, literature). To approach such a movement one must contradict oneself. The everyday is platitude (what lags and falls back, the residual life with which our trash cans and cemeteries are filled: scrap and refuse); but this banality is also what is most important, if it brings us back to existence in its very spontaneity and as it is lived—in the moment when, lived, it escapes every speculative formulation, perhaps all coherence, all regularity. Now we evoke the poetry of Chekhov or even Kafka, and affirm the depth of the superficial, the tragedy of nullity. Always the two sides meet: the daily with its tedious side, painful and sordid (the amorphous, the stagnant), and the inexhaustible, irrecusable, always unfinished daily that always escapes forms or structures (particularly those of political society: bureaucracy, the wheels of government, parties). And that there may be a certain relation of identity between these two opposites is shown by the slight displacement of emphasis that

---

2. N. B. It is by this title that Henri Lefebvre published a first book in 1947 (*Critique de la vie quotidienne* [Paris: Grasset]); then, in 1958, as a preface to another edition of this first essay, a second study of different orientation. A third volume once again took up all these questions in a new light (Paris: Editions de l'Arche). Since publishing this volume, Lefebvre has continued to extend his reflections still further. See *La Vie quotidienne dans le monde moderne* (Paris: Gallimard, 1962); *Everyday Life in the Modern World*, trans. Sacha Rabinovitch (New York: Harper and Row, 1971).

permits passage from one to the other; as when the spontaneous, the informal—that is, what escapes forms—becomes the amorphous and when, perhaps, the stagnant merges with the *current* of life, which is also the very movement of society.

Whatever its other aspects, the everyday has this essential trait: it allows no hold. It escapes. It belongs to insignificance, and the insignificant is without truth, without reality, without secret, but perhaps also the site of all possible signification. The everyday escapes. This makes its strangeness—the familiar showing itself (but already dispersing) in the guise of the astonishing. It is the unperceived, first in the sense that one has always looked past it; nor can it be introduced into a whole or "reviewed," that is to say, enclosed within a panoramic vision; for, by another trait, the everyday is what we never see for a first time, but only see again, having always already seen it by an illusion that is, as it happens, constitutive of the everyday.

Hence the exigency—apparently laughable, apparently inconsequential, but necessary—that leads us to seek an always more immediate knowledge of the everyday. Henri Lefebvre speaks of the Great Pleonasm. We want to be abreast of everything that takes place at the very instant that it passes and comes to pass. The images of events and the words that transmit them are not only inscribed instantaneously on our screens, in our ears, but in the end there is no event other than this movement of universal transmission: "the reign of an enormous tautology." The disadvantages of a life so publicly and immediately displayed are henceforth observable. The means of communication—language, culture, imaginative power—by never being taken as more than means, wear out and lose their mediating force. We believe we know things immediately, without images and without words, and in reality we are dealing with no more than an insistent prolixity that says and shows nothing. How many people turn on the radio and leave the room, satisfied with this distant and sufficient noise? Is this absurd? Not in the least. What is essential is not that one particular person speak and another hear, but that, with no one in particular speaking and no one in particular listening, there should nonetheless be speech, and a kind of undefined promise to communicate, guaranteed by the incessant coming and going of solitary words. One can say that in this attempt to recapture it at its own level, the everyday loses any power to reach us; it is no longer what is lived, but what can be seen or what shows itself, spectacle and description, without any active relation whatsoever. The whole world is offered to us, but by way of a look. We are no longer burdened by events, as soon as we behold their image with an interested, then simply curious, then empty but fascinated look. What good is it taking part in a street demonstration, since at the same moment, secure and at rest, we are at the demonstration itself, thanks to a television set? Here, produced-reproduced, offering itself to our view in its totality, it allows us to believe that it takes place only so that we might be its superior witness. Substituted for practice is the pseudo-acquaintance of an irresponsible gaze; substituted for the movement of the concept—a task and a work—is the diversion of a superficial, uncaring and satisfied contemplation. Man, well protected within the four walls of his familial existence, lets the world come to him without peril, certain of being in no way changed by what he sees and hears. "Depoliticization" is linked to this movement. And the man of government who fears the street—because the man in the street is always on the verge of becoming political man—is delighted to be no more than an entrepreneur of spectacle, skilled at putting the citizen in us to sleep, the better to keep awake, in the half-light of a half-sleep, only the tireless voyeur of images.[3]

Despite massive development of the means of communication, the everyday escapes. This is its definition. We cannot help but miss it if we seek it through knowledge, for it belongs to a region where there is still nothing to know, just as it is prior to all relation insofar as it has always already been said, even while remaining unformulated, that is to say, not yet information. It is not the implicit (of which phenomenology has made broad use); to be sure, it is always already there, but that it may be there does not guarantee its actualization. On the contrary, the everyday is always unrealized in its very actualization which no event, however important or however insignificant, can ever produce. Nothing happens; this is the everyday. But what is the meaning of this stationary movement? At what level is this "nothing happens" situated? For whom does "nothing happen" if, for me, something is necessarily always happening? In other words, what corresponds to the "who?" of the everyday? And, at the same time, why, in this "nothing happens," is there the affirmation that something essential might be allowed to happen?

What questions these are! We must at least try to hold onto them. Pascal gives a first approach, which is taken up again by the young Lukàcs and by certain philosophies of ambiguity. The everyday is life in its equivocal dissimulation, and "life is an anarchy of clair-obscur. . . .

3. See Edgar Morin's *L'Esprit du temps* (Paris: Grasset, 1975); *New Trends in the Study of Mass Communication* (Birmingham, England: University Center for Contemporary Cultural Studies, 1968). In this book, Morin does not deal directly with the problem of information, but studies what he calls Mass Culture: "that is to say, produced according to the large-scale standards of industrial output; distributed by techniques of mass circulation; addressed to a social *mass*, that is, to a gigantic agglomerate of individuals seized before and beyond the internal structures of society (class, family, etc.)." It is indeed a question of a culture with its myths, its symbols, its images. It "tends to erode, to break down other cultures. . . . It is not the only culture of the 20th century. But it is the truly massive and new current of this century." Morin sometimes opposes this culture to others, for example to humanist culture—wrongly, it seems to me. I mean that the importance of "mass culture" is to put into question the very idea of culture by producing it in such a manner as to expose it to view.

Nothing is ever completely realized and nothing proceeds to its ultimate possibilities.... Everything interpenetrates, without discretion, in an impure mix, everything is destroyed and broken, nothing blossoms into real life.... It can only be described through negations...." This is Pascalian diversion, the movement of turning this way and that; it is the perpetual alibi of an ambiguous existence that uses contradictions to escape problems, remaining undecided in a restless quietude. Such is quotidian confusion. Seeming to take up all of life, it is without limit and it strikes all other life with unreality. But there arises here a sudden clarity. "Something lights up, appears as a flash on the paths of banality . . . it is chance, the great instant, the miracle." And the miracle "penetrates life in an unforeseeable manner . . . without relation to the rest, transforming the whole into a clear and simple account."[4] By its flash, the miracle separates the indistinct moments of day-to-day life, suspends nuance, interrupts uncertainties, and reveals to us the tragic truth, that absolute and absolutely divided truth, whose two parts solicit us without pause, and from each side, each of them requiring everything of us and at every instant.

Against this movement of thought nothing can be said, except that it misses the everyday. For the ordinary of each day is not such by contrast with some extraordinary; this is not the *"nul moment"* that would await the "splendid moment" so that the latter would give it a meaning, suppress or suspend it. What is proper to the everyday is that it designates for us a region, or a level of speech, where the determinations true and false, like the opposition yes and no, do not apply—it being always before what affirms it and yet incessantly reconstituting itself beyond all that negates it. An unserious seriousness from which nothing can divert us, even when it is lived in the mode of diversion; so we experience it through the boredom that seems to be indeed the sudden, the insensible apprehension of the quotidian into which one slides in the leveling of a steady slack time, feeling oneself forever sucked in, though feeling at the same time that one has already lost it, and is henceforth incapable of deciding if there is a lack of the everyday, or if one has too much of it. Thus is one maintained in boredom by boredom, which develops, says Friedrich Schlegel, as carbon dioxide accumulates in a closed space when too many people find themselves together there.

Boredom is the everyday become manifest: as a consequence of having lost its essential—constitutive—trait of being *unperceived*. Thus the daily always sends us back to that inapparent and nonetheless unhidden part of existence: insignificant because always before what signifies it; silent, but with a silence that has already dissipated as soon as we keep still in

---

4. Georg Lukács, *L'Ame et les formes* (Paris: Gallimard, 1974), as cited by Lucien Goldmann in *Recherches dialectiques* (Paris: Gallimard, 1959); Georg Lukács, *Soul and Form*, trans. Anna Bostock (London: Merlin Press, 1971, 1974).

order to hear it, and that we hear better in idle chatter, in that unspeaking speech that is the soft human murmuring in us and around us.

The everyday is the movement by which the individual is held, as though without knowing it, in human anonymity. In the everyday we have no name, little personal reality, scarcely a face, just as we have no social determination to sustain or enclose us. To be sure, I work daily, but in the day-to-day I am not a worker belonging to the class of those who work. The everyday of work tends to keep me apart from this belonging to the collectivity of work that founds its truth; the everyday breaks down structures and undoes forms, even while ceaselessly regathering itself behind the form whose ruin it has insensibly brought about.

The everyday is human. The earth, the sea, forest, light, night, do not represent everydayness, which belongs first of all to the dense presence of great urban centers. We need these admirable deserts that are the world's cities for the experience of the everyday to begin to overtake us. The everyday is not at home in our dwelling-places, it is not in offices or churches, any more than in libraries or museums. It is in the street—if it is anywhere. Here I find again one of the beautiful moments of Lefebvre's books. The street, he notes, has the paradoxical character of having more importance than the places it connects, more living reality than the things it reflects. The street renders public. "The street tears from obscurity what is hidden, publishes what happens elsewhere, in secret; it deforms it, but inserts it in the social text." And yet what is published in the street is not really divulged; it is said, but this "is said" is borne by no word ever really pronounced, just as rumors are reported without anyone transmitting them and because the one who transmits them accepts being no one. There results from this a perilous irresponsibility. The everyday, where one lives as though outside the true and the false, is a level of life where what reigns is the refusal to be different, a yet undetermined stir: without responsibility and without authority, without direction and without decision, a storehouse of anarchy, since casting aside all beginning and dismissing all end. This is the everyday. And the man in the street is fundamentally irresponsible; while having always seen everything, he is witness to nothing. He knows all, but cannot answer for it, not through cowardice, but because he takes it all lightly and because he is not really there. Who is there when the man in the street is there? At the most a "who?," an interrogation that settles upon no one. In the same way indifferent and curious, busy and unoccupied, unstable, immobile. So he is; these opposing but juxtaposed traits do not seek reconciliation, nor do they, on the other hand, counter one another, all the while still not merging; it is the *vicissitude* itself that escapes all dialectical recovery.

To the above it must be added that the irresponsibility of rumor—where everything is said, everything is heard, incessantly and interminably, without anything being affirmed, without there being a response to anything—rapidly grows weighty when it gives rise to "public opinion," but only to the degree that what is propagated (and with what ease) becomes the movement of propaganda: that is to say, when in the passage from street to newspaper, from the everyday in perpetual becoming to the everyday transcribed (I do not say inscribed), it becomes informed, stabilized, put forth to advantage. This translation modifies everything. The everyday is without event; in the newspaper this absence of event becomes the drama of the news item. In the everyday, everything is everyday; in the newspaper everything is strange, sublime, abominable. The street is not ostentatious, passers-by go by unknown, visible-invisible, representing only the anonymous "beauty" of faces and the anonymous "truth" of people essentially destined to pass by, without a truth proper to them and without distinctive traits (when we meet someone in the street, it comes always by surprise and as if by mistake, for one does not recognize oneself there; in order to go forth to meet another, one must first tear oneself away from an existence without identity). Now in the newspaper, everything is announced, everything is denounced, everything becomes image.[5] How then does the nonostentation of the street, once published, become constantly present ostentation? This is not fortuitous. One can certainly invoke a dialectical reversal. One can say that the newspaper, incapable of seizing the insignificance of the everyday, is only able to render its value apprehensible by declaring it sensational; incapable of following the movement of the everyday insofar as it is inapparent, the newspaper seizes upon it in the dramatic form of a trial. Incapable of getting at what does not belong to the historical, but is always on the point of bursting into history, newspapers keep to the anecdotal and hold us with stories—and thus, having replaced the "nothing happens" of the everyday with the emptiness of the news item, the newspaper presents us with history's "something is happening" at the level of what it claims to be the day-to-day, and which is no more than anecdote. The newspaper is not history in the guise of the everyday, and, in the compromise it offers us, it doubtless betrays historical reality less than it misses the unqualifiable everyday, this present without particularity, that it contrives in vain to qualify, that is, to affirm and to transcribe.

The everyday escapes. Why does it escape? Because it is without a subject. When I live the everyday, it is anyone, anyone whatsoever, who does so, and this any-one is, properly speaking, neither me, nor, properly speaking, the other; he is neither the one nor the other, and he is the one and the other in

---

5. Photography—mobile, immobile—as exposition: the bringing to the fore and the preparing for appearance of a human presence (that of the street) that does not yet have a countenance, that one can neither approach, nor at which one can look full in the face. Photography, in this sense, is the truth of daily publication where everything is to be put in the limelight. See Roland Barthes's study "Le Message photographique" in *Communications*, vol. 1 (1961):127–38; "The Rhetoric of the Image," in a collection of his articles entitled *Image-Music-Text*, trans. Stephen Heath (London: Hill and Wang, 1978), 32–55.

their interchangeable presence, their annulled irreciprocity—yet without there being an "I" and an "alter ego" able to give rise to a *dialectical recognition*. At the same time, the everyday does not belong to the objective realm. To live it as what might be lived through a series of separate technical acts (represented by the vacuum cleaner, the washing machine, the refrigerator, the radio, the car), is to substitute a number of compartmentalized actions for this indefinite presence, this connected movement (which is however not a whole) by which we are *continually*, though in the mode of discontinuity, in relation with the indeterminate totality of human possibilities. Of course the everyday, since it cannot be assumed by a true subject (even putting in question the notion of subject), tends unendingly to weigh down into things. This anyone presents himself as the common man for whom all is appraised in terms of good sense. The everyday is then the medium in which, as Lefebvre notes, alienations, fetishisms, reifications produce their effects. He who, working, has no other life than everyday life, is also he for whom the everyday is the heaviest; but as soon as he complains of this, complains of the burden of the everyday in existence, the response comes back: "The everyday is the same for everyone" and even adds, like Büchner's Danton: "There is scarcely any hope that this will ever change."

There must be no doubt about the dangerous essence of the everyday, nor about this uneasiness that seizes us each time that, by an unforeseeable leap, we stand back from it and, facing it, we discover that precisely nothing faces us: "What?" "Is this my everyday life?" Not only must one not doubt it, but one must not dread it; rather one ought to seek to recapture the secret destructive capacity that is in play in it, the corrosive force of human anonymity, the infinite wearing away. The hero, while still a man of courage, is he who fears the everyday; fears it not because he is afraid of living in it with too much ease, but because he dreads meeting in it what is most fearful: a power of dissolution. The everyday challenges heroic values, but even more it impugns all values and the very idea of value, disproving always anew the unjustifiable difference between authenticity and inauthenticity. Day-to-day indifference is situated on a level at which the question of value is not posed: "il y a du quotidien" [there is everydayness], without subject, without object, and while it is there, the "he" ["il"] of the everyday does not have to be of account, and, if value nevertheless claims to step in, then "he" is worth "nothing" and "nothing" is worth anything through contact with him. To experience everydayness is to be tested by the radical nihilism that is as if its essence, and by which, in the void that animates it, it does not cease to hold the principle of its own critique.

## CONCLUSION IN THE FORM OF A DIALOGUE

"Is not the everyday, then, a utopia, the myth of an existence bereft of myth? We no more have access to the everyday than do we touch this

moment of history that could, historically, represent the end of history.
——That can, in fact, be said, but opens onto another meaning: the everyday is the inaccessible to which we have always already had access; the everyday is inaccessible, but only insofar as every mode of acceding is foreign to it. To live in the way of the quotidian is to hold oneself at a level of life that excludes the possibility of a beginning, an access. Everyday experience radically questions the initial exigency. The idea of creation is inadmissible, when it is a matter of accounting for existence as it is borne by the everyday.
——To put this another way, everyday existence never had to be *created*. This is exactly what the expression "il y a du quotidien" [there is the everyday] means. Even if the affirmation of a creating God were to be imposed, the there is (there is already when there is not yet being, what there is still when there is nothing) would remain irreducible to the principle of creation; and the there is is the human everyday.
——The everyday is our portion of eternity: the eternullity of which Laforgue speaks. So that the *Lord's Prayer* would be secretly impious: give us our daily bread, give us to live according to the daily existence that leaves no place for a relation between Creator and creature. Everyday man is the most atheist of men. He is such that no God whatsoever could stand in relation to him. And thus one understands how the man in the street escapes all authority, whether it be political, moral, or religious.
—— For in the everyday we are neither born nor do we die: hence the weight and the enigmatic force of everyday truth.
——In whose space, however, there is neither true nor false.

Translated by Susan Hanson

EDWARD BALL

# The Great Sideshow of the Situationist International

> Then appeared for the first time the disquieting figures of the "Situationist International." How many are there? Where do they come from? No one knows.
> —*Le Républicain Lorrain*, 28 June 1967

### SIRE, I AM FROM THE OTHER COUNTRY

Throughout the fifteen years of their public activity, the Situationist International—the political-artistic cell that operated in Paris and elsewhere from 1957 to 1972—refused the identities pressed upon them by the discourses around art, politics, and philosophy. The Situationists understood what Hegel called "the cunning of history"—that process by which historical actors undertake a project whose consequences result in something completely different from their intentions. History snatches defeat from the jaws of victory. As an example of this reversal it is plain to see how the Dadaist attack on the institutions of "Art" was soon assimilated and naturalized by the art-critical establishment itself. One merely has to visit a museum where Dada artifacts are on display to find them represented in a strange ideological confinement—either as another testimony to the glory of artistic expression, or as a crucial moment in the development of the modernist canon (or both). The Situationists sensed that dominant institutions control the emergence of their own opposition as a matter of course, and so like the Dadaists, they adopted tactics meant to preempt their own success on the terrain of respectable culture.

The problem of their historical representation may be more onerous in view of the fact that so few critical writings have gathered around the Situationist International since the group disbanded in 1972. In the English language, there is very little commentary on the group in either the academic or the critical press—a fact which, for the situationists stands as evidence of their aberrant success. Certainly, few anglophones are at all familiar with the some fifteen years of situationist activity in France and, to a lesser degree, in other parts of Europe and the United States. Only scattered references to that activity appeared in American journalism of the late 1960s, especially around the time of May, 1968:

Those who want to understand the ideas behind the student revolts in the Old World ought to pay serious attention not only to the writing of Adorno and of the three M's—Marx, Mao, and Marcuse—but above all to the literature of the situationists. . . . [*The New York Times*, 21 April 1968]

"Inside, in jampacked auditoriums, thousands applauded all-night debates that ranged over every conceivable topic, from the "anesthesia of influence," to the elimination of "bourgeois spectacles" and how to share their "revolution" with the mass of French workers. . . . There were Maoists, Trotskyists, ordinary communists, anarchists, and "situationists"—a tag for those without preconceived ideologies who judge each situation as it arises" (*Time*, 24 May 1968).[1] In these few sentences, one can see the situationists staring back at the puzzled gaze of American news journalism, which barely recognizes its subject.

In France, due to their leading role in the events of May 1968, the situationists have been promoted into popular memory and cant. At the end of the 1960s, situationist slogans covered the walls of Paris;[2] situationist political tactics had been popularized on the left, and the group itself was besieged by activists who wanted to sign on to its notoriety. Yet despite their strong profile, situationist writings have remained too extreme for much academic debate.[3] In the Situationist International, we are describing people who lived their history in large part outside of the legitimate press. The situationists drew the attention of the mass media, but aroused little curiosity among philosophers; they helped to shape the near revolution of 1968, but one finds them conspicuously absent from the historical narrative; they worked with activists and trade unions, but were passed over by political analysts. The history of the Situationist International is as yet unwritten.

## THE SITUATIONISTS DO PARIS

The Situationist International (the "S.I.") constituted itself and began to publish a journal of the same name in 1957. This action came after several

---

1. Cited in Ken Knabb, ed. and trans., *Situationist International Anthology* (Berkeley: Bureau of Public Secrets, 1981—no copyright).

2. The situationists were irrepressible sloganeers who seemed to submerge an entire politics in each sentence. In one phrase, "Sous les pavés, la plage" [Under the cobble stones, the beach], one can see, all at once, the political idealism of the group, its realism about transforming a society as inflexible as the street itself, and a program for street action (cobble stones are typically used against the police by demonstrators).

3. There are some exceptions to this. For example, in the handful of academic or quasi-academic accounts written by ex-members of the Situationist International, two come to mind: Jean-Jacques Raspaud and Jean-Pierre Voyer's *L'Internationale Situationniste: protagonistes, chronologie, bibliographie (avec un index des noms insultés)*, (Paris: Champ Libre, 1971); and René Vienet's *Enragés et situationnistes dans le mouvement des occupations* (Paris: Gallimard, 1968).

years of art-making, casual research, and *agit-prop* interventions on the part of its founding members. In July 1957, a handful of European avant-garde groups convened at Cosio d'Arroscia in Italy. Present were delegates from *L'Internationale Lettriste* (the Lettrist International, a cell of artists), from the German and Scandinavian movement for an Imaginist Bauhaus, and from the "London Psychogeographical Committee." These groups, which were by and large known only to their members, decided to amalgamate. They convened as *L'Internationale Situationniste*.

For the next decade and a half, the S.I. developed and practiced an aggressive critique of industrial culture of both the East (its state socialist variant) and the West (its capitalist variant). This critique pulsed into wide circulation during the dislocations in French social and economic life in the period March–June 1968. Then, situationist tactics and ideology animated the events in the universities which led to a general strike and nationwide occupation of factories and offices. Following that May, the S.I. was pushed forward to a position of romantic notoriety in the French left. The group had sought to avoid party leadership status in political life. Yet, now their ideas were "in everyone's heads," as they used to claim. The last congress of the situationists was convened in order to disband the group. In 1972, the S.I. was formally dissolved in Paris.

To approach the situationists, one cannot begin with the usual secondary source material. It does not (yet) exist. One must turn to their own self-published texts. The journal *L'Internationale Situationniste* was written and published collectively between 1958 and 1969.[4] Many of its articles appeared unsigned. This anonymity was partly collectivist in inspiration and partly an effort to produce an undifferentiated front of situationist activity. In its manifestoes, pamphlets, posters, and in the journal *L'Internationale Situationniste* itself, the S.I. copyrighted none of their writings, which were typically accompanied by an inscription encouraging the use of the text, "even without mentioning the source."

In its early years, the membership of the S.I. could gather in a small café. The cell was run, and decisions were made, by ballot. But as in most collectivities in a monadic or individualistic society (our own), the claim of equality disguised a de facto hierarchy, at the top of which was Guy Debord. Debord was to the S.I. what André Breton was to the early surrealists: its prime mover, its chief polemicist, the commissar or head of the cadre. Debord is best known today for his 1967 *Society of the Spectacle*, a bulletin of numbered theses that has received the widest circulation of any situationist text in the English-speaking world.

Situationist ideology—and we may use this word, since the writings

---

4. The journal *L'Internationale situationniste*, published irregularly in Paris between 1957 and 1969, and largely unavailable in American libraries, has been reissued in one volume, *Internationale Situationniste: 1958–69* (Paris: Champ Libre, first published by Van Gennep, Amsterdam, 1970).

supply both a diagnosis of modern social conditions and a program for their transformation—came together at the intersection of a range of discourses on art, politics, and social formations. From the Dadaist vanguard of the teens and twenties they took an urge to destroy art; from the surrealists, an aim to reconstitute it at the level of everyday life. From modernism in architecture they developed a utopian urbanism, in part derived from the Bauhaus, but superseding it in an effort to widen its formalist and populist tendencies into a general political study of urban space. Out of these positions, the S.I. developed a kind of phenomenology of urban life. One of the alternatives to the alienations of the city, they reasoned, should be the conscious construction of "situations," or theatrical environments inside the urban environment—acts of cultural sabotage or diversions that might strengthen the growing bohemian subculture. "Psychogeography" was the word introduced to foreground the whole area of mental states and spatial ambiences produced by the material arrangements of the urban scene. Guy Debord suggested that a psychogeography

> could set up for itself the study of the precise laws and specific effects of the geographical environment, consciously organized or not, on the emotion and behavior of individuals. . . . [F]rom any standpoint other than that of police control, Haussman's Paris is a city built by idiots, full of sound and fury, signifying nothing.[5]

Psychogeography provided the theoretical sanction for great delinquent play. In 1950, an event occurred in Paris that would become a legend in the ranks of the S.I. On Easter Sunday, miscreants, two of whom would later join a handful of the protosituationist Lettrist International, entered the sacristy of Notre Dame Cathedral in Paris just before high mass. There they detained the priest and donned clerical vestments. One of the group proceeded to the pulpit and, before a vast congregation on this holiest day of the Christian calendar, began to preach on Nietzsche and the death of God. After a few minutes, the gathering in the nave sensed foul play. The congregation chased the bunch of saboteurs through the cathedral and out into the streets.

In their daily lives, the situationists refined bohemian solipsism and negation into an idealist stance: they were *déclassés* intellectuals and artists, outside of the academic circuit, out of the reach of the popular press, and fiercely marginal, ". . . in the catacombs of visible culture."[6] A kind of separatist morale animates situationist writings, as if the cell is speaking from exile in its own culture. Their solidarity depended on a rigid control of membership, which gave rise to a cadre mentality common to twentieth-century avant-garde movements. Expulsion of mem-

---

5. This comes from a text which antedates the start-up of the S.I. Guy Debord, "Introduction to a Critique of Urban Geography," *Les Lèvres nues* no. 6 (September, 1955).
6. Ken Knabb, op. cit., 60.

bers was ordinary—business as usual—and helped the Situationist International to represent itself as an urban *bande à part* within the general social hegemony. This last tactic (the exclusion of members who had drifted from situationist ideology) was inherited from the surrealists as well as being a common device in leftist party politics. One can see that the situationists reached in every direction to shape an identity: toward the Bauhaus, Dada, phenomenology, and, above all in the 1960s, as we will see in a moment, toward Marxism.

It is apparent today that the story of the Situationist International is also the story of a long and wide transformation that has been making itself visible in industrialized societies since the mid 1950s. Some thirty years ago situationists announced a critique that has recently emerged as a definition of our so-called "postmodern" culture. This is not to say that the situationists were "the first postmoderns." Such a group would only be rhetorically identified by a historicism that dotes on originality. Yet the current critique adopted among political theorists, philosophers, and cultural and art historians as one or another theory of postmodernism was fully articulated in theory and practice by the S.I. long before our own allegedly postmodern times. What's more, the situationist program of cultural infidelity and sabotage has, over a relatively brief period of time, been massively incorporated into styles of discursive production (art, literature, cinema) and even, in wider areas of exchange, into methods of product development and marketing strategies in the consumer economy. It sounds like a familiar story: what was once subversive now turns a profit. Yet there is more. The situationists, as we will see, did not themselves become marketable; rather, they taught an ensuing generation how to recycle the detritus of official learning; how to reinscribe texts, figures, and artifacts so as to empower them with new meanings; and, despite their precautions, how to make new products out of the leftovers of the commodity economy.

## THE GREAT SHOW OF REIFICATION

To understand these strange reversals and their relationship to the emergence of the new industries of postmodernism, we must first look at the components of situationist politics. The greatest momentum for the mature situationist critique came from Marxism. Throughout its history, the Situationist International operated from the understanding that capitalism has established for itself a virtually totalized social field, one in which all areas of life are articulated for the survival of the given means and relations of production. This is in line with the updating or revision of the Marxist problematic generally undertaken by the Frankfurt School and many other critics since the 1930s. It is a defensive position that first arose out of the failure of the Marxist ideology to detonate the revolution in the West, a Marxism that grew up when the European left stared into the face of fascism and was forced to explain it. It is, however, not a fatalistic Marxism, but one which sees social life in a state of (putative, reversible) occupation or domination by capitalism. For the S.I., this domination has been combatted historically by insufficient and bureaucratic forms of socialist opposition, and must now be met everywhere by new forms of rebellion, new ideologies, new criticism.

The Marxism of the Situationist International developed around an idiom that has gone under the name of the critique of *reification*. The notion of reification comes strongly into view with Hegel, whose *verdinglichung* [turning into a concrete thing or object] describes the manifestation of the Idea [*Geist*] as it is realized in material forms and in social life. Marx put this concept to practical work by inverting it. For Marx, *versachlichung* [thingification: turning into an abstract thing or matter] describes the process by which the concrete products of history (social forms, commodities) are abstracted and frozen in an ideational state, where they acquire the aura of "nature" or permanence. For example, the notion of "freedom," the ideological defense for unregulated commerce which the bourgeoisie used as a weapon against the ancien régime, has since been hypostasized and raised to the status of a universal ideal.

Since Marx's day, materialist criticism has widened its discussion of reification. By reification, critical theory has tried to designate a vast operation carried out in all capitalist economies, and on the basis of this analysis has made extended claims about seemingly disconnected social facts. For a certain brand of Marxism, *versachlichung* [thingification] has meant the strategic division of lived experience into a set of neutral abstractions, as an effort undertaken so as to remove impediments to commerce and profit taking. As described by Fredric Jameson, the process of reification is:

> ... the analytical dismantling of the various traditional or "natural" [*naturwuchsige*] unities (social groups, institutions, human relationships, forms of authority, activities of a cultural and ideological as well as of a productive nature) into their component parts with a view toward their "taylorization," that is, their reorganization into more efficient systems which function according to an instrumental, or binary, means/ends logic.[7]

This version of reification identifies a massive process of post-Enlightenment times, as wide as the entire social formation, with which capitalism has sought to consolidate its position by displacing ways of life impertinent to the production and exchange of goods and services. Elsewhere, the sociologist Max Weber named a coequal phenomenon in his discussion of the dynamic of *rationalization*. Weber theorized that a systematic

---

7. Fredric Jameson, *The Political Unconscious* (Ithaca: Cornell University Press, 1981), 227.

quantification of human experience was being carried out in the terms of some newly emergent social logic. A plain example of rationalization would be the enterprise of demographics, the study of populations by means of income statistics, ethnic and gender profiles, etc. The term has elsewhere been aired in the popular critique of "dehumanization." For Weber, rationalization would in part mean the reorganization of former means of livelihood according to the needs of capitalist commerce. Cottage industry, or domestic production, then, was easily dismantled (but not eradicated) by capitalism, which has instead rearticulated it into a new social value or instrument ("folk art," crafts, etc.), with its own limited sphere of operation alongside other spheres. Leisure, labor, sport, religion, the intellect—these rough market-capitalist divisions eventually give way to the razorsharp specializations of our time, where each activity is cut off from the one next to it, while the broader movement of their relations in the totality cannot be seen from any one site in the social field.

In one definition, then, reification (to return to the Marxist vocabulary), is the division of human experience gone haywire. Social life is shattered into an ensemble of hermetic points for the purpose of organizing a higher unity, that is, the analytic arrangement of experience that capitalism requires for its smoothest operation. As a consequence of this enterprise, reification redefines earlier social forms and ways of life so that they appear to us in a diminished state, as a kind of image or frozen tableau. This remarkable feature of reification, its cannibalization of history, is paramount to understanding the work of the Situationist International.

The situationists built their critique on the theory of reification, a concept underestimated by proponents of a more traditional historical materialism. We have tried to describe this transformation as the fracturing and rearticulation (the 'thingification') of the social field for the historical purpose of enabling the hegemony of the capitalist mode of production—a process which, it must be said, is never completed. To strengthen their analysis and popularize its rhetoric, the situationists reached into the body of consumer culture to explore two symptoms of its disease: alienation and commodification.

In France during the 1950s and 1960s, the notion of alienation was mainly employed in its postwar career as the preferred term of existentialist philosophy. In fact, the journal *L'Internationale Situationniste* is rife with the cant of Marxist existentialism that was reigning at the time, with many articles given over to fierce diatribes against the new forms of alienation in social life. For the S.I., the main feature and symptom of contemporary alienation is the glorious apotheosis of the commodity form. In twentieth-century Marxist critique, reification has walked in lockstep with the concept of commodification. The two notions are integrated by a means/ends logic, the one (reification) providing a basis or precedent for the other (commodification: the translation of human experience into product form). The commodity is found in the center of the situationist critique under the disguise of a new name: the "spectacle." The first thesis of Debord's *Society of the Spectacle*, paraphrases the first sentence in Marx's chapter on "Commodities and Money" (*Capital*, volume 1), substituting for Marx's word "commodity" the revised notion of "spectacle":

> The entire life of societies in which modern conditions of production reign announces itself as an immense accumulation of *spectacles*. Everything that was directly lived has moved away into a representation.[8]

*Everything that was directly lived has moved away into a representation.* The older unities of past cultures and of lived experience appear to us today as a kind of phantasm or image. The commodity used to be a material thing; now it is a spectacular event. The *spectacle* is the commodity that has left its material body on earth and risen to a new ethereal presence. One does not buy objects; one buys images connected to them. One does not buy the utility of goods; one buys the evanescent experience of ownership. Everywhere, one buys the spectacle.

In this profile of the capitalist economy there is a sense of modern debasement that tends to mark all commentary on reification. This debasement is by and large a semiotic event. Today the widening field of commodification is commonly spoken of as the spread of so-called "consumer culture" or "media culture" since the Second World War. Yet these terms fall short of describing the phenomenon they purport to name. Debord renders this late evolution or refinement of capitalism in a memorable formula:

> The first phases of the domination of the economy over social life had brought into the definition of all human realization an obvious degradation of *being* into *having*. The present phase of total occupation of social life by the accumulated results of the economy leads to a generalized sliding of *having* into *appearing*, from which all actual "having" must draw its immediate prestige and its ultimate function.[9]

The image, severed from all reference, is the most recent (final?) form of reification, where the commodity becomes a kind of cinematic spectacle that presses back on the hard facts of simple possession. In this world, human experience is a (marketable) copy for which the original has been lost or never even existed. For Marx, writing in the 1860s, the commodity form had already begun to recast the very relations between people and things, subjects and objects. In *Capital*, volume 1, Marx writes: "The commodity is a mysterious thing. . . . There it is a definite social relation

---

8. Guy Debord, *The Society of the Spectacle*, trans. anon. (Detroit: Black and Red, 1970—no copyright), thesis no. 1.
9. Debord, ibid., thesis no. 17.

between men, that assumes, in their eyes, the fantastic form of a relation between things."[10] To this analysis the situationists would add the caveat that today's commodities bear resemblance to a language of images. "[The spectacle is] capital accumulated to such a degree that it becomes an image."[11] The material fact of a product is superseded by its ability to signify.

Jean Baudrillard, writing at the same time as Debord, discovered a similar continent in his book *Le Système des objets: la consommation des signes* (1968). For Baudrillard, commodification is at a flood mark when products begin to articulate all forms of social desire: "The system of [historical, social] needs now become less coherent than the system of objects itself . . ."[12] In Baudrillard's explanation the commodity/spectacle is the antihero in the drama of reification: even as older forms of culture are being dismantled, a new unity, the unity of the object world, rises up to displace them and take its leading historical role.

In an orthodox Marxism, the locale of power and the site of its challenge are focused in the means of production. Revisionist Marxism since 1917 has relocated its emphasis out and away from the production economy and toward a zone where the economic contradictions are represented and, in these accounts, actually come into conflict. The labels which variously describe this arena are "culture," "leisure," and the larger system of consumption and exchange. An early discussion of the question arose in German sociology at the turn of the twentieth century. *Das Alltagsleben*—everyday life—was the term applied to designate the myriad of pastimes and nonproductive activities that fill the days and nights of women and men when they are not, strictly speaking, at work selling their labor power. Another discussion of everyday life comes from the philosopher Henri Lefebvre, who first identified *la vie quotidienne* as an area for critique in *Introduction à la critique de la vie quotidienne* (1947). The very date of Lefebvre's book radiates with the aura of peacetime desire in postwar Europe for the rededication of economic energies away from the war economy and toward leisure and consumption. *La Vie quotidienne* of 1947 appears to us now as the dim prehistory of our "society of consumption," to use one of Baudrillard's phrases. In another academic tradition, *la vie quotidienne* may be familiar to English readers as the target of critique within the body of "Cultural Studies" that has grown up in Britain since the 1950s. Cultural Studies first got underway as the effort to understand the immersion of "working class culture" in the flood of postwar commodification. What was lost, the question went, in the triumph of the new consumerism?

10. Karl Marx, *Capital*, trans. Samuel Moore and Edward Aveling (New York: International Publishers, 1967), vol. 1, 72.
11. Debord, op. cit., thesis no. 34.
12. Jean Baudrillard, *Le Système des objets: la consommation des signes* (Paris: Gallimard, 1968), 222.

Among all of these treatments of the concept—German sociology, cultural studies, *la vie quotidienne*—it is Lefebvre's portrayal that frames things most handily by defining everyday life as that social experience which is left after all specialized activities (paradigmatically: labor) have been removed. Depending on one's theoretical position, these leftovers could include a great deal, or they could merely mean the unformulated social libido in a state prior to its articulation (what, in social life, is "unspecialized"?). Whatever the case, everyday life for many generations was (continues to be) the blind spot of Marxist analysis. It was rumored that nothing of importance occurs there, or anywhere in fact away from the furnaces of production.

The goal for Henri Lefebvre is to conceive everyday life in such a way as to retrieve it from its modern state of colonization by the commodity form and other modes of reification. A critique of the Everyday can be generated only by a kind of alienation effect, insofar as it is put into contact with its own radical *other*, such as an eradicated past (e.g. precapitalist or so-called "folk" culture), or an imagined future (certain utopian projections, which can be glimpsed in Lefebvre's *Le droit à la ville*). In this way, the Everyday becomes a term with a double meaning. It is at one and the same time a word of opprobrium (currently, everyday life is bad), and a naming of the place where alternative social forms might be organized: "[After the war,] alienation assumed a new and deeper significance; it deprived everyday life of its power, disregarding its productive and creative potentialities, completely devaluing it and smothering it under the spurious glamour of ideologies."[13] Unfortunately, this kind of Marxism shows signs of a prisoner's mentality, a feeling of impossible confinement which is rather common in the general theory of reification. But one would hope that critics only write about degraded realities as a polemic to empower some attempt to transform social life. Here, the reconstruction of everyday life can be seen as a potentially revolutionary project. Take Lefebvre's reading of the Paris Commune. The 1871 Commune can be viewed as a vast act of a politics from below, so to speak, which for a short time rescued quotidian experience from the grip of alienation. In the Commune one can recognize a kind of festival (Lefebvre's word) in which the reigning forms of experience (the lived relation to state power and to the urban milieu) were suddenly turned back in an explosion of disalienation and popular sovereignty. The notion of a festival or revolt returns to us today in our selective memory of the counterculture or, to use a better word, the subcultures of the 1960s. In these environs, the Situationist International was immensely important in France. For the situationists, rebellion will be a festival or it will be nothing at all.

13. Henri Lefebvre, *Everyday Life in the Modern World*, trans. Sacha Rabinovitch (New York: Harper and Row, 1971), 33.

## *DETOURNEMENT* AND THE POSTMODERN

We've taken a long detour through these debates only in order to return to the Situationist International, which realized and practiced a critique of reification that previously had lived only at the level of discourse.

It is no accident that the key figures in the S.I. during the 1950s passed under the influence of Henri Lefebvre, who briefly worked with the group and whose texts fueled the situationist writings on urban and industrial life. Situationist ideology shared with Lefebvre and others the view that consumer capitalism is a bedeviled world and an alienated spectacle, but a world in which the possibility for an alternative social life has not yet been foreclosed. The situationists knew how much capitalism had changed since Marx's time: "Not that it has become more tolerable. Revolution has to be reinvented, that's all."[14]

In the 1950s and 1960s, the S.I. developed the first explosive aesthetic politics since the surrealist experiments of the twenties. It was an "aesthetic" strategy in the sense that its opposition was raised on the terrain proposed by consumer capitalism itself, the terrain of the commodity and of reified daily experience. A pessimistic critique would abandon history to the frozen dialectic of consumerism, which is believed to arrest politics in a spectacular tableau of material abundance. But the S.I. celebrated the prospect of sustained opposition in all its forms. If a revolution of production is no longer in reach, one can begin with a revolution of consumption. The premise: politics is in part the problem of the use or reading of objects. The program: the reign of the spectacular commodity may be combatted by the intentional misrecognition of exchange values.

Beginning with this article of faith, the S.I. attempted to tease out of social life its hidden aberrations and moments of resistance. They developed the technique of the *dérive*, the day- or week-long "drift" through everyday life, a kind of roving research along the margins of dominant culture. For the situationists, *dérivisme* is an extension of the bohemian lifestyle into criticism, where the *dérive* is intended to turn up symptoms of the breakdown of reification. The *dériviste* would be a twentieth-century version of Baudelaire's *flâneur*, who has left the boulevards and taken a garret apartment on the Left Bank, and whose promenades now range all over Paris. The *dérive*, an aimless drift through the urban landscape, offers evidence that capitalism occasionally stammers in its own monologue on the proper means of living. And evidence was uncovered. This collective article dated 1962 celebrates the spreading forms of guerrilla tactics in the domain of politics and art:

14. Anon., "Instructions for Taking Up Arms," *Internationale Situationniste* no. 6 (August 1961), in Knabb, op cit., 63.

On 4 August in France, striking miners at Merlebach attacked twenty-one cars parked in front of the management buildings. . . . Who can fail to see in this—over and beyond the innumerable reasons that always justify aggression on the part of the exploited—a gesture of self-defense against the central object of consumer alienation? . . . But it isn't only industrial workers who are fighting against brutalization. The Berlin actor Wolfgang Neuss perpetrated a most suggestive act of sabotage in January by placing a notice in the paper *Der Abend* giving away the identity of the killer in a television detective serial that had been keeping the masses in suspense for weeks.[15]

For the situationists, such episodes as these were not quixotic disturbances, but potentially revolutionary acts.

Situationist practice advocates a kind of guerilla warfare that unites forms of art with collective forms of provocation: ". . . introducing the aggressivity of the delinquents onto the plane of ideas."[16] The byword for these tactics is *détournement*. The most persuasive evidence that everyday life has been homogenized is the fact that the slightest deviation sometimes reverberates far beyond its space of emergence. Clearly, any offense against the commodity form does have potentially "global implications." This state of affairs provides a warrant for the practice of *détournement*. The French *détournement* is sometimes translated as "diversion," but this rendering omits the word's connotations (in the original language) of illicit appropriation and piracy. In English, *détournement* should evoke a chain of reference that includes the metonymies of detouring, deflection, and the sudden reversal of a previous articulation or purpose.

Situationist detournement began as a theory of sabotage at the level of so-called "high" culture. Literature was its first target. In a 1957 experiment, artist Asger Jorn and Guy Debord produced a book, *Mémoires*, that consisted entirely of pirated elements. On its pages, the print ran in all directions, and the relations among the various quoted fragments were left unexplained (sentences broken off, texts superimposed, etc.). As a final gesture they bound the book with a sandpaper jacket, so that when it was shelved, it damaged other books.

In this and other projects one notices the hand of early surrealism tutoring the situationists. Take this passage, from "Methods of Detournement," a 1956 article by Guy Debord and Gil Wolman:

> Any elements, no matter where they are taken from, can serve in making new combinations. The discoveries of modern poetry regarding the analogical structure of images demonstrate that when two objects are

---

15. Anon., "The Bad Days Will End," *Internationale Situationiste* no. 7 (April 1962), in Knabb, op cit., 83–84.
16. "The Bad Days Will End," 87.

brought together, no matter how far apart their original contexts may be, a relationship is always formed. . . . Anything can be used.[17]

But the surrealist program remained an aesthete's project first and a political act only secondarily, while detournement arises out of the effort to confront systems of power with new forms of opposition, in the belief that the older forms of resistance—organized labor, party structures—have themselves become part of an expanded hegemony.

The *détourniste* begins by declaring that "culture" (in the old sense of high culture and text-making) is not an autonomous sphere of activity, separate from other kinds of commerce. In the spectacular society everything is "cultural," which is to say a potential text, an exchange value, and a commodity all at the same time. Jean Baudrillard has described these conditions as the result of a shift in capitalism from limited commodity production into a kind of hyperproduction or excessive exchange. Hyperproduction—arguably the state in which we now find ourselves—collapses the forms of the linguistic sign and the commodity onto one another for the apotheosis of unlimited commerce:

> This mutation concerns the passage from the form-commodity to the form-sign, from the abstraction of the exchange of material products under the law of general equivalence to the operationalization of all exchange value under the law of the code . . . *the political economy of the sign.*[18]

For Baudrillard, the capitalist dream of social life as a vast (semiotic) pool of exchangeable artifacts has already been realized. This same analysis rises up in recent debates surrounding the concept of the Postmodern, which, if we accept that such a social formation exists, depends upon the positioning of a break in the history of industrialism, generally set in the period 1950–60. This break marks an intense heating-up of production and consumption and the subsequent removal of a set of older prohibitions to exchange that stood in the path of the great postwar swelling in commodification. The trademark of the postmodern is the miscegenation of previously opposed levels of culture, which now become functionally equivalent: commodities/signs, high art/mass culture, news/entertainment, etc. Evidence of the postmodern is everywhere that accelerated commerce can be found. One example would be the 1960s phenomenon of Pop Art, which drew momentum from the new confusion between mass-produced items and the sacred art object with its singular aura. And then there is the (postmodern) "discipline" of semiotics: an

---

17. Guy Debord, Gil J. Wolman, "Methods of Détournement," in Knabb, op. cit., 9; first published in *Les Lèvres nues* no. 8 (May 1956).

18. Jean Baudrillard, *The Mirror of Production*, trans. Mark Poster (St. Louis: Telos Press, 1975), 121.

academic field that studies "everything that can be taken as a sign,"[19] and includes Roland Barthes's readings of fashion, food, cars, etc. as signifying systems.[20] A metadiscourse such as this has only been made possible by a new variation in the economy, a stepping up of reification that allows the process of abstraction to go forward over all obstacles.

If the situationists did not have a theory of the postmodern, it was because they practiced it. The situationist program starts up when one confuses two levels of activity: detournement makes *politics* (level one) out of *plagiarism* and *misinterpretation* (level two). The *détourniste* understands that every consumable object is imbedded in strict ensembles of interpretation and value. An automobile may be driven or it may represent its owner's class alignments (it is a commodity and a sign), but it may not be put to other uses (lived in, or destroyed before a certain amount of decay, etc.). (Fig. 1.) One kind of detournement, then, becomes the hijacking of commodities (that carry with them a prescribed reading or utility) into heavily coded, unfamiliar contexts. In a word, detournement is the reterritorialization of the object. With verbal texts, the *détourniste* gets underway by taking an overdetermined text (a cartoon, a bestseller) and subjecting it to a systematic misreading. This reinscription of texts was a favorite situationist pastime, and the S.I. may have originated (if that word can be applied here) the technique of recaptioning photographs and comics that was popularized in the pasteboard politics of the 1960s.

It would be possible, though not desirable, to understand detournement as a kind of reading procedure. In this sense, the text is any object whose use has been prescribed for it (it carries a reading that is foreclosed). Detournement would be the intentional disarticulation of the text and its rearticulation elsewhere in a new set of reading conditions. Irony would be a main feature of this practice, insofar as the text is submitted to a double reading, first in its sanctioned context (the prescribed use of the text) and next to a pirate reading that contradicts the first. Finally, this overall business would have to be distinguished from the related practice of (academic) deconstruction, which shatters the text as an intellectual exercise and offers the alternative pleasure of dispersing meaning through a gridwork of adjacent discourses.

Detournement, then, is the tactic of recycling objects for specific disjunctive effects—a method that can be repeated, and easily taught. At this point we should remind ourselves that the recycling of the object has been a standard operation, normalized in the art world since the first experiments of the twentieth-century avant-garde, from Marcel Duchamp's ready-mades on up throughout the career of Andy Warhol. The

---

19. Umberto Eco, *A Theory of Semiotics* (Bloomington: Indiana University Press, 1976), 7.

20. Cf. especially the middle section of Roland Barthes's *Elements of Semiology*, trans. Annette Lavers and Colin Smith (New York: Hill and Wang, 1967).

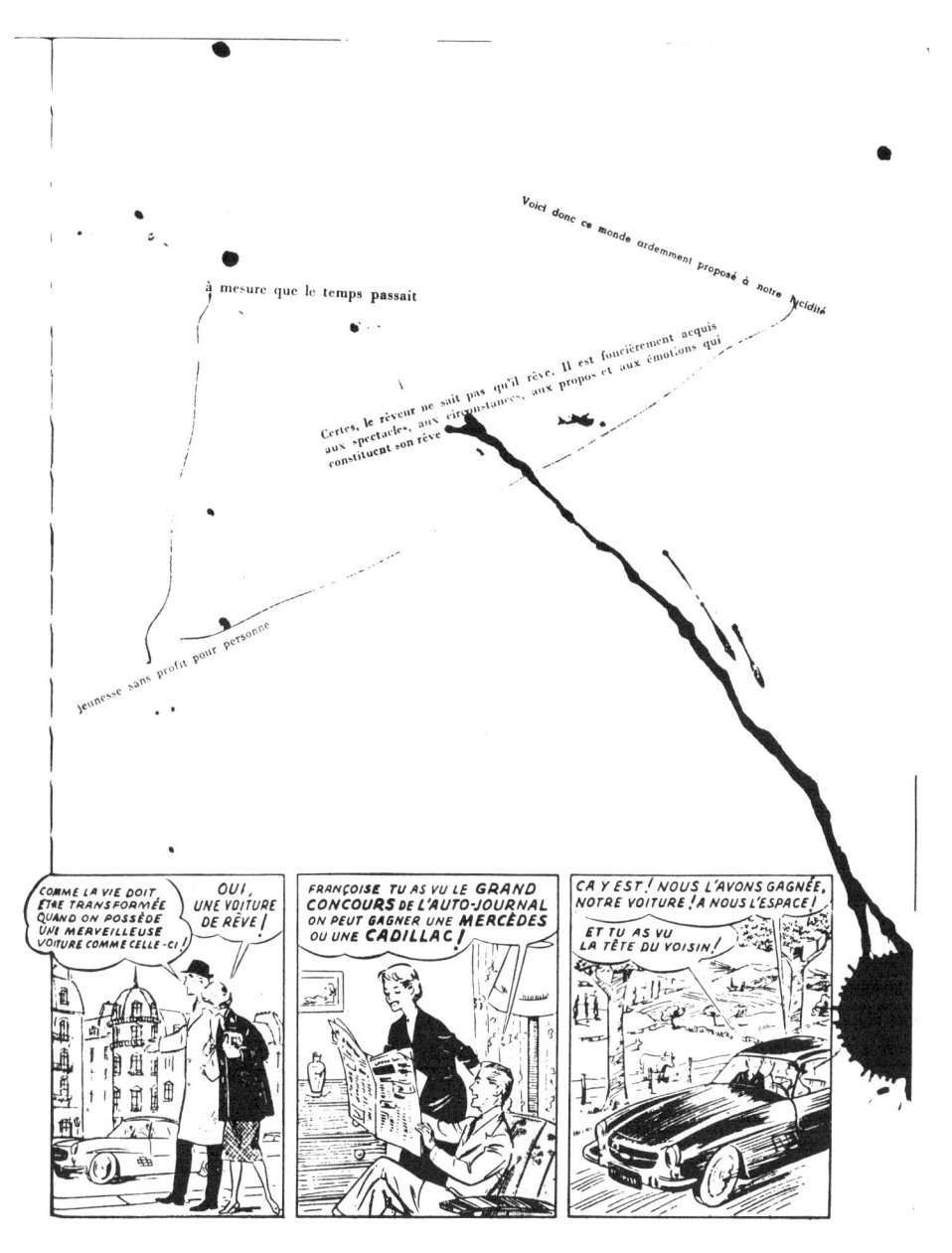

*Figure 1. Mémoires: structures portantes d'Asger Jorn.* Paris: Internationale situationniste. Distribution in the United States: Wittenborn, N.Y., 1969. No copyright. "Cet ouvrage est entièrement composé d'éléments préfabriqués."

36   *Yale French Studies*

success of the *pasticheur* in art history would seem to displace the later claims of the *détourniste*. But detournement, situationist theory claims, is not the same as pastiche or collage, since it adds two caveats for the (proper) misuse of the object, neither of which is observed by pastiche aesthetics. These are: 1) the proliferation of cultural piracy on a mass scale, and 2) this piracy as a collective and anonymous activity.

THE SOCIETY OF THE SITUATIONIST

What is to be said for this behavior? Has it arisen elsewhere, outside of the local scene of Paris, 1960–70? Yes, of course, and massively. Take the case of capitalism's "untouchables," its subcultures. In *Subculture: the Meaning of Style*, Dick Hebdige uses Lévi-Strauss's notion of *bricolage* to characterize the lifestyles and the fashions of rebellious young people in Britain from the 1950s forward. These ersatz collectivities, the Mods and the Rockers, punks and Teddy Boys, have one after another played with the style and poses of the dominant culture in aberrant ways so as to foreground their own status as misfits (detourned subjects?). The book gives an exhaustive catalog of modern gestures of transgression, which have widened in scope and appeal since the 1960s. For Hebdige, the birthmark of a subculture is its maverick use of "style":

> By repositioning and re-contextualizing commodities, by subverting their conventional uses and inventing new ones, the subcultural stylist . . . opens up the world of objects to new and covertly oppositional readings.[21]

But it is not, as *Subculture* suggests, merely in the excluded wings of societies that the bricoleur does his/her work, or at least it is not any longer. What the situationists held out as a populist revolutionary politics has now been turned into commerce, is a roaring success, a standardized format throughout the leading capitalist nations. We are now living in the society of the *détourniste*. Detournement has become axiomatic to profit-making, and like surrealism, a mass phenomenon. The cult of the displaced object has developed the contours of an industry in design, in clothing, in architecture, even food—in short, in every marketplace of postwar capitalism. Everything that was once made now reappears as a fragment in the hands of the *pasticheur*. What could not be converted into cash flow used to be expendable, but this problem has been solved: thanks to detournement, everything may stay in the stream of the economy, even the expendable. In France, one hears of *le rétro*, the dusting-off and rehabilitation of dead texts, dead commodities, dead forms in design, dead lifestyles. *Le rétro* is detournement as a bottom-line enterprise, a going concern. *Le rétro*, in a pleasant paradox, is easily recognized in the

21. Dick Hebdige, *Subculture: The Meaning of Style* (New York: Methuen, 1979), 102.

prefix "*neo-*." Neorealism, neoart deco, neogreaser, neo-1960s—soon it will be, no doubt, neo-Depression, neo-Navajo, neo-Eisenhower . . . , and there is plenty of room for more. This is not to say that the recycling of cultural elements no longer destabilizes institutions; it may still present a menace, at least in its most aggressive forms. On the other hand, a theorist of reification might have foreseen, in a kind of worst-case flash-forward, the assimilation of this explosive politics into a profitable venture, a recuperation that the situationists fiercely resisted.

How can one explain this gigantic spreading-out of detournement? To answer this question, we would do well to return to a traditional Marxist paradigm. It is necessary for capitalism to reproduce and extend itself, but this is not easily accomplished. In peacetime especially, the continuous expansion of production may pose a threat by overwhelming insufficient demand. At this point, the need for continued exchange (the only de jure axiom in capitalism: that one exchanges) arouses a search for other saleable items. The commodity form goes hunting. The marketplace throws open the doors of history to march out dead forms, so that production and consumption can once again be rejuvenated. This moment is the birth of Baudrillard's well-known simulacrum, the moment when reification and commodification meet and converge, where they had previously lived only in friendly solidarity.

One should not (as I have done just now) make a fairy tale out of these operations, which otherwise make up a highly rational, and today global, enterprise. On the other hand, the network of things under discussion here—the situationist project, the cult and the culture of the displaced object (of which detournement is merely a part), the cannibalization of history—this entire arrangement may be just the outside contour of a much larger historical process or curvature, a new social formation which is marked by the visibility of all things and by the conversion of all activity into gesture and into performance for the streamlining of exchange, an overall movement whose delirium Henri Lefebvre once sensed in "the consuming of displays, displays of consuming, consuming of displays of consuming, consuming of signs, signs of consuming." Consuming of signs of consuming.

GREGORY L. ULMER

# "A Night at the Text": Roland Barthes's Marx Brothers

ALLEGORY

Roland Barthes's approach to the gap separating the discourse of everyday life from specialized language was to enter discourse at still another level—to find a third manner of speaking capable of taking the other two into account. One of the principal tasks of my essay is to identify this alternative level, to describe the mode of entry that Barthes made possible, and to argue that it has special value for teachers.

In his search of a hybrid, "third" discourse, Barthes sometimes used artistic forms (literature, painting, music) not as objects of study in the conventional sense, but as allegories with cognitive significance. Contributing to the revalorization by modern critics of the notion of allegory,[1] Barthes tended, as his career progressed, to pay more and more attention to allegory and emblem. One of his strategies was to appropriate certain texts by the act of writing introductions or prefaces that designated them as emblems of his own concepts and concerns. The collages of Bernard Réquichot, who reworked preformed materials not as a realist would "in order to see better," but as a textualist, "in order to see something else," became, for example, according to Barthes, "the emblem of my own work now."[2]

One of the most important appropriations of this sort, in which Barthes "signed" the work of another artist, is the preface to the paintings of Arcimboldo. The innovation of Arcimboldo's portraits, Barthes said, is

---

1. See Walter Benjamin, *The Origin of German Tragic Drama*, trans. John Osborne (London: NLB, 1977). Paul de Man, *Allegories of Reading: Figural Language in Rousseau, Nietzsche, Rilke, and Proust* (New Haven, Yale University Press, 1979). On the relations among allegory, parody, and the pun (the principal modes of the method under discussion) see Lionel Duisit, *Satire, Parodie, Calembour: Esquisse d'une théorie des modes dévalués* (Saratoga, California: Anma Libri, 1978).

2. Roland Barthes, in *Bernard Réquichot* (Brussels: La Connaissance, 1973), 22, 29–30.

to devise for painting something similar to the double articulation of language (the point applies to the collage method in general, with Barthes's texts exemplifying one version of an adaptation of collage/montage writing to the critical essay): Arcimboldo's paintings function as if they were "written." "All is metaphor in Arcimboldo. Nothing is ever *denoted*, because the features (lines, forms, scrolls) which serve to compose a head have a sense already, and this sense is *détourné* toward another sense, thrown in a certain way beyond itself (that is what the word 'metaphor' means etymologically)."[3] (Detournement, as we shall see, is the central operation of the Situationists.)

Arcimboldo's portrait heads, once constructed, function allegorically, and model what Barthes meant by "third meanings." The heads are composed at the first level of sense out of "nameable things: fruit, flowers, branches, fish, plants, books, children, and so forth," which are in turn nameable (at the second level) as, on the one hand, "heads," and at the same time as something completely other—a third sense—from a different region of the lexicon: "Summer," "Winter," "Calvin," "Fire," and the like. The names for this third level of sense are derived from the viewer's general cultural codes: "I need a metonymic culture, which makes me associate certain fruits (and not others) with Summer, or, still more subtly, the austere hideousness of the visage of Calvinist puritanism: and as soon as one abandons the dictionary of words for a table of cultural meanings, of association of ideas, in short for an encyclopedia of received ideas, one enters into the infinite field of connotation" (*Arcimboldo*, 54–55).

Barthes's description of his own writing reflects an intellectual version of Arcimboldo's allegorical collages: "One could conceive *The Fashion System* as a poetic project, which consists precisely in constituting an intellectual object with nothing, or with very little, fabricating before the reader's eyes an intellectual object that develops gradually in its complexity, in the ensemble of its relations" (*Grain*, 67). What happens with the articles of clothing in *The Fashion System* is possible with any cultural object: "Where it is understood that the cultural object possesses, by its social nature, a sort of semantic vocation: in itself, the sign is quite ready to separate itself from the function and operate freely on its own, the function being reduced to the rank of artifice or alibi . . . it likewise favors the birth of more and more complex lexicons of objects" (*Fashion*, 265).

In principle, then, every object is available, capable of being separated from its original justification or context and remotivated as part of a new discourse. Thus the semiologue may draw on the encyclopedia of a society the same way a poet makes use of a dictionary. Barthes's lesson for the teacher or popularizer is a lesson in allegorical writing, in which

---

3. Roland Barthes, in *Arcimboldo* (Milan: F. M. Ricci, 1978), 37–38.

the elements of everyday life and of science may be introduced into a discourse to serve the ends of a third meaning, the nature of which was perhaps best characterized by Lacan as neither sense, nor common sense, but "jouis-sens" [bliss-sense]. What this bliss-sense teaches is the pleasure of the text, the love of learning, the subject's *desire* for knowledge.

The film or video camera makes it possible, in a sense, for anyone to be an Arcimboldo, that is, to write the objects of the world. The notion of film language, as it has been developed from Sergei Eisenstein to Stephen Heath (semioticians, opposed to realists such as Bazin who consider the film image as an analogon), involves a definition of meaning in which a photographed item (or recorded sound) is demotivated, stripped of its denotation, and remotivated, gaining its significance from its relationship with other elements in the film. What one receives in a film is not the world but a discourse on the world. We may discern in Barthes's allegorical procedure the model for an essayistic or pedagogical equivalent of filmic writing. Against the conventional pedagogy that attempts to *represent* the object of study in its discourse, an allegorical pedagogy works by *figuration*. "Similarly, and even more than the text, the film will *always* be figurative (which is why films are still worth making)—even if it represents nothing" (*Pleasure*, 56).

Barthes's best-known discussion of third meanings, in any case, concerns film stills. In the images from Eisenstein's *Ivan the Terrible* Barthes remarks not only an informational level and a symbolic level, but a third meaning, an "obtuse" meaning which "disturbs, sterilizes" metalanguage, because it is "discontinuous, indifferent to the story and to the obvious meaning (as the signification of the story)."[4] *Camera Lucida* develops the notion of the *punctum*, the wound, to work with the emotional nature of these third meanings. But the essay on Eisenstein offers several suggestions which are not pursued in the later book, but which may be equally useful for articulating that which inherently resists the naming process in the obtuse. Even though he is discussing images, Barthes indicates in a note that his third meanings have to do with the "vocal writing" mentioned in *The Pleasure of the Text*. Indeed, Barthes found that the best image for the level of writing that interested him was precisely the cinema: "A certain art of singing can give an idea of this vocal writing; but since melody is dead, we may find it more easily today at the cinema. In fact, it suffices that the cinema capture the sound of speech *close up* (this is, in fact, the generalized definition of the 'grain' of writing)" (*Pleasure*, 67). Barthes clarified the nature of this "close up" when he noted that "in the classical paradigm of the five senses, the third sense is hearing (first in importance in the Middle Ages). This is a happy coincidence, since what is here in question is indeed *listening*" (*Image*, 53).

---

4. Roland Barthes, *Image-Music-Text*, trans. Stephen Heath (New York: Hill and Wang, 1977), 61.

What one is supposed to listen for he suggests is something like the key names Saussure heard in Latin poetry. "The obtuse meaning is not situated structurally, a semantologist would not agree as to its objective existence (but then what is an objective reading?); and if to me it is clear (to me), that is *still* perhaps (for the moment) by the same 'aberration' which compelled the lone and unhappy Saussure to hear in ancient poetry the enigmatic voice of anagram, unoriginated and obsessive. . . . The obtuse meaning is a signifier without a signified, hence the difficulty in naming it" (*Image*, 60–61).

The clue here is that the obtuse meaning may be nameable if one listens in the right way, attending to the peculiar situation of the third sense: "I even accept for the obtuse meaning the word's pejorative connotation: the obtuse meaning appears to extend outside culture, knowledge, information; analytically it has something derisory about it: opening out into the infinity of language, it can come through as limited in the eyes of analytic reason; it belongs to the family of pun, buffoonery, useless expenditure. Indifferent to moral or aesthetic categories (the trivial, the futile, the false, the pastiche), it is on the side of the carnival" (*Image*, 55). This passage indicates first that the obtuse may be located, its operations identified, not only by the punctum of emotion, but also by the laughter associated with carnival. Barthes noted a model for this possibility in Bataille's approach to third meanings: "Bataille does not counter modesty with sexual freedom but . . . with *laughter*" (*Pleasure*, 55). The second point to be stressed in Barthes's notion of the obtuse as carnival is that the third meaning may be named *by means of the pun*. The pun is what one hears in the close-up of a film or text considered at the level of "vocal writing."[5]

## FROM "OPERA" TO TEXT

I want to turn to an elaboration of one particular example, to show the practical possibilities of Barthes's allegorical procedure. My point of departure is one of Barthes's own models: "*A Night at the Opera*—a work which I regard as allegorical of many a textual problem" (*Image*, 194). This Marx Brothers film, in other words, provides a model (in a humanities laboratory) for the difficult and controversial poststructuralist concept of "text." The immediate implication is that a teacher wishing to use textualist theory in a class might begin by showing *A Night at the Opera* to the students. Might we in this way begin to realize Brecht's goal

---

5. For a discussion of the notion of "inner speech" see Paul Willemen, "Cinematic Discourse—the Problem of Inner Speech," *Screen* 22 (1981). That Barthes discusses third meanings specifically in the context of Eisenstein, the principal experimenter with the possibilities of inner speech in filmic writing, suggests in itself the relevance of this notion to Barthes's thinking.

(to which Barthes frequently alluded) of integrating the realms of entertainment and intellect?

Barthes himself indicates what he has in mind with respect to this model in several asides alluding to *A Night at the Opera* as an emblem of Text, in which laughter replaces sentiment as the mark of the *punctum*.

> Emblem, gag. What a textual treasury, *A Night at the Opera!* If some critical demonstration requires an allegory in which the whole mechanics of the text-on-a-spree explodes, the film will provide it for me: the steamer cabin, the torn contract, the final chaos of opera decors—each of these episodes (among others) is the emblem of the logical subversions performed by the Text; and if these emblems are perfect, it is ultimately because they are comic, laughter being what, by a last reversal, releases demonstration from its demonstrative attribute. What liberates metaphor, symbol, emblem from poetic *mania*, what manifests its power of subversion, is the *preposterous*, that 'bewilderment' which Fourier was so good at getting into his examples, to the scorn of any theoretical respectability. The logical future of metaphor would therefore be the gag (*Barthes*, 80–81).

There are, then, at least two ways to model the operation of Text. One way, demonstrated in *Camera Lucida*, is by means of the sentiment generated by anecdotes told in association with one's family album, a level of narrative accessible to everyone.[6] The Marx Brothers' gags, of course, are equally accessible, although when it comes to his own practice (keeping in mind that the best response to a Text is another Text), Barthes never provided more than a few hints of how to operate in the dimension of the gag. The fragments of the film discussed by Barthes indicate that the aspect of Text emblematized most forcefully in *A Night at the Opera* has to do with the "fading of the subject." The "fading" refers to the current status of the problematic of the self—the shift away from a Cartesian to a Freudian notion of the person. In this context, *Camera Lucida* may be seen as a dramatic exploration of, a detournement of, the Oedipal problem.

In the Cartesian or "classical" conception, language is understood as "decoration or instrument, it is seen as a sort of parasite of the human subject, who uses it or dons it at a distance, like an ornament or tool picked up and laid down according to the needs of subjectivity or the conformities of sociality. However, another notion of writing is possible: neither decorative nor instrumental, i.e., in sum secondary but primal, antecedent to man, whom it traverses, founder of its acts like so many inscriptions" (*Sade*, 40). Barthes's own sympathy is with the "modern" understanding: "He wants to side with any writing whose principle is that the subject is merely an effect of language" (*Barthes*, 79). In the

---

6. See Mary Louise Pratt, *Toward a Speech Act Theory of Literary Discourse* (Bloomington, Indiana: Indiana University Press, 1977).

classic work the origin of the speaker is assigned to a consciousness (an author or character) or to a culture (a code). But even in a *work* the utterance may become pluralized, indeterminate: "the voice gets lost, as though it had leaked out through a hole in the discourse. The best way to conceive the classical plural is then to listen to the text as an iridescent exchange carried on by multiple voices, on different wavelengths and subject from time to time to a sudden *dissolve,* leaving a gap which enables the utterance to shift from one point of view to another without warning."[7]

Barthes finds in *A Night at the Opera* two scenes that teach this lesson "in a burlesque mode." One of the scenes emblematizes his own experience of the fading of the subject in the act of lecturing to a class:

> In the *exposé*, more aptly named than we tend to think, it is not knowledge which is exposed, it is the subject. The mirror is empty, reflecting back to me no more than the falling away of my language as it gradually unrolls. Like the Marx Brothers disguised as Russian airmen (in *A Night at the Opera*—a work which I regard as allegorical of many a textual problem), I am, at the beginning of my exposé, rigged out with a large false beard which, drenched little by little with the flood of my own words (a substitute for the jug of water from which the *Mute,* Harpo, guzzles away on the Mayor of New York's rostrum), I then feel coming unstuck piecemeal in front of everybody. [*Image,* 194]

The other scene (part of the performance of *Il Trovatore* enacted during the film) is the one in which the stage backdrops rise and fall (marking Harpo's Tarzan-like progress swinging from rope to rope above the stage, working its machinery haphazardly) during the villain Lassparri's solo: "This hubbub is crammed with emblems: the absence of background replaced by the rolling plural of sets, the codage of contexts (issue of the opera's repertoire) and their derision, the delirious polysemy, and finally the illusion of the subject, singing its imaginary while the other (the spectator) watches and who believes to be speaking backed by a unique world (a set: a complete scene of the plural which derides the subject: *dissociates* it)" (*Grain,* 111–12).

One reason why a Marx Brothers farce is a perfect emblem for the fading of the subject, for the "death of the author," has to do with the pun available in "gag" (cf. "joke" and "choke") for naming the allegorical meaning of a Marx Brothers routine. "Gag," that is, is one of those "amphibologies" that Barthes found so appealing.

> Each time he encounters one of these double words, R.B., on the contrary, insists on keeping both meanings, as if one were winking at the other and as if the word's meaning were in that wink, so that *one and the same word,* in *one and the same sentence,* means *at one and the*

---

7. Roland Barthes, *S/Z,* trans. Richard Miller (New York: Hill and Wang, 1974), 41–42.

*same time* two different things, and so that one delights, semantically, in the one by the other. This is why such words are often said to be 'preciously ambiguous': not in their lexical essence (for any word in the lexicon has several meanings), but because, by a kind of *luck*, a kind of favor not of language but of discourse, I can *actualize* their amphibology. [*Barthes*, 72]

The gags in *Night at the Opera*, then, allegorize the other gag, the gagging or choking associated with the experience of the body of desire, revealed when the subject fades or dissolves. At one level the gag is provoked by the "writing machine," with the writer's desire for certain fetish words, certain binary oppositions such as "metaphor/metonymy" that provide one with "the power of saying something": "Hence the work proceeds by conceptual infatuations, successive enthusiasms, perishable manias. Discourse advances by little fates, by amorous fits. (The cunning of language: in French the word for this infatuation is *engouement*, which means an *obstruction*: the word remains in the throat, for a certain interval)" (*Barthes*, 110).

At another level, however, the gag remarks the *disgust* experienced in the disgorging or exorcism of one's own image-repertoire (the "stupidities" of one's habits, of one's ideology): "How to question my disgust (the disgust for my own failures)? How to prepare the best reading of my self I can hope for: not to love but only to *endure tasting* what has been written?" (*Barthes*, 110–11). To work at the level of desire is to expose repulsion as well as attraction, disgust as well as pleasure, with the bliss of *jouissance* being a painful or sublime transgression of simple likes and dislikes. Against the stereotype, which is discourse "without body," the "grain" of the voice introduces the problem of judgment, of value, of taste, at the level of the inner body, emblematized for Barthes by Réquichot's collages and reliquaries (boxes representing open torsos displaying the magma of the body). Réquichot's interest in repugnance, Barthes states, resembles de Sade's, for whom "the body begins to exist there where it is revolted, disgusted, yet wanting to devour what disgusts it" (*Réquichot*, 13). Laughter, perhaps, is the only available name for the third sense of the obtuse body.[8]

An allegorical reading of the film, then, names the obtuse meanings of Text by exploiting the amphibologies of certain key words. Another such pun is available in *A Night at the Opera*, emblematizing perhaps the principal element of textuality—the sliding of the signifier under the signified, the infinite skid of meaning which replaces "signification" with "significance." If the "gag" as such emblematizes the "fading of the subject" in textuality, the specific content of the *Trovatore* sequence in *A*

---

8. Jacques Derrida, in a discussion of Kant's third *Critique*, concerning the taste and distaste of judgment, evokes the "gag" (the *vomi*) as a limit-concept transgressing the classical paradigm. See, "Economimesis," trans. Richard Klein, *Diacritics* 11 (1981).

*Night at the Opera* emblematizes the textualist sliding of the signifier: "To decondition us of all the philosophies (or theologies) of the signified, that is, of the Arrest, since we others, 'literaries', we lack any sovereign formalisms, that of mathematics, we must employ as many metaphors as possible, for the metaphor is a means of access to the signifier; lacking an algorithm, that which could discharge the signified, especially if one could manage to disoriginate it [the metaphor]. Today I propose this: the scene of the world (the world as stage) is occupied by a play of 'sets' (of texts): raise one, another appears behind it and so forth" (*Grain*, 111). The play of the "sets" or stage backdrops, as a metaphor, replace the algorithms of mathematics (set theory, for example) used in the sciences.

If we keep in mind that "opera" literally means "work," we may see that *A Night at the Opera* demonstrates the passage form "work" to "text" in the way that it *traverses* the classical opera *Il Trovatore*, by Verdi; that it shows something similar to what Barthes argues in the essay "From Work to Text": "The Text is experienced only in an activity, a production. It follows that the Text cannot stop, at the end of a library shelf, for example; the constitutive movement of the Text is a *traversal*: it can cut across a work, several works. . . . What constitutes the Text is, on the contrary (or precisely), its subversive force with regard to old classifications. . . . Whereas the Text is approached and experienced in relation to the sign, the work closes itself on a signified. . . . The Text practices the infinite deferral of the signified: The Text is *dilatory*; its field is that of the signifier."[9] The two scenes from the Opera actually performed in the film are indeed two of the most famous moments in the repertoire—the "Anvil Chorus" and the "Miserere." As one commentator put it, "*Trovatore* succeeds too well. Its melodies have been played and sung in every conceivable arrangement until their spontaneity has largely been worn away. Particularly is this true of the remarkable ensemble known as the 'Miserere', really a most telling piece of dramatic music, but heard so often, that if we do not pause to give it thought we are likely not to appreciate fully its excellent qualities."[10]

A brief plot summary is needed to reveal the emblematic gag in these scenes. The "traversal" of *Il Trovatore* begins in the second act, when Fiorello (Chico) and Tomasso (Harpo) invade the orchestra pit, inserting the sheet music for "Take me out to the ball game" into the scores on the music stands, a substitution overlooked in the distraction provided by their "refunctioning" of some of the instruments (sword fight with violin bows). The music begins, shifting suddenly, with the turning of a page, from Verdi to "Take me out to the ball game," a signal for Chico and

---

9. Roland Barthes, "From Work to Text," in Josué Harari, ed., *Textual Strategies: Perspectives in Post-Structuralist Criticism* (Ithaca: Cornell University Press, 1979), 75–76.

10. Charles O'Connell, ed., *The Victor Book of the Opera* (Camden: RCA Manufacturing Co., Inc., 1936), 509.

46  *Yale French Studies*

Harpo to produce a ball and gloves and play catch while Groucho sells peanuts.

To evade the Opera Director, Gottlieb, and the policemen sent to arrest them, Chico and Harpo move onto the stage, mingling with the actors, costumed as Gypsies, performing the "Anvil Chorus" ("Who cheers the life of the roving gypsy?/ The gypsy maiden! The gypsy maiden!"). A constrained chase scene follows, mixing the plot of the film with the plot of the Opera, leading to the hubbub of rising and descending decors to which Barthes referred. Gottlieb and the detective Henderson don costumes and join the scene themselves, hoping to disturb the action as little as possible. As Lassparri sings the effect of the chase is registered in the changing sets—the Gypsy camp is replaced first by a forest scene, then a railroad, a fruit wagon, the Battleship Potemkin, and so on.

The motivation within the film for the disruption of the performance has to do with the attempt by the Brothers to force the Director to give the leading role to their friend Baroni, a talented but young and unknown tenor, in place of the famous Lassparri, hired by Gottlieb. At the beginning of the film Groucho's plan to exploit Mrs. Claypool (Margaret Dumont), playing on her desire to enter high society by promising to arrange for her to be a sponsor for the New York Opera Company, is threatened by Gottlieb who secures her agreement to fund the hiring of Lassparri, reputed to be the "world's greatest tenor." Groucho, impressed by Lassparri's fee ($1,000 a night) and wanting a piece of the action, makes a deal with Chic, Baroni's agent, to sign Baroni for ten dollars a night, the remainder of the nightly fee put up by Mrs. Claypool to be split by the agents ("we are entitled to a small profit"). The invasion of the stage during the performance of *Il Trovatore* (near the conclusion of the film) is the final strategy to get Baroni into the leading role for which Lassparri has been hired. The Marx Brothers refuse to quit the stage until Lassparri is dismissed and Baroni hired to take over the part of "Manrico."

The allegorical significance of the *Trovatore* sequence is signalled by the pun available in the word "tenor." Chico, Harpo, and Groucho may be read as *personifications* of the signifier (their antics represent the "field of play" mentioned in the definition of Text). This "signifier," of course, may be translated into the rhetorical terminology of Ogden and Richards (*The Meaning of Meaning* being more or less contemporary with *A Night at the Opera*), who classified the parts of a metaphor as "vehicle" and "tenor" (comparable to "signifier" and "signified"). The Marx Brothers, that is, are the agents or vehicles (signifiers) "representing" the *tenor* (signified) Baroni. Their disruption of the performance, substituting one tenor for the other (forcing Gottlieb to substitute Baroni for Lassparri in the middle of the Opera), is an allegory of the sliding of the signifier constitutive of Text. Here is the scene of displacement:

STAGE MANAGER: Herr Gottlieb! Lassparri's disappeared.
GOTTLIEB: What?

(Gypsy Woman Onstage): *She's confused, trying to figure out what happened to* Lassparri.
(Tomasso /Harpo/): *In the wings, he pulls on a rope which hoists* Lassparri *upward in a piece of scenery, a scenery box.*
(Conductor): *He* taps *his baton in a futile attempt to regain order.*
(Stage Manager and Gottlieb in the Wings):
GOTTLIEB: But we haven't even a tenor![11]

The gag, for which this entire article is but a frame, depends on the amphibology in "tenor," at once "singer" and "signified," with "sing" being the anagram of sign.

I have noted that the allegorical reading of *A Night at the Opera* is directed by two puns—*gag*, which names the fading of the subject and the emergence of the body of desire; and *tenor*, associated with the sliding of the signified (displacement), the Marx Brothers personifying the drive of the signifier. That Barthes would prefer *A Night at the Opera* to one of the other Marx Brothers films must be due in part to the operatic element, the same theme informing "Sarrasine," the story analyzed in *S/Z*. Such patterns refer finally to Barthes as subject, to his idiolect. Suffice it to say here that the musical score as such served Barthes as a metaphor for the interaction of the codes or "voices" of the Text, with the readerly or classic work being compared to tonal music, and the writerly or modern Text being compared to atonal, serial music. More specifically, Italian opera is charged for Barthes with sexual connotation, associated with the theme of castration: "Italian music, an object well defined historically, culturally, mythically (Rousseau, Gluckists-and-Piccinists, Stendhal, etc.), connotes a "sensual" art, an art of the voice. An erotic substance, the Italian voice was produced *a contrario* (according to a strictly symbolic inversion) by singers without sex" (*S/Z*, 109–10).

Barthes selected "Sarrasine" as a tutor-text because it possessed that double structure he required for his allegories, defined as "double" work, "a work apparently naive and in fact very cunning, as would be the story of a battle made conjointly and with a single voice by Stendhal's Fabrice and General Clausewitz" (*Grain*, 51). The intertextual analysis of codes reveals how this double form occurs in "Sarrasine": the hermeneutic code, conveying the story of the castrato, Zambinella, manifests literally the symbolic code (involving the psychoanalytic, Lacanian theory of the entry into language figured in the Oedipal stage and the castration complex). The discourse mixes two codes: "Of these two codes, simultaneously referred to in the same words (the same signifier)," it is impossible to decide which one has priority, which one determines the meaning of the other. "Tenor" functions in *A Night at the Opera* in the same way that "castration" functions in "Sarrasine," as an amphibology joining two codes (the codes being in this instance the action code and the

---

11. The screenplay is published by Viking (New York, 1972).

48  *Yale French Studies*

cultural code). The principle for using a story as an emblem for a theoretical concept is, then, an extension of Barthes's metaphorical approach, with the "double" structure of an exemplary work being achieved by the projection of any one of the vertical codes (semic—the voice of the person; cultural—the voice of science as received knowledge; symbolic) onto either of the horizontal codes (action, hermeneutic), based on Jakobson's notion of poetry as the projection of the paradigm onto the syntagm. "Just as a successful metaphor affords, between its terms, no hierarchy and removes all hindrances from the polysemic chain (in contrast to the comparison, an originated figure), so a 'good' narrative fulfills both the plurality and the circularity of the codes" (*S/Z*, 77).

The peculiar effect of such conjunctions distinguishes Barthes's allegorical procedure from that of "illustration," "demonstration," and the like.

> To make *being-castrated*, an anecdotal condition, coincide with *castration*, a symbolic structure, is the task successfully carried out by the performer (Balzac), since the former does not necessarily entail the latter.... This success hinges on a structural artifice: identifying the symbolic and the hermeneutic, making the search for truth (hermeneutic structure) into the search for castration (symbolic structure), making the truth be *anecdotally* (and no longer symbolically) the absent phallus.... Which accounts for this story's perhaps unique value: "illustrating" castration by being-castrated, like with like, it mocks the notion of illustration, it abolishes both sides of the equivalence (letter and symbol) without advantage to either one; the latent here occupies the line of the manifest from the start, the sign is flattened out: there is no longer any "representation." [*S/Z*, 163–64]

*A Night at the Opera* includes this same flattening, such that it functions not as a sign but as a catachresis. Barthes avoids the logocentric trap of representation—the charge Derrida brought against Lacan when the latter used Poe's "Purloined Letter" to teach the truth of psychoanalysis—by stressing that his allegories are obtuse, structured not representationally as signs but as metaphors, metaphors that do not refer to preestablished truths, but themselves constitute the *significance* of Barthes's own Text. His discourse, that is, is composed not as metalanguage but as Text. "*Let the commentary be itself a text:* that is, in brief, what the theory of the text demands. The subject of the analysis (the critic, the philologist, the scholar) cannot in fact, without bad faith and smugness, believe he is external to the language he is describing."[12] It is this relation of the writer to the text that results in third meanings, whose sense finally is the subject of knowledge. "We can put it still more precisely,"

---

12. Barthes, "Theory of the Text," in Robert Young, ed., *Untying the Text: A Post-Structuralist Reader* (Boston: Routledge and Kegan, 1981), 44.

Barthes adds: "from its very principles, the theory of the text can produce only theoreticians or practitioners (writers), but absolutely not 'specialists' (critics or teachers); as a practice, then, it participates itself in the subversion of the genres which as a theory it studies" (*Untying*, 44).

One conclusion might be that in order to teach textually one must be a Situationist.

## A SITUATIONIST PEDAGOGY

The caveat that must accompany this discussion is that there is no situationism, according to the situationists, who condemned as recuperation any attempt to learn from them by people not officially recognized as "situationist." They were right, of course, given their rejection of the institutions of bourgeois culture. In this respect the situationists reflect the arrogance of militancy for which Barthes sought an alternative. This militancy may be observed in the hyperbolic tone with which they scorned the intellectuals of Europe, including Barthes himself:

> In the present cultural and social crisis those who do not know how to use intelligence have in fact no discernible intelligence of any kind. Stop talking to us about unused intelligence and you'll make us happy. Poor Heidegger! Poor Lukács! Poor Sartre! Poor Barthes! Poor Lefebvre! Poor Cardan! Tics, tics, and tics. Without the method for using intelligence, they have nothing but caricatural fragments of the innovating ideas that can truly comprehend the totality of our epoch in the same movement that they contest it.[13]

This condemnation includes not only prominent "former thinkers," but all academics, all those hopelessly ensnared in the specialization that makes the present educational apparatus dysfunctional. "It is only the specialists, whose power is geared to a society of specialization, who have abandoned the *critical* truth of their disciplines in order to preserve the personal advantage of their *function*" (*Situationist*, 85). Barthes and the other "former thinkers,"

> are not only incapable of developing ideas, they don't even know how to skillfully plagiarize ideas developed by others. Once the specialized thinkers step out of their own domain, they can only be the dumbfounded spectators of some neighboring and equally bankrupt specialization which they are ignorant of but which has become fashionable. . . . All the specializations of illusion can be taught and discussed by the tenured thinkers. But the situationists take their stand in the

---

13. Ken Knabb, ed., *Situationist International Anthology* (Berkeley: Bureau of Public Secrets, 1981), 137.

knowledge that is outside this spectacle: we are not thinkers sponsored by the state." [*Situationist*, 137][14]

The situationist attitude toward academics provides a glimpse of the way in which the problematics of pedagogy and of popularization converge.

> The lecture, the exposition of certain intellectual considerations to an audience, being an extremely commonplace form of human relations in a rather large sector of society, itself forms a part of the everyday life that must be criticized. Sociologists, for example, are only too inclined to remove from everyday life things that happen to them every day, and to transfer them to separated and supposedly superior spheres. In this way habit in all its forms—beginning with the habit of handling a few *professional* concepts (concepts produced by the division of labor)—masks reality behind privileged conventions. It is thus desirable to demonstrate, by a slight alteration of the usual procedure [the lecture is being delivered by a tape recording rather than by a person], that everyday life is right here. [*Situationist*, 68]

The situationist remedy for the cretinism they find rampant in the universities (causing them to "condemn all the ado of the lecture halls and classrooms as mere *noise*, verbal pollution"), is their own version of popularization, a merger of intellectual and life activities the goal of which is not so much to create a dialogue between discredited academics and "white-collar sheep," but to transform daily life itself (including the classroom). Before reviewing the principal technique of their program, I should note that if the modality in which the situationists pose their suggestions were altered, if the "apocalyptic" tone were removed, we would be left with a program of great interest for anyone concerned with the potentials of a postmodernized pedagogy. The combative, sarcastic tone of situationist writing is specific to the genre of the manifesto, characteristic of the terrorist postures of much European intellectual politics. However much I enjoy the hyperbole of that style, I also believe that this tone is not translatable into, is irrelevant to, the American intellectual scene. But the situationists can teach us something about the psychogeography of the academy: the situation to be constructed is the environment of the university.

The first principle of this program is termed the "realization of art," and concerns our relationship to our traditional object of study (literature and the arts), which will no longer be contemplative but active. The traditional "speculative" approach to learning in the university, that is, marks the complicity of education with the society of the spectacle in

---

14. Cf. Derrida's critique of the State's role in education in "Otobiographie de Nietzsche," in *L'Oreille de l'autre: Textes et débats avec Jacques Derrida*, ed. Claude Lévesque, Cristie V. McDonald (Montréal: V.L.B. Editeur, 1982).

which the *appearance* of education replaces the reality, in which the pursuit of degrees, the accumulation of credentials, take priority over a direct engagement with the learning process. "The spectacle presents itself as an enormous unutterable and inaccessible actuality. It says nothing more than 'that which appears is good, that which is good appears'. The attitude which it demands in principle is this passive acceptance, which in fact it has already obtained by its manner of appearing without reply, but its monopoly of appearance."[15] Since the spectacle "is the opposite of dialogue," situationists begin by replying to the spectacle.

The only means available for this dialogue, however, may be loosely described as "deconstructive" (there is no position outside the spectacle). "When analyzing the spectacle one speaks, to some extent, the language of the spectacle itself in the sense that one moves across the methodological terrain of the society which expresses itself in the spectacle" (Debord, no. 11). "In its very style, the exposition of dialectical theory is a scandal and an abomination in terms of the rules of the dominant language and for the taste which they have educated, because in the positive use of existing concepts it at the same time includes the knowledge of their rediscovered *fluidity*, of their necessary destruction" (Debord, no. 205).

The approach to teaching this dialectic, this response to the spectacle, will not be that of orthodox Marxism, since that ideology "rediscovers the confidence in pedagogical demonstrations which had characterized utopian socialism, but nixes it with a *contemplative* reference to the course of history" (Debord, no. 95). Debord and the situationists, that is, believe that modern events have refuted the original Marxist goal of rendering the workers theoreticians (Debord, no. 97). Hence, they propose an alternative approach to an education for revolution: "Our practical conclusion is the following: we are abandoning all efforts at pedagogical action and moving toward experimental activity" (*Situationist*, 17). Moreover, the goal will be not to make the people philosophers, but artists. "Thus, just as in the first half of the nineteenth century revolutionary theory arose out of philosophy (out of critical reflection on philosophy, out of the crisis and death of philosophy), so now it is going to rise again out of modern art—out of poetry—out of its suppression, out of what modern art has sought and *provided*, out of the clean sweep it has made of all the values and rules of everyday behavior" (*Situationist*, 106).

Poetry, then, the quintessential object of study in the humanities establishment, becomes the material of revolution. The poets admired by the situationists, however, are by and large dadaist and surrealist, and they conceive of poetry in a way quite alien to the tenured thinkers, a transformation identified as the *realization* of art, synonymous with the "overcoming of art." (Debord, no. 191). This realization essentially car-

---

15. Guy Debord, *Society of the Spectacle* (Detroit: Red and Black, 1970), no. 12.

ries over into performance, into action, the "insubordination of words" ("words embody forces that can upset the most careful calculations") which poets "from Baudelaire to the dadaists to Joyce" were largely content to confine to literature:

> Whereas surrealism in the heyday of its assault against the oppressive order of culture and daily life could rightly define its arsenal as 'poetry without poems if necessary,' it is now a matter for the SI of a poetry *necessarily* without poems. . . . Realizing poetry means nothing less than simultaneously and inseparably creating events and their language. . . . The same judgment leads us to announce the total disappearance of poetry in the old forms in which it was produced and consumed and to announce its return in effective and unexpected forms. Our era no longer has to *write out poetic orders;* it has to carry them out (*Situationist,* 115, 116).

Or, to put it another way, "Since understanding resides in praxis alone, one can really comprehend the nature of the enemy only in the process of fighting it . . . of introducing the *aggressivity of the delinquent onto the plane of ideas*" (*Situationist,* 87). The principal device, indeed *the* device, of this insubordination or delinquency is "detournement," the situationist "signature." Past, preexisting art in this operation (a version of collage/montage) is not abandoned but reused, refunctioned. "The two fundamental laws of detournement are the loss of importance of each *détourné* autonomous element—which may go so far as to lose its original sense completely—and at the same time the organization of another meaningful ensemble that confers on each element its new scope and effect. . . . Detournement is thus first of all negation of the value of the previous organization of expression" (*Situationist,* 55).

The laws for the use of detournement are: 1) "It is the most distant detourned element which contributes most sharply to the overall impression, and not the elements that directly determine the nature of the impression"; 2) "The distortions introduced in the detourned elements must be as simplified as possible, since the main force of a detournement is directly related to the conscious or vague recollection of the original contexts of the elements"; 3) "Detournement is less effective the more it approaches a rational reply"; 4) Detournement by simple reversal is always the most direct and the least effective" (*Situationist,* 10–11).

Techniques and examples include "experimentation in the detournement of romantic photo-comics as well as of 'pornographic' photos, and that we bluntly impose their real truth by restoring real dialogues by adding or altering speech bubbles. . . . In the same spirit, it is also possible to detourn *any* advertising billboards—particularly those in subway corridors, which form remarkable sequences—by pasting over pre-prepared placards" (*Situationist,* 213–14). Their suggestions for the use of "guerrilla tactics" in the mass media included everything from taking over an electronic newspaper in order to broadcast one's own slogans or other messages, to issuing counterfeit copies of a periodical. But of all the possibilities discussed, "it is obviously in the realm of the cinema that detournement can attain its greatest efficacity" (*Situationist*, 12). Examples include adding to Griffith's *Birth of a Nation* "a soundtrack that made a powerful denunciation of the horrors of imperialist war and of the activities of the Ku Klux Klan." Old historical epics could be reedited, and history rewritten, to "have Robespierre say, before his execution," for example, " 'in spite of so many trials, my experience and the grandeur of my task convinces me that all is well.' " Or, conversely, "a neorealist sort of sequence, at the counter of a truckstop bar, for example, with one of the truckdrivers saying seriously to another: 'Ethics was in the books of the philosophers; we have introduced it into the governing of nations' " (alluding to the "idea of a dictatorship of the proletariat").[16]

The situationist approach to the collage/montage form foregrounds the parodic tone inherent in the refunctioning strategy. What remains to be seen is whether a new pedagogy might not benefit from the situationist experience, might bring to bear on the everyday life of the university the same critique the situationists applied to the culture as a whole at the level of the mass media.[17] It should not be forgotten that the situationist call for "all power to the imagination" provided the principal slogan for the May '68 student rebellion. It is possible now, in the 1980s, to benefit from the lessons of those years, from the successes and the abuses alike, to recover some of the dynamics of change and innovation manifested in the troubles of the late sixties and early seventies, now nearly forgotten even though that generation of students now staffs the academy. Barthes was sensitive to the opportunities or new possibilities offered to teachers even in the failures of May '68. "May '68 has revealed the crisis of our teaching. The old values are no longer transmitted, no longer circulate, no longer impress; literature is desacralized, institutions are impotent to defend and impose it as the implicit model of the human. . . . Literary semiology is, as it were, that journey which lands us in a country free by default. . . . It is a moment at once decadent and prophetic, a moment of gentle apocalypse, a historical moment of the greatest possible pleasure."[18]

16. The situationists allude to Eisenstein's plan to make a film of Marx's *Capital* as a model for their own emphasis on the film medium. While a theoretical analysis of ideology is inaccessible to the layman, the same analysis, if filmed, "would become much less complicated." "I am confident that I could film *The Decline and Fall of the Spectacle-Commodity Economy* in a way that would be immediately understandable to the proletarians of Watts who are ignorant of the concepts implied in that title" (*Situationist*, 215).

17. One recent sign that the time has come to reconsider the lessons of the sixties is, *The '60s Without Apology*, ed. Sohnya Sayres et al. (Minneapolis: University of Minnesota Press, 1984).

18. Roland Barthes, "Lecture in Inauguration of the Chair of Literary Semiology, Collège de France," trans. Richard Howard, *October* 8 (1979): 14.

If we take Barthes seriously when he says that "writing makes knowledge festive" ("Lecture," 7), we may begin to appreciate the similarities relating a textualist with a situationist pedagogy. The link is not only that Barthes opposed specialization, calling for the revalorization of the status of the "amateur" against the confinement of writing to "a caste of technicians" ("Text," 42), but that he sympathized with the parodic mode of detournement.[19]

> The revolutionary task of writing is not to evict but to transgress. Now, to transgress is at once to recognize and to invert; it is necessary to present the object to be destroyed and at the same time to negate it; writing is precisely that which permits this logical contradiction. . . . Only an 'inverted' writing, presenting at once the correct language and its contestation (let us say, in short, its parody), can be revolutionary." [*Grain*, 49]

In the fragment entitled "Play, parody," Barthes noted that the only parody he ever wrote was of Plato's *Crito*, done when he was a student, "though he often wanted to" (*Barthes*, 142). His plan for the "perfect book," thus, reflects the double structure of parody: "A book of learning and of writing, at once a perfect system and the mockery of all systems, a summa of intelligence and of pleasure, a vengeful and tender book, corrosive and pacific" (*Barthes*, 173). Barthes's textuality in principle shares the disrespectful, devaluing mode of parody: "The text is (should be) that uninhibited person who shows his behind to the *Political Father*" (*Pleasure*, 53). This disrespectfulness marks the politics of Text: "I would say that etymologically, yes, I try to subvert. That is to say I come beneath a conformism, beneath a fashion of thinking that exists and to displace it a bit. No revolution, no, but to hedge things a little. To unthicken them. To render them more mobile. To introduce a doubt. Thus, always to unsettle the supposedly natural, the installed thing" (*Grain*, 268).

Parody is a desirable mode to work in because meaning and mythologies cannot be confronted directly, frontally. Textual subversion "must still be done with the appearance of communication, since the social, historical conditions for a liberation of language (in relation to the signifieds, to the *property* of discourse) are nowhere yet in place. Hence

---

19. Barthes's sympathy with the situationist attack on the society of the spectacle may be seen in this remark: "This very important theme at the level of practice I convert to theory, to the degree that I am able to imagine a society to come, totally disalienated, which, on the level of writing, would know nothing but the amateur's activities. Notably in the order of the text. People would write, make texts, for pleasure, would profit from the bliss of writing without worrying about the image they might rouse in someone else. . . . But there one encounters a problem of civilization. The technical development, the development of mass culture accentuates terribly the divorce between doers and consumers. We are a society of consumption, if I dare say so, playing on the stereotype, and not at all a society of amateurs" (*Grain*, 205). Barthes's notion of the amateur, putting the person in contact with the production of texts, has important implications for pedagogy.

the present importance of the theoretical (directive) concepts of paragram, plagiarism, intertextuality, false readability" (*Grain*, 114–15). The goal of textuality, however, is not to win the war of discourse, but to escape from it, or to neutralize it. "A ruthless *topic* rules the life of language; language always comes from someplace, it is a warrior *topos*" (*Pleasure*, 28). Against this *topos*, the text scandalizes by attempting to be *atopic*: "It is not a jargon, a fiction, in it the system is overcome, undone (this overcoming, this defection, is signification). From this atopia the text catches and communicates to its reader a strange condition: at once excluded and at peace. There can be tranquil moments in the war of languages, and these moments are texts" (*Pleasure*, 29).

Here we begin to see more precisely the nature of the position Barthes defined alternative to the opposition between doxa and science: "The Neutral is therefore not the third term—the zero degree—of an opposition which is both semantic and conflictual; it is, *at another link of the infinite chain of language*, the second term of a new paradigm, of which violence (combat, victory, theater, arrogance) is the primary term" (*Barthes*, 132). Three strategies are mentioned by which the text gets out of the war of sociolects: "First, the text liquidates all metalanguage, whereby it is text.... Next, the text destroys utterly, to the point of contradiction, its own discursive category, its sociolinguistic reference (its 'genre'): it is 'the comical that does not make us laugh', the irony which does not subjugate.... Lastly, the text can, if it wants, attack the canonical structure of the language itself" (*Pleasure*, 30–31).

In these strategies, particularly in the second one (the comical that does not make us laugh) we find the key to the status of parody or detournement as a textualist device. The problem with irony or parody as traditionally understood is that it involves an *explicit* quotation, necessarily *signals* the source of its allusion, and hence reduces its multivalence. Barthes insists on the necessity of abolishing these quotation marks: "The wall of voices must be passed through to reach the writing: this latter eschews any designation of ownership and thus can never be *ironic*.... What could a parody be that did not advertise itself as such? This is the problem facing modern writing: how to breach the wall of utterance, the wall of origin, the wall of ownership?" (*S/Z*, 45).

To identify the parodic potential of Barthes's writerly mode reveals the versatility of the double-collapsed, allegorical texts that Barthes sought out in the canon ("Sarrasine," "The Case of M. Valdemar," "The Sorrows of Young Werther," and even *A Night at the Opera*). Even if Barthes's own sensibility was, finally, melancholic, exploring the profundities of love and death, he also directed us to another side of his operation, the parodic dimension, in which laughter organizes the effect of third meanings. Part of the interest of this other side of the double inscription is that it opens an alternative operation with which to apply Barthes's lessons to critical writing and to the classroom.

56  Yale French Studies

The situationists provide the clue indicating how Barthes's project to breach the wall of ownership might be "realized," keeping in mind the amphibology in "proper" (property and propriety), by suggesting a style of *improper* behavior. The essence of *their* lesson is the introduction of "carnival" ("metaphorical revolution") into academics as an antidote to alienation. We may see in this context that, when the situationists argued that Marxism itself needed to be detourned (*Situationist,* 171), the Marx *Brothers* provide at least an allegory for this detournement (recalling that the Yippees were said to be Groucho-Marxists). The situationists claimed that their strategy of a *realized* poetry represented "a new kind of humor," one which had to be taken "literally and seriously." The structure of comedy without the laugh might refer, then, to the detournement of parody to other ends, to the politics of pedagogy, for example.

The formation of a new pedagogy, based on textuality and the situationist experience, will require taking seriously the program of a realized art and the practice of detournement. Again, *A Night at the Opera* provides the model for such a project, *in a realized form*. The point would be not simply to watch the film and discuss its allegorical possibilities, but to adopt its operations as an experimental performance activity, detourning other "works" the way Verdi's Work (Opera) was detourned in the film. The wall of utterance will be broken, thus, because one would not refer to the Marx Brothers' one would perform them without quotation marx (idea for a situationist film: the life of Karl Marx with the leading role acted in the manner of Groucho). And what the Marx Brothers show us is that the third meaning, neither common sense nor science, is *nonsense,* the nonsense of the gag that subverts the rule of usage. That nonsense may be the best modality for teaching (at least for a teaching made festive) has been known since ancient times. "All the sources of arguments," Quintillian noted, "can also furnish jokes."[20]

Let the playfulness of the Marx Brothers' relationship with language and objects serve as an emblem for what teachers may do to *realize* the classroom as Text. And let Groucho, in his role as Professor Quincy Adams Wagstaff, shown at the beginning of *Horsefeathers* being welcomed as incoming President of Huxley College, serve as a model for the administrators textualist teachers will need: "Members of the faculty,

---

20. Lucie Olbrechts-Tyteca, *Le Comique du discours* (Brussels: Editions de l'University de Bruxelles, 1974), 24. Cf. Susan Stewart, *Nonsense: Aspects of Intertextuality in Folklore and Literature* (Baltimore: Johns Hopkins University Press, 1978), 206. The whole of Stewart's excellent study provides a major argument for the development of pedagogical nonsense. Cf. Wendy Steiner, *The Colors of Rhetoric: Problems in the Relation between Modern Literature and Painting* (Chicago: University of Chicago Press, 1982). For discussions of parody as the predominant mode of our paradigm, see Margaret A. Rose, *Parody/Meta-fiction* (London: Croom Helm, 1979), and Claude Bouché, *Lautréamont: du lieu commun à la parodie* (Paris: Larousse, 1974). Cf. Theodor Verweyen, Gunther Witting, *Die Parodie in der Neueren Deutschen Literatur: Eine Systematische Einführung* (Darmstadt: Wissenschäftliche Buchges, 1979).

faculty members; students of Huxley and Huxley students," Wagstaff says in his address. "I guess that covers everything. Well, I thought my razor was dull until I heard this speech, and that reminds me of a story that's so dirty I'm ashamed to think of it myself. As I look out over your eager faces I can readily understand why this college is flat on its back. The last college I presided over things were slightly different. I was flat on my back. Things kept going from bad to worse, but we all put our shoulders to the wheel, and it wasn't long before I was flat on my back again. Any questions? Any answers? Any rags, any bones, any bottles today?"[21] Of course, some would say that we have such administrators already; so what are we waiting for?

21. Richard J. Anobile, ed., *Why a Duck? Visual and Verbal Gems from the Marx Brothers Movies* (New York: Avon, 1972), 98.

## II. Social Space

WOLFGANG SCHIVELBUSCH

# The Policing of Street Lighting*

In the medieval community, all connections with the surrounding world were thoroughly severed after sunset. The City gates which had been opened at sunrise were closed and the individual houses shut tight—their doors locked, their windows shuttered. The town as a whole, as well as the individual houses, prepared for the night not unlike a ship that prepares for a storm. Doesn't the night-guard patrol the empty streets just as the night-watch patrols the ship while the rest of the crew (or citizens) are safely asleep under deck? Indeed, in mythological imagination, darkness and water are usually seen as the same original force, emanating from a state of the world before the Creation.

The period between sunset and sunrise was called by the same name that in present time is reserved for situations of civil unrest: CURFEW. In the middle ages no one was allowed to be outside his home, unless he was making himself clearly visible and identifiable. The means of identification was a light. "And no man walke after IX of the belle streken in the nyght without lyght or without cause reasonable in payne of empresonment."[1] There were similar provisions all over Europe. Parisians in the sixteenth century had to carry a lantern, if not they risked being arrested by the bourgeois police patrols and sent to prison.[2]

This state of affairs gradually began to change in the sixteenth century, when the first attempts were made to introduce a fixed public lighting system—i.e. a system in which light was displayed in a fixed

\* This article, part of an American translation, *A Slash of Light* forthcoming from the University of California Press, is here reprinted with the permission of the author.

1. English ordinance no. 1463, quoted in G. T. Salsbury Jones, *Street Life in Medieval England* (1939; Brighton: Harvester Press, rpt. 1975), 139.
2. Auguste Philippe Herlaut, "L'Éclairage des rues à Paris à la fin du XVIIe et au XVIIIe siècles" in *Extraits des Mémoires de la Société de l'histoire de Paris et de l'Ile-de-France* (Paris: P. Renouard, 1916), vol. 43. Except where otherwise indicated, all the English translations were done by the editors.

61

position rather than in motion. Citizens still carried a light with them while moving outdoors, but house owners now had to put up some sort of light on their premises.

This obligation represented a first attempt to establish orientation points of light in the dark city, thereby structuring what hitherto had been totally chaotic. (One might compare this luminous structuring of the dark city to that of the absolute prince, who, by means of fireworks, inscribed his powers onto the dark sky.)

Early ordinances to light the private houses were accompanied by other measures taken to create order and lawful conditions in the streets, such as pavement, prohibitions to dump garbage and anything else that might inhibit traffic. Through these reforms emerged the street, in its modern sense: a public place for the flow of traffic. In other words, the street ceased to be primarily an extension of the space of the people who lived in the houses adjoining it. This appropriation of the street by the modern state can be paradigmatically described in stages by looking at the different spheres of influence that can still be detected in it today. The sidewalk is the responsibility of the adjoining house-owner who has to clear it of snow and ice, whereas the bordering area of the street proper concerns only the municipality.

The early process of introducing law and order in the streets—as in so many other developments of this nature—can most clearly be observed in the capital of classical European absolutism, Paris. It was in Paris, at the end of the seventeenth century, that administrative public lighting was introduced. No longer were private premises ordered by the authorities to expose lights. Instead a truly public, state owned and state run lighting system was installed. This occured fourteen years after the defeat of the Fronde by Louis XIV, in 1667. It was also a direct result of the organization of police the year before through the appointment of the first police chief, La Reynie. "Police" in that period still had the old function of general administrators, but soon, and particularly in France, they were to be seen as the executors of absolutist power, control, and repression. Thus all the "technical" measures taken by the police to create hygienic and orderly conditions in the city became as closely associated in the popular mind with the repressive function of the police as did the police repression of other kinds of popular traditions. Public lighting service as conducted by the police soon became one of the symbols of the new state. This becomes clear if we look at the density, position, and capacity of the lanterns about which, sadly enough, there exists only dim and controversial information. According to Eugène Defrance, there were 2,736 lanterns distributed over the 912 streets in Paris, one at each end of the street, with an additional lantern in the middle if the street superseded a certain length.[3] This seems to be an improbably even distribution. It is

---

3. Eugène Defrance, *Histoire de l'éclairage des rues de Paris* (Paris: Imprimerie nationale, 1904).

more likely that lanterns in this early period were installed only in the busiest streets, but in greater density. According to Herlaut, who has provided the most reliable account of early Paris street lighting, the first phase of installation consisted of one thousand lanterns in intervals of ten *toises* (ca. twenty yards) apart from each other.[4] The actual means of lighting consisted of a simple candle enclosed in the glass cage of the lantern. The position of the lanterns in relation to the street and the houses was curious. As Martin Lister, an English visitor, described them in 1698, the lanterns "hang down in the very middle of all the streets, about twenty paces distance, and twenty foot high."[5] This position in the middle of the street is noteworthy because it represents a radical departure from the former "private" position lights of the houses. If we turn to the way public lighting emerged in London, we see that there, the old form of providing lights from the houses was effectively preserved in the position of their public successors. These were installed as extensions of the houses—on poles, or hanging from little gallows from the house walls. If the English lantern can be described as an extension of the old house light into the street, the French version must be understood as an extension of royal representation in the street. A symbolic presence of the *roi soleil* incorporated in the artificial "sun," a lantern, the French light exposes the street to control by making it visible in the dark.

Having observed how public lighting slowly emerged from the originally "private" position lights of the houses, let us now see how the lighting density increased in the course of time.

The first generation of lanterns installed in Paris consisted of nothing but candles that were placed in the glass cages of the lanterns. These candles were lit at nightfall and simply burned down within the next few hours. About midnight, when the flame tapered off, darkness spread out again. Apart from this brief period of light, there were other limitations. The lanterns were not lit at all during the periods of a full moon or during the summer months. The lighting period lasted only from October to April.

If we take all these limitations together—the weak source of one candle every twenty yards, the few hours it actually burned, the very limited time period during the year that these lanterns were lighted—we can hardly regard this system as an effective way of actually illuminating space. Despite the many enthusiastic poems and other statements celebrating the new lanterns as a kind of artificial sun rising over the city, these should not be taken literally as realistic descriptions. The fact is that the older mobile form of street illumination survived until the arrival of gas lighting well into the nineteenth century. This was the institution of the torchbearer, who was stationed at most street corners in the

4. Herlaut, op. cit.
5. Martin Lister, *A Journey to Paris in the Year 1689* (1890; New York: Arno, rpt. 1971), 17.

city and whose services could be rented. The purpose of these mobile light sources shifted from identifying its bearers to actually illuminating their way down the street. Identification, on the other hand, was now the function of the fixed public lanterns, more useful for revealing selected spots than for illuminating real spaces. Lanterns became beacons in the city, representing law and order. The night walker still needed a torch in order to avoid holes or other obstacles, but at least he was able to orient himself in the dark labyrinth of streets on the basis of these position lights.

After this basic system was established, subsequent development consisted in an expansion of these points of orientation into wholly lighted spaces. Obviously, that necessitated light technologies which were more powerful and efficient than candles. Gas and electric lighting carried out this task during the nineteenth century. The tendency towards a light-flooded space could already be seen in the eighteenth century with the emergence in Paris of the *lanterne à réverbère* (approximately 1760). With the introduction of the concave reflector, we witness the direction or management of light in a way quite different from the one described above. This new type of lantern collected light, making previously unused light available, and thus disciplined light into heretofore inconceivable functions. Lavoisier, a participant in the contests for new lanterns that were organized by the Academy and initiated by the police chief, gives the following definition of the reflector:

> A concave metal mirror, of whatever shape, placed in order to capture that part of the light which would have been lost without it, and in order to direct it toward the scheme or object one wants to light up. In this way all the rays emanating from the light source favor that object; none of them are dissipated or turned toward another.[6]

In addition to the improvement brought about by the reflector, the replacement of the candle by the oil lamp represented a substantial improvement of the burner or actual light source. But there is one curious thing about the use of these new highly improved lanterns. Their increased lighting power was not used to increase the amount of light in the street. Rather, the number of *réverbères* was reduced by approximately the same degree by which their intensity had increased. Instead of the 6,000 to 8,000 lanterns there were now only about 1,200 *réverbères* installed, and instead of the distance of 20 yards between each one, the distance now became about 60 yards. In other words, the lighting intensity had tripled in inverse proportion to the actual number of lanterns. One is tempted to see in this a confirmation of the original function of public lighting—at least in Paris—to be more a symbolic representative than a realistic light source.

6. Antoine Laurent Lavoisier, *Oeuvres* (Paris: Imprimerie impériale, 1865, rpt. New York: Johnson Reprint Co., 1965), vol. 3, 86.

As we have argued above, public lighting was closely connected with the police. Surveillance and light, visibility and control: these pairs complement each other, as much as crime/conspiracy and darkness/night are paired in myth and psychology. Further clues show with greater specificity how closely public light was linked in the popular mind of the ancien régime with the increasingly hated police. One of these is the fact that the commercial torchbearers in the eighteenth century often served simultaneously as police informants.[7] Another one has to do with the service duty of lighting the lanterns. Well into the eighteenth century this was the responsibility of the citizens of each street, who assembled each year to elect someone to perform the duty. Since this duty was highly unpopular, the petty bourgeois usually elected a person of rank, a decision that frequently was reversed by the police commissioner of the precinct upon the request of that person. This in turn aroused the anger and protests of the petit-bourgeois. On the basis of this frequent class friction, public lighting was increasingly looked at as something unpleasant and unnecessary to the simple people. From a pamphlet in the year 1749:

> If there were anyone for whom that public task could be of little interest it would be the artisan: the day's exhaustion doesn't allow him to enjoy nightime comforts.[8]

The skepticism, hostility, and anger with which public lighting was regarded in the eighteenth century, assumed a new quality during the revolutionary periods of the nineteenth century. Eighteenth-century accounts testify to the attraction that smashing a burning lantern, hearing the satisfying noise of breaking glass, and feeling the power of extinguishing the light of authority and creating darkness had always held for night people. (Such acts committed in England resulted in minor fines, whereas they were punishable by the galleys in France—as though the destruction of a French lantern were tantamount to a crime against His Majesty.) But in the rebellions and revolutions in the nineteenth century, smashing lanterns became a landmark ritual.

A prelude to the role the lantern plays in nineteenth-century Paris rebellions can be seen in its use in the 1789 revolution. Before revolutionary executions became routinely mechanized through the guillotine, justice took place by popular lynching. Its instrument was the lantern. In July of 1789, two of the most unpopular representatives of the old regime, Foulon and Berthier, were killed by being hanged on the lantern at the Place de Grève, the traditional execution square in Paris. The lantern's physical shape made it useful as a gallow, while other pieces of public furniture available for that purpose—trees, shop signs, and inn signs— went unused. There is some proof for the assumption that to "lantern-

---

7. Louis Sébastien Mercier, *Tableau de Paris* (Paris: Dentu, 1889).
8. Pamphlet quoted by Herlaut, op. cit.

ize" the victims—as it became known—was an act of symbolic revenge: the inversion of an instrument of police control into an instrument of revenge. The revolutionary song "Ça ira" contains in its refrain the line: "Les aristocrates à la lanterne." And it is hardly by chance that one of Desmoulins's decisive addresses of the early days of the revolution was published and widely circulated under the title of "Discours de la lanterne aux Parisiens," referring to that same lantern at the Place de Grève.

For specific acts of destroying lanterns in the nineteenth century, let us listen to Maxime du Camp's summary of this popular action, given in retrospect during the Second Empire:

> Pendant les jours d'émeute—ils furent nombreux sous la Restauration et le gouvernement de Louis-Philippe—les réverbères étaient le point de mire de tous les incorrigibles gamins qu'on cherche à poétiser aujourd'hui, qui ne méritent que le fouet, et qui bourdonnent autour des émotions populaires comme des mouches autour d'un levain de fermentation. A coups de pierre ils cassaient les verres des lanternes; les plus lestes grimpaient sur les épaules de leurs camarades, coupaient la corde, et se sauvaient ensuite à toutes jambes pour éviter les patrouilles qui arrivaient au bruit de la lourde machine rebondissant et se brisant sur le pavé. Il suffisait parfois d'un quart d'heure à ces drôles pour mettre une rue dans l'obscurité.[9]

> During the days of the rioting—which were numerous under the Restoration and the government of Louis-Philippe—the reflector lanterns were the focal point for all the incorrigible street kids that people try to romanticize today, who only deserve the whip and who buzz around popular emotions like flies around fermenting yeast. They broke the lanterns' glass with stones; the most agile climbed on their comrades' shoulders, cut the cords, and ran away as fast as their legs could carry them to avoid the patrols who arrived when they heard the heavy machines toppling over and breaking on the pavement. Sometimes it only took fifteen minutes for those rascals to reduce a street to darkness.

From a German eyewitness account of the July revolution in 1830, we hear that "the people raged through the streets, smashing the lanterns, calling upon the citizens to take part in the fight, swearing revenge."[10] A little later in the same account a description of the scenery after these rampages: "All the lanterns were broken, the streets with their pavement torn out were covered with the dead and the wounded." In another German observation of the same events by Schnitzler, the

---

9. Maxime Du Camp, *Paris, ses organes, ses fonctions et sa vie dans la seconde moitié du XIXe siècle* (Paris: Hachette, 1875), vol. 5, 285.

10. *Briefe aus Paris Geschrieben während der grossen Volkswoche im Juli 1830, von einem deutschen Augenzeugen an seinem Freud in Deutschland* (Hamburg: Hoffman and Sonn, 1831), 47, trans. author.

routine of revolutionary street fighting includes "the barricading of streets with wooden objects, planks and stones as well as the removal and destruction of the lanterns."[11] This desecration has a practical and a symbolic meaning. The phrase "since the lanterns were broken and darkness occurred, the royal troops were ordered to withdraw from the insecure streets," clearly states the practical purpose of the recreated darkness. A contemporary French author explains it as follows:

> Along with the reflector lanterns all the other emblems of the treacherous king were smashed—no one wanted to put up with even one effigy of him any longer.[12]

Schnitzler's account mentions a remarkable encounter of two kinds of representative symbols of the regime against which the revolution was directed: "Royal crests after having first been draped with black flour, were then removed or smashed and hoisted to the lanterns." On the other side of the revolutionary confrontation, the old guard tried to preserve law and order against this assault by upholding order with identification using lights. Whenever lanterns were smashed, there was a return to the state of public lighting as we remember it from the sixteenth century, i.e. the lighting of the individual premise by its owner. From an ordinance by the Paris police prefect in the days of July 1830: "People of Paris! keep away from those criminal elements . . . stay in your houses and during the night put a light in the window in order to light the street. . . ."[13]

Let us now turn to a literary treatment of this phenomenon because it further develops motives in the historical accounts and, so to speak, concludes them. Hugo develops lantern destruction and its meaning in *Les Misérables* in several scenes. In a chapter entitled "Gavroche the enemy of lamps," the perpetrator is the street boy or *gamin* Gavroche; the context is the uprising of 1830. During the uprising, Gavroche encounters a lantern that is still intact, and the following dialogue begins:

> —Tiens, dit-il, vous avez encore vos lanternes ici. Vous n'êtes pas en règle, mes amis. C'est du désordre. Cassez-moi ça.
>
> Et il jeta la pierre dans le réverbère dont la vitre tomba avec un tel fracas que des bourgeois, blottis sous leurs rideaux dans la maison d'en face, crièrent: "Voilà Quatre-vingt-treize!"
>
> Le réverbère oscilla violemment et s'éteignit. La rue devint brusquement noire.

11. Johann Heinrich Schnitzler, *Ausführlicher Bericht eines Augenzeugen über die letzten Auftritt der französischen Revolution während der zwei Wochen vom 26. Juli bis zum 9 August 1830* (Stuttgart: J. G. Cotta, 1830), 37, trans. author.

12. J. P. R. Cuisin, *Les Barricades immortelles du peuple de Paris, relation historique . . .* (Paris: Chez le roi, 1830), 130.

13. Author's personal archives.

—C'est ça, la vieille rue, fit Gavroche, mets ton bonnet de nuit.[14]

"Hey," he said, "you still have your lanterns on here. That's against the rules, my friends. That's unruly. Break that one for me."

And he threw the stone at the reflector lamp; its glass fell with such a fracas that some townspeople pressed up against their curtains in the house across the way yelled out " '93 all over again!' "

The reflector lamp swayed violently and went out. Suddenly the street was dark.

"Now here," offered Gavroche, "is the old street. Put on your nightcap."

Light being the representative of law and order in well-policed civil society, darkness thus becomes the medium of the counterorder of the rebellion. This is the thesis in Les Misérables, distilled from the revolutionary experience as seen in the empirical accounts. In another night scene in Hugo's novel, the hero Marius walks from a section of town which has not been part of the uprising, to the seditious area. As he walks, a lit landscape slowly gives way to darkness. Lights become ever scarcer, until "at the corner of the rue de la Bourdonnais, the lanterns ceased": that is to say, a no man's land and then a rebellious area begins. The area controlled by the rebels is totally dark. Hugo presents it from his favorite perspective, the bird's eye view. To a bat or an owl sweeping overhead, that neighborhood would have looked:

> ... comme un énorme trou sombre creusé au centre de Paris. Là le regard tombait dans un abîme. Grâce aux réverbères brisés, grâce aux fenêtres fermées là cessait tout rayonnement, toute vie, toute rumeur, tout mouvement. L'invisible police de l'émeute veillait partout, et maintenait l'ordre, c'est-à-dire la nuit. Noyer le petit nombre dans une vaste obscurité, multiplier chaque combattant par les possibilités que cette obscurité contient, c'est la tactique nécessaire de l'insurrection. A la chute du jour, toute croisée où une chandelle s'allumait avait reçu une balle. La lumière était éteinte, quelquefois l'habitant tué. Aussi rien ne bougeait. Il n'y avait rien là que l'effroi, le deuil, la stupeur dans les maisons; dans les rues une sorte d'horreur sacrée.[15]

> ... like an enormous dark hole dug in the center of Paris. There the eyes plunged into an abyss. Thanks to the broken reflector lanterns and the shut windows, all glimmer, all life, all noise, all movement had ended. The invisible guardians of the riot maintained their watch everywhere and safeguarded order—that is to say, the night. The tactic required for

---

14. Victor Hugo, Les Misérables (Paris: Editions Rencontre, 1967, rpt. of 1865 edition), vol. 4, book 15, chapter 2, 105.
15. Hugo, vol. 4, book 13, chapter 2, 58.

insurrection was to drown small numbers in a vast darkness and to enhance each fighter with the possibilities that darkness contains. At dusk, every corner with a lit candle had been shot at. The lights were out, and sometimes the person who lived near them killed. So nothing budged. There was nothing but fright, grief, stupor in the houses; in the streets there was a kind of sacred horror.

Compare this fictional text with another real eyewitness account of such darkness in the rebellious city:

> On se peindrait difficilement l'obscurité sepulchrale que produisit la destruction de tout éclairage de cette ville immense; les portes des magasins, des boutiques, des hôtels fermés, les persiennes de toutes les fenêtres, faisaient ressembler Paris à une cité désertée, dévastée par la peste; un silence effrayant achevait de rendre ce tableau horrible et douloureux.[16]

> It would be difficult to depict the sepulchral darkness brought about by the destruction of all the lighting of that immense city; the closed doorways of stores, of boutiques, of hotels, shutters on all the windows, made Paris look like a deserted city devastated by the plague; a frightening silence completed this tableau of horror and pain.

It would be tempting to chart out the political psychology of the middle classes against those of the lower classes on the basis of different attitudes towards lighting. After all, it is the same Victor Hugo who sympathized politically with the revolutionaries of 1848 whom we see here in abhorrence of the darkness created by the lower orders of society. The abolishment of public light is an act by which the real popular upheaval separates itself from the enlightened fathers of the revolution and their bourgeois background.

Let us now procede to the next Paris revolution, 1848, eighteen years after the 1830 revolution. At first glance, the same kind of lantern destruction seems to occur.

> Au centre de Paris, le peuple brise les réverbères et les lanternes du gaz. Les boutiques sont fermées; aucune lumière n'en sort. L'obscurité est complète; elle couvre l'invasion des magasins d'armes et facilite les barricades.[17]

> In the center of Paris the people break reflectors and gas lanterns. The shops are closed; no light shines from them. The darkness is complete; it conceals people breaking into gun stores and facilitates barricades.

16. Cuisin, p. 130.
17. Louis Antoine Garnier-Pagès, *Histoire de la Révolution de 1848* (Paris: Pagnerre, 1861–7?), vol. 4:305–06.

And Victor Hugo, now an autobiographical observer of events writes:

> L'aspect du Marais est lugubre. . . . Les réverbères sont brisées et éteints sur le boulevard fort bien nommé *le boulevard noir*.[18]

> The Marais has a lugubrious air. . . . The reflector lamps, extinguished, have been smashed on the boulevard so appropriately called *black boulevard*.

On closer examination however, lantern destruction in 1848 is no longer such a constituent action as it was in 1830. At least, it is not as routinely reported as it was eighteen years earlier. Whereas we find smashed lanterns mentioned in almost every account of the 1830 events, the two from 1848 quoted above have been the only ones I was able to find out of a great number of accounts of the events in 1848.

If we look for an explanation of this remarkable change in rebellious behavior, what comes to mind is the technical change in public illumination that occurred in the period between 1830 and 1848. In 1830 public lighting was still largely based on the traditional *réverbères* system, i.e. oil lamps. It was only in the 1830s—and then very slowly—that gaslight was introduced in Paris. In 1835 there were only 203 gas candelabres in Paris as against several thousand oil lanterns, and it was only in the '40s that the gas lanterns outnumbered the oil lamps. What does this technical change mean in terms of possible popular attitudes? An oil lamp is a self-sufficient light machine feeding itself from its own fuel reservoir, while a gas light is only an extension or an outlet of a large system that comprises the gas works and the pipe-systems network. An English gas engineer describes the difference in an 1849 account: "A gas-work, like a railway, must be viewed as one entire and indivisible machine; the mains in one case being analogous to the rails in the other."[19] In terms of destruction, this technical difference may well have a meaning. A lamp that is an autonomous unit may be more attractive and rewarding to smash than the mere outlet of a system. The individual that acts as the destroyer acts against an "individual" lamp. Gaston Bachelard has stressed this quality of the lamp in his psychological poetics. Man will either perceive the lamp as a mirror of his inner self, or he will suspect it as a threatening agent of surveillance. Bachelard describes the first situation of identification taking place through a reverie in front of the lamp:

> Avec une rêverie de la petite lumière, le rêveur se sent chez soi, l'inconscient du rêveur est un chez soi pour le rêveur.[20]

---

18. Victor Hugo, "23 février 1843" in *Choses vues* (Paris: Ollendorff, 1913), vol. 2:33.
19. John Obadish Newell Rutter, *Gas Lighting: Its Progress and Its Prospects . . .* (London: J. W. Parker, 1849), 54.
20. Gaston Bachelard, *La Flamme d'une chandelle* (Paris: Presses Universitaires de France, 1980), 7.

With the dim light reverie, the dreamer feels at home, the dreamer's unconscious is a home for the dreamer.

According to Bachelard, electric light no longer has this magic ability to evoke a reverie:

> L'ampoule electrique ne nous donnera jamais les rêveries de cette lampe vivante qui, *avec de l'huile,* faisait de la lumière. Nous sommes entrés dans l'ère de la lumière administrée. Notre seul rôle est de tourner un commutateur. Nous ne sommes plus que le sujet mécanique d'un geste mécanique.[21]

> The electric bulb will never provide the same reveries as this living lamp, which used to produce light *out of oil.* We've entered the era of administered light. Our only role is to turn on the switch. We are but the mechanical subjects of a mechanical gesture.

It is the oil in the fuel container that makes the lamp an individual entity rather than an administered producer of administered light.

Because the gas light system centralized services that had formerly been technologically autonomous, gas light required different forms of destruction. We are, with gas light, at the dawn of new forms of revolutionary tactics: no more are individual acts of destruction sufficient; it is incumbant upon the revolutionary to occupy the *centers* of those collective technological systems. Originally this meant the gasworks, later the electric power stations, railway stations, radio and tv stations. If 1848 still witnessed acts of lantern destruction, these were no longer part of the tactics of revolution so much as ritualistic residues from 1830. That the 1848 revolution also indicated the arrival of a modern form of urban revolutionary tactics is stated here by an American observer:

> Great anxiety was felt as night fell, relative to the gas, which it was feared would be cut off by the insurrection; but by the concentration of a large military force around the works this fear was removed, and the lamps were all lit, with the exception of those on the Champs Elysées, which had been broken by the rioters.[22]

So far we have only looked at the events in Paris. If we now turn to other European centers of insurrection in the revolutionary year 1848, we find that nowhere is the practice of lantern destruction performed, or at least we find no recorded information on this subject. This can in part be explained by what we have already said about the 1830 revolution in Paris: the dependence of lantern destruction on the state of lighting technology at that time. Since there were no comparable insurrections in the year 1830 in other cities, it is hard to tell what might have happened to

21. Bachelard, 90. The emphasis is the author's.
22. Percy Bolinbroke St. John, *French Revolution in 1848: The Three Days of February* (New York: G. P. Putnam, 1848), 90.

lanterns in Vienna and Berlin, had there been rebellions there. Certainly of some significance is the revolutionary tradition or practice of the Parisians, whose experience in urban upheaval was totally missing from the streets and populations in Berlin and Vienna. It is due to this ignorance of how to organize an effective resistance that a scene like the following was possible in Berlin in the March events in 1848:

> About half past nine P.M. the windows were illuminated in all the streets where one expected the military to attack. This illumination, aggravated by the additional light of a full moon, was extremely disadvantageous to the insurgents. Due to it nobody escaped the shots of the soldiers.[23]

Note that these windows were not illuminated by peaceful and orderly bourgeois trying to demonstrate their loyalty to the military (as had been demanded of townspeople by the Paris police prefect in 1830), but by the insurgents themselves. Their seemingly foolish motives remain unknown. On the other hand, illuminations *after* the revolutionary victory (however short-lived a victory and however illusory it was) became much more frequent an occurence.

In these latter light displays we can see a popular revival of the bonfires of archaic and medieval times, as well as of the illuminations once conducted in honor of festive events such as royal weddings, entries of princes into towns and the like. The illumination of this old type, emerging from the bonfire, marks a kind of saturnalia in light. The popular illumination celebrating the victory of the revolution distinguishes itself from the supervised illumination of the ancien régime by its disorder. There is a whole scale of degrees of anarchism displayed in these events. Let us look at a few recorded examples. An Austrian witness writes of March 1848 in Vienna, "today the city was illuminated as never before. The people celebrated its victory by marching along with torches and illuminating brilliantly. There was no window in the city nor in the suburbs that was not illuminated."[24]

Such exhibitions were enforced by popular demand, often against the will of those officially in charge of lights. Valentin, historian of the 1848 Revolution, writes, "There was no end to the rejoicing. The masses enforced the illumination of all houses." He reports the same from Berlin, where the Russian embassy was made to take part in the popular light fest:

> In the evening the masses celebrated their victory with a great illumination. . . . A group of citizens and workers showed up at the Russian embassy and demanded that it be illuminated. Meyendorff (the ambas-

23. Adolf Wolf, *Berliner Revolutions-Chronik* (Berlin, 1851), vol. 1: 169.
24. Friedrich Unterreither, *Die Revolution in Wien vom März und Mai 1848* (Vienna: Gedruckt bei C. Uebereuter, 1848), vol. 1: 43.

sador) finally had to agree—had he declined, the consequences would have been considerable.[25]

If these illuminations were of an apparently traditional character (putting candles in windows, etc.), revolutionary only in that they involved coercion by the masses, other kinds of illumination were more obviously anarchistic in character. Paris gave birth to the phenomenon of lantern destruction in order to create revolutionary darkness, but it was in Vienna that the new generation of lantern destruction emerged. For example: "Everywhere on the Glacis the iron lamp poles were torn out and destroyed, releasing gigantic jets of burning gas flames."[26] Or: "The gas pipes between the Kaeruten gate and the Burg were destroyed, releasing the gas in flames as thick as a man's arm, uncannily illuminating the night."[27] An illustration of the latter scene is accompanied by the following text: "Many people, mostly of the lower classes, had assembled on the Glacis, smashing the gas lanterns, destroying the lantern poles. . . . Out of the pipes came the gas and produced gigantic red columns of fire."

We do not know what the motives were for this way of dealing with gas candelabres. Was it the direct continuation of the old practice of lantern destruction—the will to create darkness—resulting in an unexpected outburst of light? Or was this gigantic outburst of flame and light intended to "liberate" the normally regulated fire of the gas system, and with it, the people who were regimented into work and other structures of domination? Since there are no recorded descriptions of what these people had in mind, we don't know.

We don't have accounts from the Paris '48 revolution of "liberated" gas lanterns. What we have instead are accounts of the kind of illumination that took place in Paris after the victory—however illusory—of the insurgents there. Much like the German ones quoted earlier, these accounts describe traditional illuminations of buildings. With a dramatic difference. The illumination of Paris after the three days of fighting in February was the second part of a double movement that began with the destruction of lanterns. It was the same clan of people that had first destroyed the public lighting who now enforced the revolutionary illumination: the street kids or *gamins* we met in Hugo's novel.

> Des bandes, composées en majeure partie de gamins, circulaient dans tous les quartiers, dans toutes les rue, et forçaient les habitants à illuminer sur-le-champ, devant elles. Les uns s'y prêtaient de bonne grâce, les autres avec colère. Ce cri connu *'Des lampions! Des lam-*

25. Veit Valentin, *Geschichte der deutschen Revolution von 1848–49* (Berlin: Ullstein, 1930–31; reprint Cologne, 1970), vol. 1: 448.
26. Adolf Pichler, *Aus den März- und Oktobertagen zu Wien 1848* (Innsbruck: Wagner'schen buchhandlung, 1850), 8.
27. Valentin, loc. cit.

*pions!'* retentissait sur tous les tons devant les croisées rebelles, jusqu'à ce qu'une clarté quelconque vint donner satisfaction.[28]

Street gangs, mostly young kids, stalked each neighborhood, each street, and forced the inhabitants to rekindle the lamps right then and there. Some went about it willingly, others angrily. This well-known cry *"Des lampions! Des lampions!"* rang out in every key at the rebellious crossroads, until some sort of light came on to give satisfaction.

**Extinguished and relit by the same people, public lighting underwent a kind of revolutionary ellipsis.**

28. Garnier-Pagès, vol 6: 299–300.

PIERRE BOURDIEU

# The Invention of the Artist's Life*

To ascertain that "Frédéric Moreau obviously owes much to autobiography" is inadequate; this received idea results in dissimulating the fact that Frédéric is not a kind of imaginary portrait painted by Flaubert to resemble Gustave. Frédéric is an indeterminate being, in the two senses the term, or rather one subjectively and objectively determined by indetermination. Settled into the passive liberty assured by his status as annuitant, he is governed, even in the feelings which he appears to experience, by the fluctuations of his investments, which determine the successive orientations of his choices. His annuity is embodied for a long time by his mother, "who cultivates lofty ambitions for him" and who reminds him of the strategies (especially matrimonial ones) necessary to assure the maintenance of his position. This "young man of eighteen with long hair," "a recent graduate," "[whose] mother sent him to Le Havre with the necessary funds to visit an uncle from whom she hoped he would inherit," this bourgeois adolescent, who muses upon "the plot of a drama, subjects of paintings, future passions," has arrived at that point in his career where those whom Sartre calls "the juniors of the dominant class" can embrace in a single glance all of the constitutive "positions" of the field of power and of the avenues that lead there: "For me there yet remain the great highways, the ready-made roads, clothes to sell, positions, a thousand holes plugged by imbeciles. Then I will be a hole-plugger in society. That is how I will serve my time. I will be a decent man, proper and all the rest if you will. I will be like another, correct, *like everyone*, simply a lawyer, a doctor, a magistrate, a solicitor, a *judge*, an idiocy like all idiocies, a man of the world or of the chamber, which is even more ridiculous. Indeed one has to be something in all of that, and there is

* Translated from "L'Invention de la vie d'artiste," *Actes de la recherche en sciences sociales*, 2 March 1975 with the kind permission of the author.

## Field of the Dominant Class according to L'Education Sentimentale

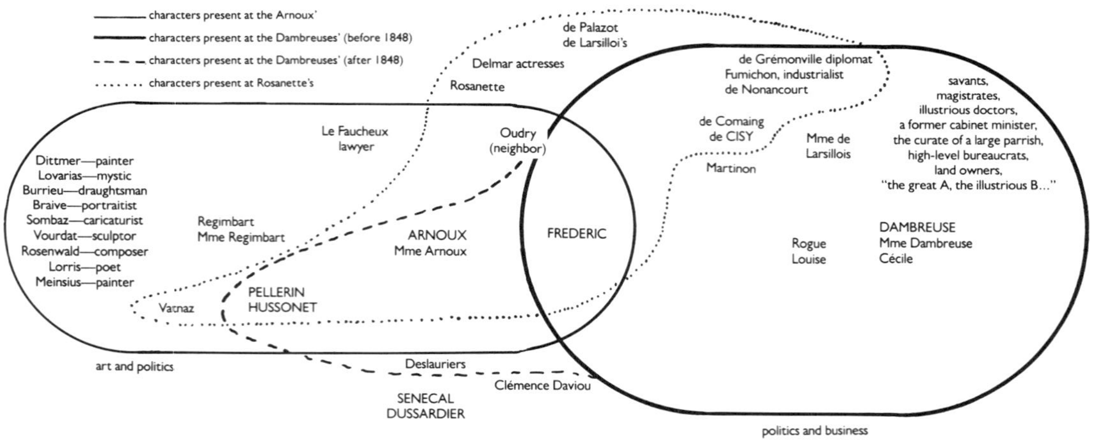

——— characters present at the Arnoux'
———— characters present at the Dambreuses' (before 1848)
– – – – characters present at the Dambreuses' (after 1848)
·········· characters present at Rosanette's

**art and politics**

Dittmer—painter
Lovarias—mystic
Burrieu—draughtsman
Braive—portraitist
Sombaz—caricaturist
Vourdat—sculptor
Rosenwald—composer
Lorris—poet
Meinsius—painter

Regimbart
Mme Regimbart

Le Faucheux
lawyer

Vatnaz

PELLERIN
HUSSONET

Delmar actresses
Rosanette

de Palazot
de Larsillois'

Oudry
(neighbor)

FREDERIC

ARNOUX
Mme Arnoux

Deslauriers
SENECAL
DUSSARDIER

Clémence Daviou

de Grémonville diplomat
Fumichon, industrialist
de Nonancourt

de Comaing
de CISY
Martinon

Mme de
Larsillois

Rogue
Louise

savants,
magistrates,
illustrious doctors,
a former cabinet minister,
the curate of a large parish,
high-level bureaucrats,
land owners,
"the great A, the illustrious B..."

DAMBREUSE
Mme Dambreuse
Cécile

**politics and business**

At the three dinners given by the Arnoux (E.S., Pl. 65, 77, 114; F. 52, 64, 101), we meet, in addition to the pillars of *L'Art Industriel*, Hussonnet, Pellerin, Regimbart. At the first dinner there is Mlle Vatnaz, and among the "regulars" are Dittmer and Burrieu—both painters—Rosenwald the composer, Sombaz the caricaturist, and the "mystic" Lovarias (all of them present twice). Finally there are the occasional guests, the portraitist Anténor Braive, the poet Théophile Lorris, the sculptor Vourdat, the painter Pierre Paul Meinsius. And to these must be added, from one such dinner, the lawyer Maître Lefaucheux, two art critics who are friends of Hussonnet, a paper manufacturer and Father Oury. In the opposite sphere are the receptions and dinners at the Dambreuse's (E.S., Pl. 187, 266, 371, 393; F. 178, 259, 368, 390). The first two of these are separated from the rest by the Revolution of 1848. They include a number of characters defined generically: a former cabinet minister, the curate in charge of a large parish, two high-level bureaucrats, some landowners and figures of notoriety in the arts, the sciences and in politics ("the geat Monsieur A, the illustrious B, the profound C, the eloquent Z, the immense Y, the grand old men of the moderate left, the knights errant of the right, the centrist commanders"). And, by name, they include Paul de Grémonville, diplomat, Fumichon, industrialist, Mme de Larsillois, wife of the prefect, the Duchess of Montreuil, M. de Nononcourt, and finally—in addition to Frédéric—Martinon, Cisy, M. Roque and his daughter. After 1848 we will also see at the Dambreuse's M. and Mme Arnoux, Hussonnet and Pellerin—the converts—and finally Deslauriers, whom Frédéric has introduced onto the staff of M. Dambreuse. At the two receptions given by Rosanette, one during the period of her liaison with Arnoux (E.S., PL. 145, F. 135), the other at the end of the novel when she is planning to marry Frédéric (E.S., Pl. 421, F. 418), we meet, apart from some actresses, the author Delmar, Mlle Vatnaz, Frédéric and certain of his friends, Pellerin, Hussonnet, Arnoux, Cisy, and finally, in addition to the Count of Palazot, some of the characters also seen at the Dambreuse's: Paul de Grémonville, Fumichon, M. de Nononcourt and M. de Larsillois, whose wife frequented Mme Dambreuse's salon. Cisy's guests are all nobility (M. de Comaing, also a regular at Rosanette's, etc.), with the exception of his tutor and of Frédéric (E.S., Pl. 249, F. 241). At Frédéric's soirées one always finds Deslauriers accompanied by Sénécal, Dussardier, Pellerin, Hussonnet, Cisy, Regimbart and Martinon (the latter two, however, are absent from the final soirée). (E.S., Pl. 88, 119, 167; F. 75, 106, 157). Last of all, Dussardier brings Frédéric together with the petty bourgeois faction of his friends—Deslauriers, Sénécal, and an architect, a pharmacist, a wine distributor and an insurance agent (E.S., Pl. 292, F. 285).

*Figure 1.* Field of the dominant class according to Flaubert's *Sentimental Education*.

no middle ground. Well I have made my choice, I have made up my mind, I will study law, which leads to nothing instead of leading to everything" (To Ernest Chevalier, 23 July 1839) [Bourdieu's emphasis].

## THE BOURGEOIS ADOLESCENT AND POSSIBILITIES

This description of the field of positions objectively offered to the adolescent bourgeois of the 1840s owes its objectivist rigor to an indifference, a dissatisfaction, and an "impatience for limits," that are hardly compatible with the enchanted experience of a "vocation": "I will become a lawyer, but I find it hard to believe that I would ever plead for a dividing wall or for some unfortunate family father who was defrauded by a rich, ambitious man. When people speak to me about the bar by saying that this good fellow will plead well because he has broad shoulders and a vibrant voice, I admit that I am inwardly revolted and that I do not feel that I'm made for this material and trivial life" (To Gourgaud-Dugazon, 22 January 1842). It would be vain to expect Frédéric to declare so openly his refusal of any "condition." Indeed the "disdain" (E.S., Pl. 55, F. 41)[1] that he shows towards other students and their common preoccupations derives, like his indifference to the success of fools, from "loftier ambitions" (E.S., Pl. 93–94, F. 80). Nevertheless he considers a future as an official of the government or a parliamentary orator with neither revulsion nor bitterness.

But, like his sometimes evident indifference for the common objects of bourgeois ambition, ambitious reverie is but a secondary effect of his idealized love for Mme Arnoux, a sort of imaginary support of his indetermination. "What is there for me to do in the world? The others do their utmost for wealth, fame, and power! As for me, I have no condition; you are my exclusive occupation, my entire fortune, my goal, the center of my existence, of my thoughts" (E.S., Pl. 300–01, F. 293). As for the artistic interests that he expresses less and less frequently, they do not have enough constancy and consistency to serve as the stepping stone to a higher ambition that is capable of countering, in a positive way, common ambitions: Frédéric, who at first "mused upon the plot of a drama and the subjects for paintings," who at another time "dreamed of symphonies," "wanted to paint," and wrote poetry, one day began "to write a novel entitled *Sylvio, the Son of the Fisherman*" in which he depicted himself with Mme Arnoux, then he "rented a piano and composed German walzes," turned next to painting, which brought him closer to Mme Arnoux, and finally returned to his ambition to write, this time a *History of the Renaissance* (E.S., Pl. 34, 47, 56, 57, 82, 216; F. 20, 33, 42, 43, 68, 207).

1. Pl. refers here and henceforth to the edition of *l'Education sentimentale* (hereafter *E.S.*) published in the Pleiade collection (Paris: Gallimard, 1948). F. refers to the edition published in the Folio collection (Paris: Gallimard, 1972). All translations are Erec Koch's.

The indeterminate artist's doubly indeterminate status thus appears as the most accomplished way to affirm (and not just in a negative and provisional way, like the student) the refusal of every condition; however, the indetermination of the artistic project strips of its reality the negation of every social determination affirmed in the artist's choice of a pure condition. The refusal of every position and of every social bond, which for Gustave is but the other side of the ambition to affirm oneself as an artist with neither ties nor roots, is never constituted for Frédéric as a positive project nor presented as the explicit principle of all actions, in daily life as in art. This refusal is affirmed only negatively by the series of passively endured determinations that, at the end of a long series of setbacks, will turn Frédéric into a *failure*, defined, by default, in a purely negative fashion by the absence of all the positive determinations that were objectively attached, as abstract potential, to the person of the bourgeois adolescent's being by means of all those opportunities that he "did not know how to take advantage of," that he missed or refused.

In a way, Flaubert has only converted into explicit and systematic intention Frédéric's "inactive passion,"[2] which represents less a copy of himself than another possibility of himself. He made a "system," a "doctrine" of the refusal of social determinations, whether they be those associated with belonging to a social class, those of all the bourgeois maledictions, or even those of properly intellectual signs. "No, by God! No! I will not try to publish in any revue. It seems to me, as time goes on, that everything is so base that *to belong to anything*, to belong to any organization, any brotherhood or 'boutique' is to dishonor oneself, to demean oneself" (To Louise Colet, 3–4 May 1853). *L'Education sentimentale* marks a privileged moment in this work of conversion since the esthetic intention and the neutralization that it implies are applied in the novel to the very possibility that Gustave had been obliged to deny—while conserving this possibility—in order to constitute himself, that is, Frédéric's passive indetermination, the spontaneous equivalent of artistic style, and thus its failed equivalent. Frédéric is indeed one of Gustave's possibles, never completely left behind: through him and everything he represents, we are reminded that esthetic disinterestedness is rooted in practical disinterest and indetermination chosen as a style of life in indetermination suffered as a destiny. What if intellectual ambition were only the imaginary inversion of the failure of temporal ambitions?

Undoubtedly because Flaubert strives to invent this new way of living the bourgeois condition that defines the modern intellectual and artist, while still sufficiently recognizing the axioms implicit in the style that have the objectivity, the opacity, and the permanence of reality and

---

2. "I want to write the moral history of men of my generation; a 'sentimental' history would be more exact. It is a book about love, passion, but passion as it can exist today, that is to say inactive" (To Mlle Leroyer de Chantepie, 6 October 1864).

of bourgeois life to think of imposing its recognition, he feels even more particularly the anxiety that forces interrogation (today socially repressed, that is, *censored* by intellectual propriety) about the social determinants of the writer's career and about the intellectual's position in the social structure and, more precisely, in the dominant class's structure.

How could the writer not ask himself whether his contempt for the bourgeois and the temporal possessions that imprison him—properties, titles, decorations—doesn't owe something to the resentment of the failed bourgeois, driven to convert his failure into the aristocratism of voluntary renunciation? As for the autonomy that is supposed to justify this renunciation, might it not be the conditional liberty, limited to the separate universe to which the bourgeois assigns it? Isn't the revolt against the "bourgeois" still commanded by that which it contests as long as it neglects the properly reactional principle of its existence: how can one be sure that it is not the "bourgeois" still who, in keeping the writer at bay, permits the writer to take his distance from the "bourgeois"? Let us consider the reflection, worthy of Gustave, elicited in Frédéric by Martinon's success: "Nothing is more humiliating than seeing a fool succeed in enterprises where one fails" (*E.S.*, Pl. 93, F. 80). All the ambivalence of the subjective relation that the intellectual maintains with the factions of the dominant class and their usurped powers is illustrated in the illogicality of this statement. The contempt shown for success, for what it procures and for those who know how to obtain it, coexists with the shameful realization that shame and envy betray before the success of others or the effort to transform failure into refusal. "Do not stand before a court whose verdict you do not recognize," said Kafka. Unable to refuse the court, Frédéric is just as incapable of recognizing its verdict.

The compossibility of all possibles, even contradictory, that properly defines the imaginary is in the social order the immediate compatibility of all social positions that, in ordinary existence, can only be occupied simultaneously or even successively, among which one has to choose, by which one is chosen, to Gustave's despair, whether one wants it or not. "This is why I love Art. Because there, at least, all is liberty, in this world of fictions. There one satisfies everything, one does everything, one is at once his own king and people, active and passive, victim and priest. No limits; humanity is for you a jingling puppet that one rings at the end of a sentence like a jester at the end of one's foot" (To Louise Colet, 15–16 May 1852). What the magic of writing abolishes are all determinations, constraints, and limits that constitute social existence: to exist socially is to be socially situated and dated, to occupy a position in the social structure and to bear its marks, in the form of verbal automatisms or of mental mechanisms and of the entire habitus that the constitutive conditionings of a condition produce; it is also to be dependent, to hold and to be held, in short to *belong* and to be forced into the web of social relations that are elicited in the form of obligations, debts, duties, in short of determinations and constraints.

The idealism of the social world is only the systematic formulation of the relation that Frédéric maintains with the universe of social positions objectively offered to his "reasonable" aspirations. Inscribed henceforth in the social definition of the intellectual's profession, the idealist representation of the "creator" as pure subject, with neither attachments nor roots, finds its spontaneous equivalent in the bourgeois adolescent's dilettantism, provisionally freed of social determinisms, "with no boots to lick; homeless, faithless, and lawless," as the Sartre of *La Mort dans l'âme* said.

## THE HEIR INHERITED

The transmission of power between generation always represents a critical moment in the history of domestic unities. Among other reasons because the relation of *reciprocal appropriation* between the material, cultural, and symbolic patrimony and the biological individuals shaped by and for the appropriation finds itself temporarily put into question. The tendency of the patrimony (and hence of the entire social structure) to persevere in itself can only be realized if the inheritance inherits the heir, if the patrimony manages to appropriate for itself possessors both disposed and apt to enter into a relation of reciprocal appropriation.

Of all the exigencies required by inheriting, the most absolute is that the heir take these exigencies seriously. Frédéric doesn't meet these conditions: a possessor who doesn't intend to allow himself to be possessed by his possession—without renouncing it, at any rate—he refuses to settle, to tear himself from indetermination, to bear socially recognized, distinctive properties by allowing himself to be appropriated by the two properties which alone, in this time and in this "milieu," would confer on him the instruments and the distinguishing marks of social existence, namely a "condition" and an appropriate spouse with an annuity. In short, Frédéric behaves like an "heir" who wants to inherit without being inherited. He lacks what the bourgeois call "le sérieux," that aptitude to be what one is: the social form of the principle of identity that alone can found an unequivocal social identity. Furthermore, by being unable to take himself seriously, by revealing himself incapable of identifying himself by anticipation with the social being that awaits him (for example, as the future husband of Mlle Louise (*E.S.*, Pl. 275, F. 267), and in this way to give guarantees to his future "sérieux," he derealizes "le sérieux" and all the "domestic and democratic virtues" (To Louise Colet, 7 March 1847) of those who identify themselves with what they are, who, as they say, are what they do, do what they must, "bourgeois" and "socialist" alike.

Frédéric's disdain for appropriated individuals, always disposed, like Martinon, to adopt enthusiastically the condition to which they are destined and the spouses whom they are promised, has as its counterpart the irresolution and psychological—and intermittently material—insecurity that a universe without fixed goals and firm points of reference creates and that are the price of taking liberties with the rules of bourgeois existence.[3] Frédéric incarnates one of the ways, and not the rarest one, to realize a bourgeois adolescence that can be lived and express itself, according to the moments of an individual life or the periods of History, in the language of aristocratism or the phraseology of populism, both of them strongly colored with estheticism in both cases. Latent bourgeois and provisional intellectual, the heir awaiting his heritage, whose student status obliges him to adopt or mimic for a time the dispositions and poses of the intellectual, is predisposed to indetermination by this double and contradictory indetermination: placed in the middle of a field of forces that owes its structure to the opposition between the pole of economic or political power and the pole of intellectual or artistic prestige (whose force of attraction receives reinforcement from the very logic of the student's "milieu"), he is situated in the zone of social weightlessness where the forces that will carry him in one or the other direction provisionally compensate and balance one another. But disinterest and detachment, the flight from the real and the taste for the imaginary, the passive availability and the contradictory ambitions that characterize Frédéric derive from a being without internal force or, if one prefers, without *gravity* (another way of saying "le sérieux"), incapable of offering the least resistance to social forces.

The conflicting ambitions of Frédéric (or of Gustave), who brings to the faculty of law[4] the aspirations of a student of letters or of fine arts, and the oscillations that bring these aspirations from one extreme to the other in the field of power—from minister to writer, from banker to artist—are better understood if one brings them to bear upon the relative indetermination (from this point of view) of that segment of the dominant class to which he belongs by birth. The "capacités," as they said in Flaubert's time, that is the liberal professions, today occupy an intermediary position between economic power and intellectual prestige (as they undoubtedly did in Flaubert's time. Indeed, the propensity of his

    3. Besides the fact that it constitutes in itself a symbolic negation of the bourgeois mode of existence, the "genre" of the artist's life, estheticism converted into a life's project, constitutes one of the conditions for the proper usage of the annuity that makes it possible. The dispositions to onirism that lead to prefering the plenitudes of imaginary satisfactions to the uncertain and relative gratifications of real life undoubtedly contribute to determining the powerlessness to place oneself in the social world and all of the (relative) privations that result from it; but this asceticism of luxury provides, on the other hand, the interior resources that permit "restraining expenditures" by fleeing what's lacking in the present or accommodating oneself to what's lacking by reconciling it with art.
    4. All of the positions in the field of higher education are not equivalent: they are also distributed between the two opposite poles (marked today for example by the ENA and the ENS), each one of them being closely tied to a class of positions of families of origin in the field of power and to a class (the same one) of positions anticipated in this field.

father Achilles-Cléophas, to invest at the same time in the education of his children and in landed property clearly shows this): this position, whose occupants are relatively rich in both economic capital and cultural capital, constitutes a sort of crossroad from which to direct oneself, with more or less equal probability and in conjunction with secondary variables such as rank of birth and sex, towards those segments of the dominant class supremely dominant or themselves dominated.

The objective relation that is established between the "capacités" and the other segments of the dominant class (not to mention the other classes) commands the unconscious dispositions of the members of the Flaubert family with respect to the different positions that they could seek and also structures the representation that they consciously make of it: thus one is necessarily struck in reading Gustave's correspondence by the precocious appearance of oratorical precautions so characteristic of his relation to writing and by which Flaubert will distance himself from commonplaces and sententiousness. And it is not without surprise that the reader of *L'Idiot de la famille*[5] discovers the same stereotyped horror of the stereotypical in a letter from Doctor Achille-Cléophas to his son, in which the ritual musings—on the virtues of travel—not without intellectual pretention suddenly assume a typically Flaubertian tone in their vituperation against the shopkeeper: "Profit from your journey and remember your friend Montaigne who wishes that one travel primarily to bring back the humors of nations and their ways, and 'to rub and polish our brains against those of others.' Look, observe, and take notes; do not travel like a shopkeeper or like a traveling salesman" (29 August 1840). This project for a literary voyage that writers and especially followers of art for art's sake have so often made ("Look, observe, and take notes; do not travel like a shopkeeper") and perhaps the form of the reference to Montaigne ("your friend"), leads to believe that Gustave was informing his father of his literary tastes. And it shows that if, as Sartre suggests, Flaubert's literary "vocation" originated in the "paternal malediction" and in his relation to his older brother—in what is after all a certain division of the work of reproduction—his vocation undoubtedly met early on with the understanding and the support of Doctor Flaubert. Doctor Flaubert, if we are to believe his letter of 29 August 1840 as well as the frequency with which he refers to poets in his medical thesis—among other indications—must not have been insensitive to the prestige of the literary enterprise.

One begins to make out the relation of homology that unites the structure of the social field within which Gustave's position defines itself, and the structure of the social space of *L'Education sentimentale*: in transfering Gustave's dispositions to Frédéric, Flaubert has uncon-

5. J. P. Sartre, *L'Idiot de la famille, Gustave Flaubert de 1821 à 1857* (Paris: Gallimard, 1971), vol. 1, 226–330.

sciously reproduced, in the imaginary space of the novel, the structure of the relation that Gustave maintains with the universe of constitutive positions of the field of power in the form of the relation between Frédéric and the universe of characters functioning as symbols responsible for marking or representing the pertinent positions of the social space. Flaubert's characters are not "caractères" in La Bruyère's fashion, as Thibaudet thought, even if Flaubert conceived them as such, but rather they are symbols of a social condition, obtained by the intensification of sociologically pertinent traits: thus the different reunions and receptions of *L'Education* are entirely signified, intrinsically and differentially, by the beverages that are served there, from Deslauriers's beer to the Dambreuse's "grands vins" of Bordeaux, via Arnoux's "extraordinary wines," lip-fraoli and tokay, and Rosanette's champagne. This structure that the novelist has unconsciously produced in an effort to construct a social universe endowed with the appearances of reality is hidden, as in reality, under the interactions that it structures. And as the most intense of these interactions are sentimental relations, underscored from the start by the author himself, it is understandable that they have completely hidden the true principle of their own intelligibility from the eyes of readers and commentators whose "literary sentiment" hardly predisposed them to discover the truth of the sentiments in the social structures.

## THE CONSTITUTION OF THE SPACE OF SOCIAL POSITIONS

To construct the social space of *L'Education sentimentale*, one need only refer to the definitions the different groups give themselves through social practices of co-optation such as receptions, soirées, and friendly gatherings. Frédéric's existence and the entire universe of the novel are organized around two homes represented by the Arnouxs and the Dambreuses: "art and politics" on the one hand, "politics and business" on the other. Besides Frédéric himself, only old Oudry, who is invited to the Arnoux's but simply as a neighbor, finds himself at the intersection of these two universes, at least in the beginning, before the revolution of '48. The Dambreuses mark the pole of political and economic power. From the start, they are made up of the supreme goals of political and amorous ambition: "A man with millions, think of it! Contrive to please him, and his wife too! Become her lover" (*E.S.*, Pl. 49, F. 35). Their home welcomes "men and women well versed in life," that is the dominant segments of the dominant class, and before '48, it totally excludes artists and journalists. The conversation there is serious, tedious, and conservative: guests declare the Republic impossible in France; they want to muzzle journalists; they want to decentralize, to scatter the city's surplus population in the country; they condemn the vices and needs of "the lower classes"; they discuss votes, amendments, and counteramendments;

they have prejudices against artists. The rooms are filled to excess with art objects. The finest delicacies are served there—dolphin, venison, lobster—on the most beautiful settings and accompanied by the finest wines. After dinner, the men stand and talk among themselves; the women sit in the background.

It is not a great artist, either revolutionary or established, but Arnoux the art dealer who marks the other pole, and as such he is the representative of money and business at the heart of the universe of art. Flaubert is perfectly clear in his notebooks: M. Moreau (Arnoux) is an "industrialist of art," then "a pure industrialist." In the title of his newspaper, *l'Art industriel*, as much as in the designation of his profession, the alliance of these words exists to underscore the double negation which is inscribed in the formula of this double being. Indeterminate like Frédéric, Arnoux is hence doomed to his own ruin: "His intelligence wasn't great enough to achieve Art, nor bourgeois enough to aim exclusively at profit, and hence he ruined himself without satisfying anyone" (*E.S.*, Pl. 226, F. 217). "The neutral ground on which conflicting rivalries mingled casually," *l'Art industriel* is where artists who hold opposing intellectual views, such as partisans of "social art," supporters of art for art's sake, and artists sanctioned by the bourgeois public, can meet. Conversation there is "free," apt to be obscene ("Frédéric was astonished by the cynicism of these men"), and always paradoxical; manners are "simple," but "posturing" isn't forbidden. Members of this group eat exotic dishes and drink "extraordinary wines." Esthetic and political theories excite them. Politically, they are rather Republican, like Arnoux himself, to the left, even socialist.

But *l'Art industriel* is also an artistic industry capable of economically exploiting artists' work *because it is* inevitably—and not "although" it is—an instance of properly intellectual and artistic power which can direct writers' and artists' production through its consecration. In a way, Arnoux was predisposed to serve the double function of the art dealer who can assure the success of his business only by hiding its truth, namely exploitation, through the permanent interplay of art and money ("*l'Art industriel* seemed more like a 'salon' than a shop" (*E.S.*, Pl. 52, F. 38)): on the market for symbolic goods, there is only room for that gentle form of violence which is symbolic violence ("Arnoux liked Pellerin, even while exploiting him" (*E.S.*, Pl. 78, F. 64). This double being is an "alloy of mercantilism and ingenuousness" (*E.S.*, Pl. 425, F. 422), of calculated avarice and "madness" (in Mme Arnoux's sense—(*E.S.*, Pl. 201, F. 191)—but also in Rosanette's—(*E.S.*, Pl. 177, F. 167), meaning extravagance and generosity as well as impudence and impropriety. Arnoux can turn to his advantage the strengths of these two antithetical logics, that of disinterested art which knows only symbolic profits and that of commerce, only because his duality, which is deeper than all duplicities, allows him to beat the artists at their own game of disinterestdedness, trust, generosity, and friendship. Arnoux leaves the artists the better part, the symbolic profits which they themselves call "fame," and takes the material profits gained from their work. A businessman among men who must refuse to acknowledge, or perhaps even know, their material interests, Arnoux is fated to seem a bourgeois to the artists and an artist to the bourgeois. Between Bohemia and high society, there lies the "demi-monde," represented by Rosanette's "salon," which simultaneously draws its members from the two opposite groups: "The young women's 'salons' (their importance dates from this time) were the *neutral ground* on which reactionaries of both extremes met" (*E.S.*, Pl. 421, F. 418). These girls of luxury—and even of art, like the dancers and actress, or the half-kept woman, half-woman of letters Vatnaz—are also "good-natured girls" (*E.S.*, Pl. 145, F. 134), as Arnoux says of Rosanette. Often from the "lower classes," they don't worry about fine manners and don't burden others with them. Paid to be frivolous, they dismiss everything serious and dull with their caprices and extravagance. They are free and engender liberty and liberties. In their circle, everything that would be unthinkable elsewhere, even at Arnoux's not to mention at the Dambreuses', is permissible: all the bourgeois rules and virtues are banished from here, with the exception of respect for money, which can prevent love as virtue does elsewhere. This environment created for pleasure takes the advantages of the two opposite groups of society, preserving the freedom of one and the extravagance of the other, but it doesn't suffer the disadvantages, since some abandon their forced asceticism, and others their mask of virtue.

It would seem that Flaubert had consciously selected, from within the social space he experienced directly or immediately, all the necessary and sufficient positions for constructing the social field that he needed to establish the conditions for this sort of sociological experimentation which he calls "sentimental education." Temporarily joined by their shared status, but fated to follow divergent paths in their future careers as in their past, Frédéric and his classmates indeed will have to define themselves in terms of the constituent forces of this quasi-experimental field.

## SOCIAL AGING

By intending to produce an ensemble of individuals endowed with their separate talents (talents which, in his eyes, represented the conditions for social success), Flaubert is led to create a group of four adolescents, Frédéric, Deslauriers, Martinon, and Cisy (five, if Hussonnet is included, although he is treated seperately), such that each member is united to each of the others, and separated from all of the others, by a set of similitudes and differences which are distributed more or less systematically: Cisy is very rich, noble, and distinguished (handsome?) but not very intelligent nor ambitious; Deslauriers is intelligent and driven by a forceful will to succeed, but he is poor and not handsome; Martinon is wealthy enough, handsome enough (so he boasts at any rate), intelligent enough, and eager to succeed; Frédéric, as they say, has everything needed to succeed—a fair amount of wealth, charm, and intelligence—everything, that is except the will to succeed. The principle of ulterior differences among the classmates is already inscribed in their different dispositions, due to their different origins: on the one hand, Hussonnet, Deslauriers, and his friend Sénécal (and also the only laborer, Dussardier), the "petits bourgeois," as Frédéric later calls them; on the other, those whom Frédéric will later find at the Dambreuses' 'salon,' either because they, like Cisy, "the child of a great family" and distinguished patrician, already belong to high society by birth, or because their gravity makes them worthy of admission, like Martinon, "whose father, a successful farmer, destined him for the magistrature."

This formulation may appear mechanical and simplistic, although it is really more methodical than the "literary" formulas in which scholarly commentary tries to capture the essence or the essentiality of a character. At any rate, it serves its function which is to make *L'Education sentimentale* appear like the necessary story of a group—taken in the sociological and also, very freely, in the mathematical sense—whose elements, united by quasi-systematic combination, are subject to the systematic whole of repellent and attractive forces which the power field, that is the field of the dominant class's constitutive positions, exerts on them. What removes the abstract appearance of parametric combinations from these characters is paradoxically the narrowness of the social space in which they are placed. In this closed and finite universe, similar despite appearances, to that of mystery novels where all the characters are confined on an island, an ocean liner, or an isolated estate, the twenty protagonists are likely to meet, for better or worse. Thus they develop, in the course of a necessary adventure and deducible story, the implications of their respective "formulas" and of their combined formula, which from the outset includes the vicissitudes of their interaction: for example, the rivalry for a woman (between Frédéric and Cisy for Rosanette, or between Martinon and Cisy for Cécile) or for a position (between Frédéric and Martinon for protector of M. Dambreuse). Each of the protagonists is defined by a sort of generative formula, which need not be elaborated and much less formalized, to direct the novelist's choices. This formula functions more or less like practical intuition about the habitus, which allows one, in everyday life, to predict or at least to understand the behavior of those familiar to us. From this principle, the characters' actions, opinions, and interactions are organized necessarily and systematically both in themselves and with respect to the actions and reactions of the group's other members. Each of them is present entirely in each of his manifestations. Thus Martinon's trimmed fringe of beard is an immediately intelligible sign of all ulterior manifestations of his habitus: from the palor, sighs, and lamentations which betray his fear of being compromised during the uprising, or his prudent contradiction of his friends when they criticize Louis-Philippe (this is an attitude which Flaubert himself explains by Martinon's docility, which enabled him to escape punishment during his secondary education and now allows him to please his Law professors); to the gravity he displays in his conduct, as well as in his ostentatiously conservative statements at the Dambreuses' "soirées."

With the different players' capacities defined, as well as the stakes and the space of the game, it suffices to observe them busily realizing the destiny that is objectively enclosed in the fixed relation between objective structures and their dispositions. In short, one need only observe the player's age, in the sociological sense of the term. Social aging certainly is measured by the number of changes in position within the social structure, and these changes result in restricting the range of initially acceptable possibilities; or, in other words, it is measured by the bifurcations of the tree which, with its innumerable dead branches, represents a career or retrospectively, a curriculum vitae.[6] Because a change of position can result from the absence of any displacement in the social space—as when, for example, an individual or group marches in place while their peers or competitors continue to advance—Frédéric paradoxically will age and be held in check through his inability to leave the neutral point which he, like his classmates, occupies from the start, to go beyond the state of indifferentiation which defines adolescence, to "seriously" undertake one career or another which he is offered, in short, to accept growing old.

The story is but the time needed to develop the formula. For the novelist, placed in the position of divine spectator, the actions—and particularly interactions—, the relationships of rivalry and conflict, and even good and bad fortune, which seem to determine the course of the biographical story, are but so many opportunities to expose the characters' essence by deploying them temporally in the form of (a) (hi)story.

---

6. This is hardly the place to develop all the implications of this definition of social aging as objective displacements within the social structure. Trying to understand a career or a biography as a unique story sufficient in itself is almost as absurd as attempting to explain a determined route in the subway without taking into account the structure of the system, that is the matrice of objective relations among the different stations. Each individual trajectory must be understood as a particular way of traversing the social space, which is made up of all positions joined by determined relations of compatibility and incompatibility, of domination and subordination, etc. . . . In theory, these positions can be occupied by any agent, or more specifically, by any agent belonging to the same class. This means that social age can never be defined independently of the position occupied within the field of class relations and, more precisely, independently of the position within the field of power when it comes to members of the dominant class.

Two principles of differentiation suffice to produce the formula which allows the development of the generative formulas for each of the group's five members: heritage and the heir's disposition to it, and these two only. An inheritance distinguishes the heirs from those "petits bourgeois," like Deslauriers and Hussonnet, whose only capital is the will to succeed. Among the heirs, those, represented by Frédéric, who refuse their inheritance are opposed to those who accept it and, like Cisy, are content to maintain it or, like Martinon, strive to augment it. This last opposition shows that the future objectively attached to each social position is presented as a distribution of probabilities, as a group of trajectories of which the highest, and most improbable, marks the upper limit (for example, Frédéric as minister, as Mme Dambreuse's lover) and the lowest, the bottom limit (for Frédéric again, clerk for a country lawyer, married to Mlle Roque). Thus, Cisy's only raison d'être, in the logic of the novel, is to represent one of the possible dispositions towards inheriting and, more generally, towards the system of dispositions to inherit, namely towards the leading class and its interests: he is the heir without a story; given the nature of his heritage, his holdings, his titles, and also his intelligence, he is content to inherit because he has nothing else to do, and nothing else to do to earn it, either.

At the end of the first comparative summation of the trajectories, we learn that "Cisy will not complete his studies in Law." And why would he? Having spent his Parisian adolescence, as tradition expects, involved with heretical people, morals, and ideas, he doesn't hesitate to return to the straight and narrow path which leads to the future implied by his past, namely to the "castle of his ancestors" where he ends his days, as he must, "ensconced in religion and the father of eight children." A pure example of simple reproduction, Cisy is opposed to Frédéric, the heir who refuses his heritage, as well as to Martinon, who does everything to increase his, and who puts at the service of his inherited capital (holdings and connections, beauty and intelligence) a will to succeed which is matched only by the "petits bourgeois" and which assures him the highest trajectory objectively possible. To attribute this result to the power alone of a will capable of mobilizing all means at its disposal in order to succeed, including the most inadmissible, would be to forget that Martinon's determination—like Frédéric's indetermination, which is its precise opposite—owes much of its efficacy to the symbolic effects which accompany every action marked by determination: the particular modality of the practices which reveals the disposition with regards to the stakes, namely "gravity," constitutes the most certain guarantee of adhering to the objectives and of recognizing the coveted positions; in short, of submitting to the order to be joined, which is precisely what everybody requires of anyone who would recreate it.

Frédéric and Deslauriers's relationship sketches the opposition of those who receive an inheritance and those who inherit only the aspiration to possess, that is, of "bourgeois" and "petit bourgeois".[7] Through one of those necessary accidents which direct biographies, the question of inheriting is what checks Deslauriers's educational ambitions: having arrived at his "agrégation" "with a thesis on the right of will-making, in which he argued that it must be limited as much as possible," "fate dictated that he should draw Prescription as his subject," which gave him the opportunity to continue his diatribe against inheriting and heirs. Strengthened by his failure of the exam with respect to the "deplorable theories" that led to this failure, he advocates the abolition of collateral succession, excepting only the case of Frédéric ... (*E.S.*, Pl. 141–42, F. 130–31).

## THE DIALECTIC OF RESENTMENT

But the sovereign ease of the prestigious heir, who can waste his fortune or afford to refuse it, doesn't exist to abbreviate the distance between Frédéric and Deslauriers:[8] this implicit condemnation of uneasy and anxious opportunism can only add unadmitted envy to shameful hatred. Deslauriers's deliberations, at the time when he tries to appropriate Frédéric's two opportunities, M. Dambreuse and Mme Arnoux, and to *take his place* by identifying with him, express in the manner of the parable *this desperate hope to be someone else,* which is the entire content of the petty bourgeoisie's specific alienation: "If I were Frédéric!," this is the generative formula of interaction between the two characters. Deslauriers's propensity to take himself for Frédéric and to "almost imagine

---

7. The social distance which separates them is brought up many times, and particularly through the opposition of their tastes. Deslauriers has esthetic aspirations of the first order and ignores the refinement of snobism ("poor, he coveted wealth in its clearest form" *E.S.*, Pl. 276, F. 268): "in your place, says Deslauriers, I would buy silver instead, and conceal the man of humble origins by this love of luxury" (*E.S.*, Pl. 144, F. 133). In fact, "he desires wealth as a means of power over men, whereas Frédéric sees his future as an esthete" (*E.S.*, Pl. 85, F. 72). Furthermore, Frédéric several times expresses his shame at his relationship with Deslauriers (*E.S.*, Pl. 185, F. 175) and even openly shows him his disdain (*E.S.*, Pl. 185, F. 175).

8. The objective relationship between the two classes is not reducible to a psychological relationship, which is fundamentally *ambivalent,* like the petty bourgeoisie's position in the social structure, in which it can express itself. We eliminate any chance of determining the true principle of a relationship between two individuals when we begin by reducing it to its psychological or even "sentimental" dimension: certain commentators—including Sartre himself—have inquired quite seriously about the existence of a homosexual relationship between Frédéric and Deslauriers precisely because of one of the passages in *L' Education sentimentale* in which the interaction between individuals most clearly shows the objective structure of the relationship between classes: "Then he thought of Frédéric himself who had always exercised an almost feminine charm on him" (*E.S.*, Pl. 276, F. 268). This is, in fact, only a relatively stereotypical way of speaking, since elegance and charm are traditionally associated with women, as this other passage shows: "At school, he had made the acquaintance of another person, M. de Cisy, the child of a great family, whose gracious manner made him seem like a woman" (*E.S.*, Pl. 53, F. 39).

to be him by a peculiar intellectual evolution which simultaneously combined vengeance and compassion, imitation and audacity" (*E.S.*, Pl. 276, F. 269), presupposes an acute awareness of the difference which separates him from Frédéric, a *sense* of the social distance which forces him to keep his distance even in imagining. Knowing that what is good for one is not necessarily good for the other, he keeps to his place even when he puts himself in Frédéric's: "in ten years, Frédéric had to be a *député*; in fifteen, a minister; why not? With the patrimony that he would soon get his hands on he could first found a newspaper; that would be the beginning; and then, time would tell. As for himself, he still wanted a chair at the School of Law" (*E.S.*, Pl. 118, F. 106). If he ties his ambitions to Frédéric's, his realistic and limited plans are always subordinated: "you must go into the world; you'll take me there later" (*E.S.*, Pl. 49, F. 35). He has ambitions *for* Frédéric: but this means that he *gives* Frédéric not *his own* ambitions strictly speaking, but those he would feel fully justified in having *if only* he had Frédéric's means at his disposal: "he had an idea: to go to M. Dambreuse and ask for the position of secretary. Of course, this position could not be obtained without buying a certain number of shares. He recognized the *madness* of his project and said to himself: 'Oh no! That would never do'. Then he thought about how to retrieve the fifteen thousand francs. Such a sum was *nothing for Frédéric!* But if *he'd had it*, what a lever!" (*E.S.*, Pl. 275–76, F. 268, emphasis mine).

Desperate hope to be another can easily turn into despair at not being another. *Moral indignation* completes ambition by proxy: with what he possesses, Frédéric should have Deslauriers's ambitions himself; or Deslauriers, being what he is, should have Frédéric's means. Here we come to the principle of the *dialectic of resentment*, which condemns in another the possession desired for oneself. "Why did he lend them? Because of Mme Arnoux's beautiful eyes. She was his mistress!' Deslauriers had no doubts whatsoever. 'There's yet another thing that money is good for!' He was seized by *hateful* thoughts." When it comes to the unnamable "thing" desired and denied, resentment borders on hatred.

Such is petty bourgeois resentment, that unfortunate passion for inaccessible possessions, that extorted admiration which is destined to become hatred of the other. This is the only way to escape self-hatred when envy turns to characteristics, especially *incorporeal* ones like manners, which one is unable to appropriate without also being able to abolish all desire to appropriate. But resentment isn't the only result; it develops in conjunction with willfulness, of which it represents the passive or, perhaps, defeated form: "nevertheless, isn't the will the capital element of all affairs? After all, doesn't it overcome everything . . ." (*E.S.*, Pl. 276, F. 268). What Frédéric need only desire, Deslauriers wants to obtain by force of will, even if he would become like Frédéric.

This typically petty bourgeois vision which makes social success dependent on the individual's will and goodwill, this extorted ethic of effort and merit which carries resentment with it, logically extends to a view of the social world which combines the practice of artifice with cryptocratic obsession: it is part optimistic, since dedication and intrigue can achieve anything, and part desperate, since the secret mechanisms of the machine are accessible only to the plots of the initiated. *"Having never seen the world*, he *pictured it* as an *artificial creation* which functioned according to mathematical laws. Dinner in the city, encountering a man in a high position, a pretty woman's smile could all yield tremendous results through a deducible chain of events. Some Parisian 'salons' were like those *machines* that centuple the value of raw materials. He believed in courtesans advising diplomats, in profitable marriages obtained through intrigue, in the genius of convicts, in the docility of fate in the hands of the powerful" (*E.S.*, Pl. 111, F. 98, emphasis mine). This is how the world of power appears when viewed from outside, from afar and below, by someone who aspires to enter it: in the world of politics as elsewhere, the petty bourgeois is condemned to *allodoxia*, an error in perception and understanding which consists of taking one thing for another. For this reason, Deslauriers's Mme Arnoux represents "the woman of the world": "the woman of the world (or what he took for this) dazzled the lawyer like the summary or symbol of a thousand unknown pleasures" (*E.S.*, Pl. 276, F. 268).

Resentment is a suppressed rebellion. The deception and the ambition thus exposed constitute an admission of defeat and of acknowledgment, an admission of failure with respect to criteria that an ultimate defeat compels to be recognized. Conservatism was never fooled: it was able to discern there the greatest homage paid to a social order which provoked no other rebellion save that of spite, of deception, in short of frustrated ambition, just as it was able to discern the truth of more than one juvenile rebellion in its *criss-crossed trajectory* leading from adolescence's rebellious Bohemianism to maturity's disabused conservatism or reactionary fanaticism. Hussonnet goes from failure to failure, from an unsuccessful newspaper to an indefinitely planned periodical (*E.S.*, Pl. 184, 245; F. 174, 236). And so, this slightly utopist adolescent, who has neither the material nor the intellectual means to stave off failure and to await public acclaim, becomes an embittered Bohemian: he is ready to criticize everything in the art of his contemporaries as well as in revolutionary action (*E.S.*, Pl. 344, F. 340). And he will find himself placed in the position of the consummate leader of a reactionary circle (*E.S.*, Pl. 377, F. 373), of the disillusioned intellectual, particularly on intellectual matters, who is ready for anything, even for writing biographies of the captains of industry. Hussonnet will do all of this to gain the temporal compensation for his unsuccessful attempts at imposing his dominance through appropriated means: to earn the "lofty position" from which to command "all of the theaters and all of the presses" (E.S., Pl. 453–54, F. 452).

Now we can return to Frédéric: because of the systematic relation which unites him to the other members of the group as a whole, he is defined by the system of differences which opposes him to each of them. Fundamentally, he is the heir who uses his inheritance to defer the moment when he inherits in order to prolong the state of indetermination which defines him. In short, he maintains with social possibilities a unique relationship, which is as radically opposed to that of the heirs who accept conformity as to that of the disinherited who are stripped of the means to avoid the irreversible choices which determine social aging.[9]

## NECESSARY ACCIDENTS

If it is true that every determination is negation, it is clear that Frédéric is indetermination itself, and in both senses of the term. Indeed, he is the one who can attach himself to all the characters by all possible forms of relation, like love, friendship, amorous rivalry, and competition, and can even successively and simultaneously tie his future to almost all of them. If Frédéric's story is one of missed opportunities and of accidents, of unfortunate encounters of independent causal series which put an end to his indecisiveness and vacillation, it is because he wants to play the game in every field and to hold together within undifferentiated projects and enterprises real or imagined possibilities, which are more or less incompatible. He should be taken literally when, at the end of the novel, he attributes his failure to "the lack of a straight line": his incessant comings and goings among positions in the social space which are as distant as *l'Art industriel* and the Dambreuses' 'salon' are only the passive forms of the ambition to possess the gift of social ubiquity. And Frédéric's failure is the necessary culmination of the inability to choose among incompatible possibilities, which is the passive equivalent of the Flaubertian ambition to lead all lives, and his failure carries with it the condemnation of social idealism which is only livable in the imaginary universe of writing.

Frédéric's story is inscribed in the relation between his disposition

---

9. "Ruined, despoiled, lost," Frédéric had to renounce Paris and all that bound him there, including "art, science, and love," to resign himself to working for M. Prouharam. He returns to this plan—which at the time seemed like "madness, absurdity" to his mother, responsible for reminding him of his place—, when he inherits from his uncle (E.S., Pl. 130, F. 118). It is a new foundering of his investments which again determines his return to the country, the family home, and Mlle Roque, that is to his "natural place" in the social order. "At the end of July, there was an inexplicable fall in stocks in the North. Frédéric hadn't sold his; he lost sixty thousand francs at once. His revenues were substantially diminished: he had to either restrict his expenditures, find a profession, or make a good marriage" (E.S., Pl. 273, F. 265).

towards his inheritance—which is itself tied, as we have seen, to the nature of the inheritance, balancing between economic and cultural capital—and the structure of the social space in which he is located. The two characters, Arnoux and Dambreuse, who mark the opposite poles of this social field, each have a feminine doublet, which, in the case of Arnoux, a double being, is itself double. As a result, a business or amorous relationship with one of the occupants of these positions cannot exist without inevitably creating a homologous social relationship with the other. "From that day forward, Arnoux was more cordial than ever, he invited him to dine at his mistress's, and soon he frequented both homes" (*E.S.*, Pl. 174, F. 164). It follows that the affairs of ambition, whose stakes are art or money and power, can only interfere for better or worse with the sentimental affairs that are their double: the coexistence of independent series, which are always on the verge of interfering with one another, imply the simple misunderstandings, fortunate and unfortunate coincidences, which are endured passively or consciously exploited, and particularly the *necessary accidents* which gradually annihilate all theoretically compatible but practically incompatible lateral possibilities; they also imply the indecisiveness and vacillation of the "double existence" (*E.S.*, Pl. 417, F. 415), which permit deferring the ultimate determination for a time.

A misunderstanding announces the dramatic mechanism which organizes the entire novel. Deslauriers arrives at Frédéric's home just as he is preparing to go dine in the city. The former thinks that the latter is going to the Dambreuses', and not to the Arnoux's, and jokingly states: "You look like you are going to get married!" (*E.S.*, Pl. 76, F. 62). A series of misunderstandings and switches mark out Frédéric's trajectory; the last one is orchestrated by Martinon who, with the victim's complicity, pushes Mme Dambreuse into Frédéric's arms and meanwhile courting Cécile, whom he'll marry and from whom he'll inherit Mme Dambreuse's fortune, which he sought at first through Mme Dambreuse until she was disinherited by her husband at the very moment when Frédéric "inherits" her.

This last switch should be counted among the necessary accidents which introduce *irreversibility*, that is to say history, or more precisely social aging, into Frédéric's biography through the determinations they bear: as opposed to simple coincidences, such as when Rosanette discovers Mme Arnoux with Frédéric, who ostensibly came "to discuss business with Arnoux" (*E.S.*, Pl. 389, F. 385–86), the necessary accidents in Frédéric's biography cause ambition and love—the two series on which his destiny depends—to interfere. In ambition's realm, Frédéric restricts his aspirations after vacillating between art (even its different forms) and power ("he lost his intellectual ambitions, and his fortune, he realized, was insufficient" (*E.S.*, Pl. 186, F. 176)). Nevertheless, he continues to vacillate between a position of power in the world of art and a position in government or in business ("Auditeur du Conseil d'Etat" or General Secretary of M. Dambreuse's business). In the sentimental realm, Frederic finds himself between Mme Arnoux, Rosanette, and Mme Dambreuse. Louise (Roque), the one "promised," the most probable possibility, is never more for Frédéric than a refuge and a revenge at times when financial and other activities wane. These three women represent a system of possibilities and each one of them is defined in opposition to the other two: "at her side (Mme Dambreuse's) he did not feel the complete delight that drew him to Mme Arnoux, nor the disordered happiness that Rosanette at first brought him. But he coveted her like something unusual and difficult because she was noble, because she was rich, and because she was pious" (*E.S.*, Pl. 395-96, F. 392). Rosanette is to Mme Arnoux as the accommodating girl is to the inaccessible woman, whom one refuses to possess in order to continue dreaming of her and loving her like someone from an unreal past. Rosanette is to her as "the woman with nothing" is to the sacred, "saintly" (*E.S.*, Pl. 440, F. 438), priceless woman: "one is playful, passionate, entertaining, and the other serious and almost nunlike" (*E.S.*, Pl. 175, F. 165). On the one hand, the woman whose social truth (a "whore" *E.S.*, Pl. 389, F. 386) is always evident—to the point where only a son is acceptable from such a mother, and she herself proposes to name "Frédéric" after his father, thus acknowledging her unworthiness. On the other, the woman destined to be a mother and to be the mother of a "little girl" who will resemble her (*E.S.*, Pl. 390, F. 387). Mme Dambreuse is equally different from each of them: she is the antithesis of all forms of "fruitless passions" (*E.S.*, Pl. 285, F. 278), as Frédéric says, of the "follies" or "foolish love" which drive bourgeois families to despair because they destroy ambition. With her, as with Louise but at a greater level of success the antinomies between power and love, between money and passion are abolished: Mme Moreau herself can only applaud this bourgeois love for fulfilling her greatest dreams. But if this love, characterized retrospectively by Frédéric as "a slightly ignoble speculation" (*E.S.*, Pl. 285, F. 278), yields power and money, on the contrary, it provides neither happiness nor "delight," and it must seek fulfillment in authentic love: "he made use of his old love. As if inspired by Mme Dambreuse, he recounted everything that Mme Arnoux had once made him feel, his languishing, his apprehensions, his dreams" (*E.S.*, Pl. 396, F. 393). "He realized then what he had hidden from himself: the disillusioning of his senses. Nevertheless, he feigned great passion; but he had to evoke Rosanette's or Mme Arnoux's image to feel it" (*E.S.*, Pl. 404, F. 401).

The first accident that puts an end to Frédéric's artistic aspirations occurs when he must choose among three possible destinations for the fifteen thousand francs that he has just received from his lawyer (*E.S.*, Pl. 213, F. 204): give them to Arnoux and help him escape bankruptcy (and save Mme Arnoux in the process); turn them over to Deslauriers and

Hussonnet and get involved in a literary enterprise; bring them to M. Dambreuse for his coal stocks. The impossibility of realizing the possibility which Arnoux represents will befall Frédéric by means of the relationship that ties him to Arnoux (through his wife). And the necessity of this accident is shown by the fact that it forces Frédéric to confront himself, and specifically the different possibilities that express his necessity: on one side foolish love, the principle and manifestation of the refusal to inherit; and on the other, an ambition as ambiguous as the segment of society from which he came, ambition for power in the world of art—that is in the universe of nonpower, and ambition for real power, symbolized by the Dambreuses.

The same necessity forces Frédéric to seek in strategies of dissociation the means to stay for a while in this universe which he realizes is "his true 'milieu'" (*E.S.*, Pl. 379, F. 376) and which gives him "appeasement, deep satisfaction" (*E.S.*, Pl. 403, F. 400). This is the period of his "double existence," which reconciles opposites by keeping them apart and by reserving separate times and spaces for them. When his political aspirations are rekindled, Frédéric becomes involved in a candidacy "which is upheld by a conservative and boosted by a leftist" (*E.S.*, Pl. 402, F. 399). In the sentimental realm, at the cost of a rational division of his time and of some lies, he manages to play off the noble love of Mme Dambreuse, the very incarnation of "bourgeois esteem" (*E.S.*, Pl. 394, F. 391), and the passionate love of Rosanette, overcome by passion for him and only for him at the very moment when he discovers perversity: "he repeated to one the very oath he had just sworn to the other, sent them two similar bouquets, wrote them at the same time, and he drew comparisons between them;—there was always a third woman present in his thoughts. The impossibility of having her justified his perfidies, which enlivened his pleasure through variety" (*E.S.*, Pl. 418–19, F. 416).

Like so many others, the political undertaking ends with a missed opportunity and a new accident spoils his amorous project definitively: Mme Dambreuse learns that the twelve thousand francs lent to Frédéric were destined to save Arnoux, therefore Mme Arnoux (*E.S.*, Pl. 438, F. 436). On Deslauriers's advice, she has the Arnouxs' possessions auctioned off to avenge herself; Frédéric breaks with Rosanette, whom he suspects of this action. And it is their final encounter, an archetypal manifestation of the structure, which brings Mme Dambreuse and Rosanette together around the "relics" of Mme Arnoux. When Mme Dambreuse buys Mme Arnoux's jewelry box, which reduces the symbol and the love symbolized to its monetary value of one thousand francs, Frédéric answers by breaking with her and reinstates Mme Arnoux to the status of priceless object by "sacrificing his fortune to her" (*E.S.*, Pl. 446, F. 444). Foolish love is art for the art of love's sake. Frédéric is placed between the woman who buys love and the one who sells it, between two incarnations of bourgeois love, the legitimate spouse and the mistress—

and incidentally these are complementary and hierarchical, like the "monde" [high society] and demi-monde"—and he affirms pure love which is irreducible to money and to objects of bourgeois interest: a love for nothing and serving no end.

## PURE LOVE

Placed back in the context of the system of possible relations between love and money, the relationship that unites Frédéric with Mme Arnoux, that sentiment which knows no end but itself and which subordinates all other temporal objectives, beginning with the quest for power and money, seems the homologue, in another order, of the relationship which the writer, according to Flaubert, maintains with his art: it is an exclusive and absolute passion which presupposes the renunciation of all temporal ends, beginning with all the forms of bourgeois love.[10] The artist's exclusive dedication to his art is the precondition for art and the artist's emancipation, and in this way it is purified of all dependence and any social function. Frédéric loves Mme Arnoux, "the woman of Romantic novels" (E.S., Pl. 41, F. 27); he never finds in real happiness the happiness dreamed (E.S., Pl. 240, F. 231); he burns with a "retrospective and inexpressible concupiscence" from the literary evocation of the royal mistresses; through his awkwardness, indecisiveness, or delicacy, he conspires with the objective accidents, which delay or prevent the satisfaction of a desire or the accomplishment of an ambition, as if he wants to preserve the dreamed satisfaction which insatisfaction procures. This estheticism of love is, of course, a reminder of Gustave who writes: "reading moves me more than a real misfortune" (to Louise Colet, 6–7 August 1846). Or again: "many things that leave me cold when I see them or hear others talk of them excite me, animate me, wound me when I tell them, especially if I'm writing" (to Louise Colet, 8 October 1846). Or even better, in *L'Education sentimentale* of 1845: "Jules lived in sobriety and chastity, dreaming of love, the sensual, and orgies." Or finally, this profession of faith: "my good fellow, you will paint wine, love, women, and glory provided that you are never a drunk, a lover, a husband, and a glorymonger. When you are caught up in life, you see it poorly, you suffer and enjoy it too much" (to his mother, 15 December 1850).

Art for art's sake is the pure love of art. Pure love proclaims the irreducibility of love to money, that is of the woman to merchandise and of the lover to the "grocer" and to bourgeois interests. In sacrificing his

---

10. Direct justification for this parallel can be found in an often quoted letter where, after an exalted profession of estheticism ("For me, there is only beautiful verse in the world . . . "), Flaubert writes: "I have always separated what ordinarily touches men most deeply and what for me is secondary in physical love from the other kind of love. I heard you making fun of this view the other day in reference to J. J. That was my story. You are truly the only woman whom I've loved and whom I've had. Until then, I quelled in others the desires stirred by others" (To Louise Colet, 6–7 August 1846).

fortune, Frédéric affirms the absolute value of his love, that is of the subject and object of this love. Pure art is no different: by reserving the name "work of art" for something priceless, for the pure and disinterested work, which is not for sale or which in any case is not created *to be sold,* by writing for *nothing* and for *no one,* the artist affirms that he is irreducible to a simple producer of merchandise, to *l'Art industriel,* as well as to the bourgeois who only knows his own interests. Better yet, the real intellectual or artist is he who, like Frédéric, sacrifices a fortune to the realization of his projects, or at least he believes this and in a certain way succeeds in convincing others. "Artists: praise their disinterestedness" reads *Le Dictionnaire des idées reçues.* This is the principle of a prodigious ideological reversal which turns poverty into wealth refused, therefore spiritual wealth. The poorest of intellectual projects is worth a fortune, the one that is sacrificed to it. Better yet, there is no temporal fortune that can rival it, because it always will be the preferred of the two. . . . This paralogism, which, at the price of an imaginary renunciation of wealth, turns misery into fortune as others turn necessity into virtue, is the key to all the symbolic arms which the intellectual segment of society uses in the struggle for dominance in the dominant class.

## SOCIAL NEUTRALISM

Like Frédéric, Flaubert tried his entire life to remain in this indeterminate social position, in this *neutral place,* where one can rise above the class struggles and material conflicts of the dominant class, those that divide the different types of artists and intellectuals as well as those that oppose them to the different kinds of "men of property." But it was only with the success of *Madame Bovary,* that Flaubert was assured of occupying the sovereign position of the consecrated and accursed writer. Thus, completely reassured of the non-negative character of his determination to complete *L'Education sentimentale,* this several times abandoned novel on *social finitude,* was Flaubert able to affirm the irreducibility of the writer to social determinations by writing the story of an unsuccessful attempt to escape them. But did Flaubert really succeed where Frédéric failed? The freedom which writing allows remains limited to the universe which writing creates: nothing forbids occupying all the positions there simultaneously, but only as an actor who *plays roles* and takes different poses, not like an agent who acts only as much as he is stirred, who is taken up by his different poses.

Estheticism, which converts reality into *spectacle,* is the prototypical instrument of *social neutralism*: "caught *between two large crowds*, Frédéric didn't move. Actually, he was fascinated and was enjoying himself immensely. The wounded who fell, the stretched out dead didn't seem like they were really wounded, really dead. He felt as if he were at the theater" *(E.S.,* Pl. 318, F. 313). Flaubert's entire existence and all of his works are inspired by this will to sever all ties and roots, to place himself above the conflicts between classes and between the segments of the leading class and, at the same time, above those in the intellectual field who implicitly or explicitly take part in these conflicts. "For me, there is only beautiful verse in the world, well-turned, harmonious, singing sentences, beautiful sunsets, moonlit nights, colorful paintings, marble sculptures of antiquity, and striking faces. Beyond that, nothing. I would rather have been Talma than Mirabeau because he lived in a more pure sphere of beauty. I pity birds in a cage as much as enslaved peoples. In all of politics, there is but one thing that I understand, and that is riots. A fatalist like a Turk, I believe that all we can do for humanity's progress or nothing amounts to the same thing" (to Louise Colet, 6–7 August 1846).

When the naturalism of esthetic indifference can no longer derealize and neutralize ugliness and aggression in the world, only the lofty struggle in all directions against universal stupidity remains: "In it, I will attack everything," says Flaubert about *Le Dictionnaire des ideés reçues* (to Louis Colet, 9 December 1852). Rather, Flaubert's is a combat on two fronts, against bourgeois art and against socialist art, against bourgeois utilitarianism and against socialist materialism. The only content of estheticism and objectivism, like the Platonic Other, is the negation of all determinations. This is the reason why they are appropriate to this *utopic being*, the intellectual who strives to distance himself from social positions—except of course the position from which he establishes his distance. As a result of fleeing the commonplace and received ideas, he finds himself having no other idea save the distance from all ideas, which he marks negatively by opposing them to one another: Voltaire against Lamartine, and Homais against Bournisien.

## FLAUBERT'S FORMULA

The ambition to rise above it all, the pretention to accede to an absolute and neutral vision of the social world presuppose extraordinary optimism about the intellectual's capacities, defined solely by the function of intellection, and extraordinary pessimism about the "social order." "In this world, the most important thing is to keep one's spirit in a high region, far from the bourgeois and democratic mire. The cult of Art creates pride; there is never too much of it. This is my rule" (to Mme Gustave de Maupassant, 23 February 1872). The aristocratism, which leads Flaubert to dream of a reign of mandarins, is part of the essentialism which leads him to treat collective history as simple *stage set* of individual histories and which leads him to place himself in the role of the indifferent, detached, and quasi-divine spectator of predetermined adventures. "One must play two roles in life: live as a bourgeois and think as a demi-god" (to Louise Colet, 21–22 August 1853). This time Flaubert delivers Flaubert's *formula*.

The notebooks in which Flaubert sketched the scenarios of his novels, the tiny core of symmetries and antitheses around which he builds the space of the novel, clearly reveal the *modus operandi* that is at the root of Flaubertian creation, and also the relation between this habitus and the social conditions of its production, which is to say Flaubert's trajectory and his position in the social space. By means of the schemas which structure his perception of the social world and his discourse on this world, whose most obvious manifestation is the obsessionally repeated *chiasmatic structure* in the most varied contexts, statements, characters, and plots, Flaubert indefinitely reproduces, in his own work, the position which he occupies in the social structure, that double *relation of double negation* which opposes him as an artist to the "bourgeois" and to the "people," and pits him as a pure artist against "bourgeois art" and "social art."[11]

It is his own taste for antitheses and symmetries that Flaubert bestows on Bouvard et Pecuchet. The "antithetical parallels," that is parallels among antithetical things and antitheses among parallel things, are but so many ways to affirm by this incessant alternation of pro and con that there is always and everywhere both pro and con. And the *crisscrossed trajectories*, which lead so many of Flaubert's characters from one extreme of the social space to the other, with all the attendant political reversals and sentimental palinodes, are only the temporal elaboration of the same chiasmatic structure in the form of biographical process: in *L'Education sentimentale.* Hussonnet, the revolutionary, becomes a conservative ideologue; Sénécal, the Republican, becomes a police agent at the service of the "coup d'état" and kills his old friend Dussardier on the barricades. In Flaubert's sketches, the characters who abruptly change direction are innumerable; one need only mention the entirety of "Le serment des amis," where he presents two of those processes of reversal so dear to him, in a social space reminiscent of that of *L'Education.*

Abrupt changes and repudiations, spinnings-around and about-faces, especially the ones from left to right, in which bourgeois disenchantment delights, all of the steps towards surpassing the seemingly most insurmountable antitheses are so many ways of affirming that "opposites meet." This is the first and last word of the social philosophy made to reconcile in Flaubert the indifference of the demi-god and the pessimism of the bourgeois.

## SOCIAL SPACE AND GEOGRAPHIC SPACE IN L'EDUCATION SENTIMENTALE

In the triangle whose extremities are represented by the business world (IV, La Chaussée d'Antin, the Dambreuses' residence), the world of art

---

11. See P. Bourdieu "Champ du pouvoir, champ intellectuel et habitus de classe," *Scolies* 1, (1971):7–26.

and of successful artists (V, the Faubourg Montmartre, with *L'Art industriel* and Rosanette's successives residences), and the students' district (II, the Quartier Latin, Frederic's and Martinon's first residences), we find a structure which is none other than that of *L'Education sentimentale*.[12] On the whole, this universe itself is defined objectively by a double relation of opposition, which is never mentioned in the novel itself (indeed, its absence is very significant). On the one hand, there is the opposition to the established aristocracy of the Faubourg Saint-Germain (III), which is often mentioned in Balzac but totally absent from *L'Education sentimentale*; on the other hand, the opposition to the "popular classes" (I): the zones of Paris, where the decisive revolutionary events of 1848 took place, are excluded from Flaubert's novel (the description of the first incidents in the Quartier Latin (*E.S.*, F. 44 ff.) and the disturbances at the Palais Royal refer each time to the sections of Paris which are mentioned in the rest of the work. In the novel, the only representative of the popular classes, Dussardier, at first works on the rue de Cléry (*E.S.*, F. 47). Upon his return from Nogent to Paris, Frédéric comes to this area (rue Coq Héron).

The Quartier Latin, the area of studies and "beginnings in life," is the home of students and of "grisettes," whose special image is beginning to take form (particularly with Musset's *Contes et nouvelles*, and most notably with "Frédéric et Bernerette," published in the *Revue des deux mondes*). Frédéric's social trajectory is sketched there: he successively lives on the rue Sainte Hyacinthe (*E.S.*, F. 38), then the Quai Napoléon (*E.S.*, F. 41) and regularly dines on the rue de la Harpe (*E.S.*, F. 38). The same goes for Martinon (*E.S.*, F. 39). In the social portrait of Paris which writers are beginning to create and to which Flaubert tacitly refers, the Quartier Latin of artists and "grisettes" leading the Bohemian life is the scene of the "fêtes galantes," and it is in sharp contrast with the lofty place of aristocratic asceticism, the Faubourg Saint-Germain.

In the universe of *L'Education sentimentale*, the Chaussée d'Antin, which is the zone made up of the rues Rumfort (with Frédéric's residence), d'Anjou (Dambreuses'), and de Choiseul (Arnoux's), is the home of the dominant class's new leading segment. This new bourgeoisie is opposed to both the demi-monde of the Faubourg Montmartre and even more to the established aristocracy of the Faubourg Saint-Germain, among other things because of the composite character of the population

12. In preparing the map of Paris p. 101, we completed "Paris dans *L'Education sentimentale*," which appeared in J. L. Douchin's compilation of abstracts (Paris: Larousse, 1969). The dotted line running from north to south, which represents the limit of the zone occupied by the insurgents of 1848, was taken from Ch. Simon, *Paris 1800 à 1900* (Paris: Plon et Nourrit, 1900–01), 3 vols. The lines with arrows represent the main characters' trajectories. Their names are on their place of residence, and if need be, their successive residences are numbered in order. N. B. Because we were unable to find the "rue" des Trois Maries mentioned by Flaubert, we placed Deslauriers on the Place des Trois Maries.

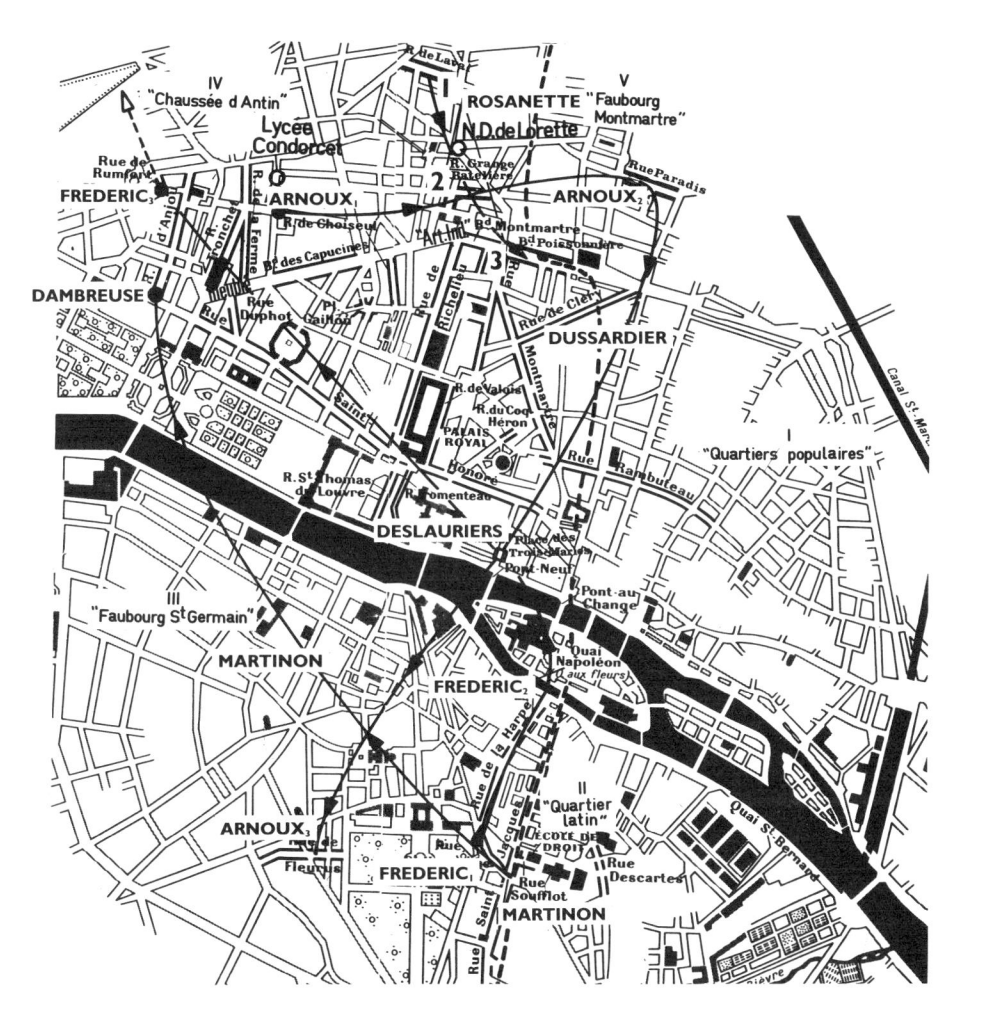

*Figure 2.* Paris in Flaubert's *Sentimental Education.*

that resides there (which is shown in the novel by the social distance among Frédéric, Dambreuse, and Arnoux) and by the mobility of its members (Dambreuse came there, Frédéric gets there after his inheritance, Martinon arrives there through his marriage, and soon Arnoux is excluded from there). This new bourgeoisie, which desires to preserve or recreate the signs of the Faubourg Saint-Germain's established train of life (for example, by giving itself extravagant residences), is undoubtedly partly the result of a *social reconversion* which is shown by a *spatial transition:* "M. Dambreuse's real name was the count d'Ambreuse; but as of 1825, as he gradually gave up his nobility and his party, he turned to industry" (*E.S.*, F. 36). And a little farther, this passage marks both the social and geographic bonds, and their severing: "In cajoling the duchesses, she [Mme Dambreuse] appeased the noble faubourg's rancor and let it be thought that M. Dambreuse could still repent and be of service to them." The Dambreuse coat of arms, which is both a heraldic mark and the trademark of a knight of industry, reveals the same system of connections and oppositions. The allusion to the "Comité de la rue Poitiers" (*E.S.*, F. 390), where all the conservative politicians met, would confirm, if necessary, that it was in this part of Paris that all subsequent action would take place.

The Faubourg Montmartre, where Flaubert situated *l'Art industriel* and Rosanette's successive homes, is recognizable as the residence of successful artists (for example this is where Gavarni lives—in 1841, he will invent the term "Lorette" to designate those members of the *demi-monde* who frequent the section of Notre Dame de Lorette and the place Saint Georges—, or also Feydeau). Like Rosanette's "salon," which in a way is its literary transfiguration, this is where the financiers, successful artists, journalists, and also actresses and "lorettes" live or meet. These members of the *demi-monde*, who, like *l'Art industriel*, are situated halfway between the bourgeois and popular sections of Paris, are opposed equally to the bourgeois of the Chaussée d'Antin as well as to the students, "grisettes," and failed artists of the Quartier Latin—Gavarni really makes fun of the last three groups in his caricatures. Because of his home (rue de Choiseul) and his place of work (boulevard Montmartre), Arnoux participates in two universes at the time of his glory, then he finds himself first sent back to the Faubourg Montmartre (rue Paradis—*E.S.*, F. 128) before being exiled to the absolute exteriority of the rue de Ficurus (*E.S.*, F. 422). Rosanette also circulates in the space reserved to the "lorettes" and her progressive slippage east, that is towards the border of the workers' section, signals her decline: rue de Laval (*E.S.*, F. 134); then rue Grange-Batelière (*E.S.*, F. 279); and finally boulevard Poissonnière (*E.S.*, F. 339).

Thus, ascending and descending social *trajectories* clearly are distinguished in this *structured and hierarchical space:* for the former, the movement is from the south towards the north-west (Martinon and, for a while, Frédéric); for the latter, it is from west towards east and north to south (Rosanette, Arnoux). Deslauriers's failure is shown by the fact that he never leaves the point of departure, the students' and artists' section (place des Trois Maries).

Translated by Erec R. Koch

KRISTIN ROSS

# Rimbaud and the Transformation of Social Space

To constitute "social space" as an object of analysis is to confront the difficulty of focusing on the ideological content of socially created space. Our tendency, that is, is to think of space as an abstract, metaphysical context, as the container for our lives rather than the structures we help create. The difficulty is also one of vocabulary, for while words like "historical" or "political" convey a dynamic of intentionality, vitality, and human motivation, "spatial," on the other hand, connotes stasis, neutrality and passivity. Space, as Feuerbach suggested, tolerates and coordinates, while time excludes and subordinates—and thus becomes the privileged category for the dialectician.

It is perhaps not so surprising then to find Marxist theory, following the example of Marx himself, somewhat lax in developing a theory of space.[1] Analogously, the current generation of Marxist critics has, for the most part, neglected to concern itself with poetry and has reasserted the traditionally dominant Marxist concern with narrative, and especially with the novel. In this essay I want to explore the advantages of a spatial comprehension of cultural production and I want to do so by looking at lyric poetry—specifically the poetry of Rimbaud.

One of the major reasons for the left's neglect of poetry has to do with the ideology of "poethood" itself, and perhaps no French poet so much as Rimbaud has suffered the effects of a massive critical mythification of that

1. The work of Henri Lefebvre, particularly the important series of works on urbanism from the late 1960s and 1970s, *Le Droit à la ville* (1968), *La Révolution urbaine* (1970), and *La Production de l'espace* (1974) remains a notable exception to this, as does the work of geographers in France and America publishing in journals like *Antipode* and *Hérodote*. Lefebvre and anyone else who shows a preoccupation with spatial categories, has run the risk of being labeled within Marxism as a "spatial fetishist"—of conceptualizing space separately from the structure of social relations and class conflict. For a brief history of spatial theory within Marxism, see Edward Soja, "The Socio-Spatial Dialectic," *Annals of the Association of American Geographers*, 70: 207–25.

"poethood"—whether it be the boy genius, the mystical or hallucinogenic "voyant," or the solitary adventurer. Recent critical work which reacted against the biographical mythification, has produced a textual Rimbaud exemplary of the most progressive strains of a polysemic and counterdiscursive modernism. One of my tasks in this essay is to try to rescue the peculiar and repressed strain of Rimbaud's modernism from this generalized "politics" of the signifier—and this will entail a different perspective on both the biographical (historical) data and the information to be gleaned from textual interpretation. I want to show how the expansive, centrifugal energy of Rimbaud's brief production not only resists a purely linguistic analysis, but opens up onto a whole synchronic history of his particular moment. This task is made all the more necessary by Rimbaud's theoretical comprehension *of* that moment--one which marks two distinct spatial impulses or events. The first of these, which will concern us here, is the Paris Commune, the construction of the revolutionary city, or what the Situationists were to single out in the 1950s as "the only realization of a revolutionary urbanism to date." And the second, on a global scale, is the passage from market capitalism into a farflung and geographic world system, the "spatialization of history" into what would become the Imperialist heyday of the late nineteenth century.[2]

Certainly the renewed fascination with the Paris Commune on the part of the Situationists, Henri Lefebvre, and other participants in proto- and post- May '68 culture, has something to do with the Commune as spatial "event"—its privileged status as a utopian moment of spatial transformation and reorganization.[3] To mention just a few of the spatial problems posed by the Commune, consider, for example, the relationship of Paris to the provinces, the post-Haussman social division of the city and the question of who, among its citizens, has a "right to the city," the military and tactical use of city space during the fighting. But it is important to avoid granting either the Commune or Rimbaud the status of privileged object for theoretical analysis. Space, in other words, as a social fact, and as an instance of society, is always political and strategic. (And because it is characterized, among other things, by the difference in age of the elements which form it—the sum of the action of successive modernizations—spatial structure cannot be understood according to an old "history vs. structure or logic" opposition). But one of the particularities of social relations within capitalist culture is its ability to persuade us

___

2. This essay forms part of a forthcoming book on Rimbaud and the political language of the 1870s. There I treat the question of Rimbaud and geography; see also Fredric Jameson, "Rimbaud and the Spatial Text," in *Re-writing Literary History*, ed. Tak-Wai Wong and M. A. Abbas (Hong Kong: Hong Kong University Press, 1984), 66–93.

3. See Lefebvre, *La Proclamation de la Commune* (Paris: Gallimard, 1965); and the Situationist theses on the Commune in *Internationale Situationniste 1958–69* (Paris: Editions Champ-Libre, 1975), 109–12: English version, *Situationist International Anthology*, ed. and trans. Ken Knabb (Berkeley: Bureau of Public Secrets, 1981), 314–16.

that space is not a dimension of the mechanisms of transformation but is instead natural, physical—our unchanged and unchanging surroundings. While people's experience of their bodies in space, their physical perceptions, their entrances and exits, their minds' attention, are all *social* facts, the particular way in which social relations are reproduced and organized through repeated daily practices dulls the perception of that social aspect, and subsumes it into a biological or natural given.

I hope then to suggest larger methodological advantages for the critical concept of social space beyond its particular efficacy for writing about the 1870s in France. Social space can help us avoid the pitfalls of so much of the social or "contextual" analysis of art—the kind of analysis which would attempt, say, to decode a single "masterwork" by Rimbaud, for example, in such a way that it reveals all of the social relations of the 1870s. The restrictions and political drawbacks of such analyses are numerous—not the least of which is their leaving unquestioned the cult of the masterpiece in a way that is singularly not in keeping with either Rimbaud or the people who pulled down the Vendôme Column. Secondly, the "social history" which emerges full blown from such interpretations of the masterwork tends itself to be left unanalyzed—as if the deconstruction of a text offered up a social context which did not in turn have to be deconstructed! My aim, rather, is something like "synchronic history": considering cultural production, in this case Rimbaud, as one "phoneme," so to speak, among many in the political language of the 1870s.

I.

Attempts to discuss Rimbaud in terms of the events of 1871 have for the most part been limited to frenzied interrogations by literary historians and biographers anxious to ascertain the precise physical whereabouts of Rimbaud during the months of March to May 1871.[4] The actual, complex links binding Rimbaud to the events in Paris are not to be established by measuring geographic distance. Or, if they are, it is perhaps by considering Rimbaud's poetry, produced at least in part within the rarified situation of his isolation in Charleville, as one creative response to the same objective situation to which the insurrection in Paris was another. In what way does Rimbaud figure or prefigure an adjacent—side-by-side rather than analogous—social space to the one activated by the insurgents in the heart of Paris?

4. The one notable exception is Steve Murphy, in his "Rimbaud et la Commune?", *Rimbaud Multiple*, ed. Bedou and Touzot (Gourdon: Dominique Bedou, 1985), 50–65. Murphy addresses the biographical question intelligently and with much relevant erudition, situating Rimbaud in terms of Communard culture: Vermersch, Vallès, Rochefort, political journals of the time, political and sexual slang—establishing, in other words, a sphere of influence and interaction distinct from the Parnassian, or Symbolist context with which Rimbaud's production is usually placed in dialogue.

To begin to answer this question I propose bypassing Rimbaud's most explicitly "political" poems—poems like "Les Mains de Jeanne-Marie" which praises the revolutionary actions of women during the Commune, or like "Chant de guerre parisien"—this latter announced by Rimbaud under the rubric of a "psaume d'actualité" and featuring verbal caricatures of Favre and Thiers lifted straight from the political cartoons and *gravures* of the early months of 1871. Such overtly political verse is important for an ideological reading of Rimbaud, but no more so, I hope to show, than the early Charleville erotic verse (or, for that matter, than the late "hermetic" prose poems): in Rimbaud there is little distance between political economy and libidinal economy. And the significance of the Commune is most evident in what Marx called its "working existence": in its *displacement* of the political onto seemingly peripheral areas of everyday life—the organization of space and time, changes in lived rhythms and social ambiances. The insurgents' brief mastery of their own history is perceptible, in other words, not so much on the level of governmental politics as on the level of their daily life. Taking seriously such a "displacement of the political" points us in the direction of certain of Rimbaud's poems thematically at a distance from the turbulence in Paris: the early ironic and erotic everyday Rimbaud of kisses, beer, and country walks.

Like much of Rimbaud's early lyric poetry, "Rêvé pour l'hiver" (1870) puts forth a particular imagination of the nineteenth-century commonplace of "the voyage." The poem opens with the dream of an enclosed, infantile universe:

> L'hiver, nous irons dans un petit wagon rose
>    Avec des coussins bleus.
> Nous serons bien. Un nid de baisers fous repose
>    Dans chaque coin moelleux.
>
> In winter we shall travel in a little pink railway
>    carriage
> With blue cushions.
> We'll be comfortable. A nest of mad kisses lies in wait
>    In each soft corner.[5]

The interior of the carriage is created oppositionally to the winter outside; inside is warmth, well-being and comfort—the simplicity of "Nous serons bien"—repose and restfulness. The muted pastel colors suggest a child's nursery; the carriage is a nest where the violence and jolts of the voyage are cushioned and where all sensation or sound of moving through space is dulled. The passage will not be noticed.

---

5. Arthur Rimbaud. *Oeuvres complètes,* ed. de Renéville and Mouquet (Paris: Gallimard, Pléiade, 1967), 65. All future references to Rimbaud will be to this edition; translations from the French, here and elsewhere, are mine.

But if the carriage is a nest, it is also the container of nests—a potential disturbance in the nursery is suggested by the adjective "mad," whose threat is for the moment attenuated by the verb "repose." Madness is there, a violence oddly separated and detached from the actors and seemingly part of the environment, but it is, at least at present, a sleeping *folie.*

> Tu fermeras l'oeil, pour ne point voir, par la glace,
>   Grimacer les ombres des soirs,
> Ces monstruosités hargneuses, populace
>   De démons noirs et de loups noirs.
>
> You will close your eyes, so as not to see through
>   the window
>   The evening shadows grimacing,
> Those snarling monsters, a swarm
>   Of black devils and black wolves.

The second stanza opens out onto the landscape, continuing the childlike tone whereby shadows are frozen into grimaces not unlike the anthropomorphized nature illustrations in the popular children's books ("petits livres d'enfance") Rimbaud mentions in "Alchimie du verbe." Still, it is the gesture of cushioning, or refusing the experience of voyaging, which appears to hold sway. You will close your eyes to the outside, shutting off vision—that which continually makes and undoes relations between the voyager and the outer world. You will believe yourself intact because surrounded by the walls of the carriage. But the refusal of vision is double-edged: it is also a relinquishing of the mastery involved in any viewer/viewed relation: the domination of the look. To stop seeing the horrifying exterior through the window is, by the same token, to shut off the possibility of defining the interior by its contrary. Gone then is the protection of being distanced from the outside world which would remain there, detached, frozen into an illustration. The closing of the eyes makes the illustration come alive and awakens the sleeping madness:

> Puis tu te sentiras la joue égratignée ...
> Un petit baiser, comme une folle araignée,
>   Te courra par le cou ...
>
> Et tu me diras: "Cherche!" en inclinant la tête,
> —Et nous prendrons du temps à trouver cette bête
>   —Qui voyage beaucoup ...
>
> Then you will feel your cheek scratched ...
> A little kiss, like a mad spider
>   Will run about your neck ...

> And you'll say to me "Find it!" bending your head,
> —And we'll take a long time to find that creature
> —Who travels far . . .

A kiss begins its journey; as a spider, it shares with the outer world the quality of darkness; its threatening aspect is underlined by the repetition of the adjective "mad." The outside invades the inside, the nursery is threatened by erotic madness. Closing the eyes awakens the possibility of haptic perception—touch rather than an abstracted and distanced mastery of the scenery. The word "égratignée" signals the movement from *voir* to *faire*; the violence of contact is reminiscent of key moments in many of the poems of *opening*, moments when seams are exposed, the instant of scratching the surface: the fingernails on the child's scalp in "Les Chercheuses de poux," the "picotement" of "Sensation," the holes in the pockets and trousers in "Ma Bohème;" "A blast of air pierces gaps in the partitions, . . . blows away the limits of homes" ("Nocturne vulgaire"). Rimbaud's poetry as a poetry of transformation is crystallized in this moment: the phenomenon of an absolutely commanding perception of the transformation brought on in us by the event of "contact," "opening," "rupture." Thus the importance of the reflexive form in many of these movements: "Puis tu *te* sentiras . . .".

The adjective "petit" used to describe the carriage in the first verse is repeated a propos of the kiss; the kiss shares with the carriage the properties of motion and time as well. The movement of the poem follows the invisible silent machine, the carriage, tracing its passage through space, and the spider/kiss, tracing its passage along the microgeography of the woman's body. These two transgressive movements become one, and what has initially functioned as a mode of separation, an enclosed module transporting its passengers through space, becomes in the intruding spider/kiss what articulates or breaks down the division between interior and exterior. Roland Barthes, speaking of the more extensive and dramatic play with the boundary between inner and outer space which occurs in Rimbaud's "Bateau ivre," calls this the move beyond a psychoanalysis of the cavern to a true poetics of exploration. And indeed, the lover's exclamation, "Cherche!", the only sound in the poem, becomes a true "invitation au voyage"—the invitation to conceive of space *not* as a static reality, but as active, generative; to experience space as created by an interaction, as something which our bodies reactivate, and which through this reactivation, in turn modifies and transforms us. The space of the voyage, whose unmapped itinerary lies in the dashes and ellipses which crowd the end of the poem, merges with a temporal passage ("And we'll take a long time . . .") which guarantees that the voyagers will not be the same individuals at the end of the trip that they were at the beginning.

The poem, as such, constitutes a movement and not a tableau, a *récit* rather than a map. Instead of the abstract visual constructions proper to the stasis of a geographic notion of space, the poem creates a "non-passive" spatiality—space as a specific form of operations and interactions. In the late 1860s the expression "chercher la petite bête" was a prevalent popular slang expression for wanting to know the inner workings of a thing, the hidden reasons of an affair—like a child wanting to know what lies beneath a watch face. But it was also a slang expression popular among literati, who used it to signify amusing oneself on the level of stylistics instead of bearing down on serious matters of content.[6] The turns and detours of the spider—ruse, madness, desire, passage—are at once the turns and detours of figures of style, an erotics, and a manner of moving through the world. It is this prefiguration of a reactivated space that in turn becomes transformative which we will take as our point of access to the event or "working existence" of the Commune.

II.

In his *Mémoires*, Gustave-Paul Cluseret, the Commune's first Delegate of War, reflects on the lessons to be learned from the street fighting at the end of the Commune, and, in the process, details the philosophy and strategic use of that topographically persistent insurgent construction, the barricade. The building of barricades was, first of all, to be carried out as quickly as possible; in contrast to the unique, well-situated and centralized civic monument, whose aura derives from its isolation and stability, barricades were not designed around the notion of a unique "proper place": street platoons were to set up as many barricades as they could as quickly as possible. Their construction was, consequently, haphazard and makeshift:

> It is therefore not necessary for these barricades to be perfectly constructed; they can very well be made of overturned carriages, doors torn off their hinges, furniture thrown out of windows, cobble-stones where these are available, beams, barrels, etc.[7]

Monumental ideals of formal perfection, duration or immortality, quality of material and integrity of design are replaced by a special kind of *bricolage*—the wrenching of everyday objects from their habitual context to be used in a radically different way. A similar awareness of the tactical mission of the commonplace can be found in Rimbaud's parodic "Ce qu'on dit au poète à propos de fleurs" where standard Parnassian "tools" are rendered *truly* utilitarian: "Trouve, ô Chasseur, nous le

---

6. Alfred Delvau, *Dictionnaire de la langue verte* (Paris: C. Marpon and E. Flammarion, 1883), 87.
7. Gustave-Paul Cluseret, *Mémoires* (Paris: Jules Levy, 1887), vol. 2: 274–87.

voulons,/ Quelques garances parfumées / Que la Nature en pantalons / Fasse éclore!—pour nos Armées! . . . Trouve des Fleurs qui soient des chaises!" [Find, O Hunter, we desire it, / One or two scented madder plants / Which Nature may cause to bloom into trousers / --For our Armies! . . . Find Flowers which are chairs!]. In this poem and elsewhere Rimbaud's paradoxical solution to the sterility of Parnassian imagery is, on the one hand, an unqualified return to the full range of ordinary experience—everyday life—at its most banal and, on the other hand, a breakthrough to a distinctly utopian space. Similarly, anything, writes Cluseret, can serve as building material, anything can be a weapon— "explosives, furniture, and in general, anything that can be used as a projectile"—and any person can be a soldier:

> Passers-by were stopped to help construct the barricades. A battalion of National Guards occupied the area, and the sentries called on everyone passing to contribute their cobble-stone willy-nilly to the defense effort.[8]

But perhaps the most crucial point to emphasize concerning the barricades was their strategic use: they were *not*, as Auguste Blanqui also makes clear in his *Instructions pour une prise d'armes*, to be used as shelter. Barricades, writes Cluseret, "are not intended to shelter their defenders, since these people will be inside the houses, but to prevent enemy forces from circulating, to bring them to a halt and to enable the insurrectionists to pelt them with . . . anything that can be used as a projectile." The immediate function of the barricades, then, was to prevent the free circulation of the enemy through the city—to "halt" them or immobilize them so that they, the enemy, could become targets. The insurgents, meanwhile, who have mobility on their side, offer no targets: "offering them no targets. . . . No one is in sight. This is the crucial point." To this end Blanqui outlines the strategy known as "le percement des maisons":

> When, on the line of defense, a house is particularly threatened, we demolish the staircase from the ground floor, and open up holes in the floorboards of the next floor, in order to be able to fire on the soldiers invading the ground floor.[9]

Cluseret writes of a "lateral piercing" of the houses: "Troops guard the ground floor while others climb quickly to the next floor and immediately break through the wall to the adjoining house and so on and so forth as far as possible." Houses are gutted in such a way that the insurgents can move freely in all directions through passageways and networks of com-

---
8. L.-N. Rossel, *Mémoires, procès et correspondance* (Paris: J. J. Pauvert, 1960), 276.
9. Auguste Blanqui, *Instructions pour une prise d'armes* (Paris: Editions de la tête de feuilles, 1972), 61.

munication joining houses together; the enemy on the street is rendered frozen and stationary. "Street fighting does not take place in the streets but in the houses, not in the open but undercover." Street fighting depends on a practice of mobility or permanent displacement. It depends on changing houses into passageways—reversing or suspending the division between public and private space. Walter Benjamin writes that for the *flâneur*, the city is metamorphosed into an interior; for the Communards the reverse is true: the interior becomes a street.

### III.

Commentators on the Commune from Marx and Engels on have singled out the failure on the part of the Communards to attack that most obvious of monumental targets, the Bank of France:

> The hardest thing to understand is certainly the holy awe with which they remained outside the gates of the Bank of France. This was also a serious political mistake. The Bank in the hands of the Commune— this would have been worth more than 10,000 hostages.[10]

Engels evaluates the "serious political mistake" by calculating a rate of exchange between bank and hostages. Not surprisingly, his analysis is situated soundly in the realm of political economy. In the early 1960s the Situationists—a group whose project lay at the intersection of the revolutionary workers' movement and the artistic "avant-garde"—proposed another sort of analysis: one which altered the sphere of political economy by bringing transformations on the level of everyday life from the peripheries of its analysis to the center. To the extent that the Situationist critique of everyday life was inseparable from the project of intervening into, transforming lived experience, the activities of the group can be seen to fall under the dual banner of Engels's "making conscious the unconscious tendencies of the Commune" and Rimbaud's "changer la vie." In the failure of the Commune—its failure, that is, in the classical terms of the workers' movement, to produce what the more "successful" revolutions succeeding it produced, namely a state bureaucracy—in that failure the Situationists saw its success. To view the Commune from the perspective of the transformation of everyday life would demand, then, that we juxtapose the Communards' political failure or mistake—the leaving intact of the Bank of France—with one of their (what we really oughtn't to call) "monumental" achievements: the pulling down of the Vendôme Column, built by Napoleon to glorify the victories of the Grand Army. On the one hand, a reticence, a refusal to act; on the other, violence and destruction as complete reappropriation: the creation, through

---

10. Friedrich Engels, introduction, Karl Marx and V. I. Lenin, *The Civil War in France: The Paris Commune* (New York: International Publishers, 1940), 18.

destruction, of a positive social void, the refusal of the dominant organization of social space and the supposed neutrality of monuments. The failure of the Communards in the "mature" realm of military and politicoeconomic efficacy is balanced by their accomplishments in the Imaginary or preconscious space which lies outside specific and directly representable class functions—the space that could be said to constitute the realm of political desire rather than need.

What monuments are to the Communards—petrified signs of the dominant social order—the canon is to Rimbaud:

> Les blancs débarquent. Le canon! Il faut se soumettre au baptême, s'habiller, travailler.
> J'ai reçu au coeur le coup de grâce. Ah! je ne l'avais pas prévu!
>
> The whites are landing. The cannon! We will have to submit to baptism, get dressed, and work.
> I have received in my heart the stroke of mercy.
> Ah! I had not foreseen it!

This imaginary historical reconstruction, which occurs near the middle of the "Mauvais Sang" section of *Une Saison en enfer*, depicts a scene in the colonization of everyday life. The narrator, in his attempt to rewrite his genealogy, to find another history, another language, has adopted the persona of a black African. Precisely at that moment, the colonists arrive. The "coup de grâce" is also the shot of the cannon: in this context, the word "canon" should be taken, as Rimbaud said elsewhere, "littéralement et dans tous les sens"—not only as a piece of artillery or as a law of the Church, but as the group of books admitted as being divinely inspired. The cannon is also an arm which implies an economic investment that only a State apparatus can make.

(The issue of canonization should play an important role in any discussion of Rimbaud *today*, given the ideologically significant modification of the "place" of Rimbaud in the literary canon which has occurred over the last twenty years. Dominant methodological or theoretical concerns have always generated a list of chosen texts which best suit their mode of analysis. Literary theory of the last twenty years—from structuralism to deconstruction—is no exception. It has, to a certain extent, brought about a rewriting of the canon which has elevated Mallarmé while visibly neglecting Rimbaud; this rewriting in and of itself attests to Rimbaud's resistance to a purely linguistic or "textual" reading.)

It is, however, the most extended sense of the word "canon"—the set of rules or norms used to determine an ideal of beauty in the Beaux Arts—which dominates *Une Saison en enfer*. Beauty appears in the opening lines of the poem, capitalized and personified, seated on the knees of the narrator and cursed by him: "Un soir, j'ai assis la Beauté sur mes genoux.—Et je l'ai trouvée amère.—Et je l'ai injuriée." [One evening I sat Beauty on my knees. And I found her bitter. And I cursed her.] It is the transformation of this idealized beauty into a "decanonized," lower case form by the end of the narrative—"Je sais aujourd'hui saluer la beauté— which constitutes, along with the gradual construction of a plural subject, the primary direction and movement of the poem. But the decanonization of beauty is not just a change in the object; it is a transformation in the relation of the narrator to the object—a transformation signaled by the verb "saluer" (a greeting which is both a hello and a farewell): thus, a relation to beauty which is no longer timeless or immortal, but transitory, acknowledging change and death.

The verb "saluer" appears again near the conclusion in one of the poem's most celebrated passages:

> Quand irons-nous, par delà les grèves et les monts, saluer la naissance du travail nouveau, la sagesse nouvelle, la fuite des tyrans et des démons, la fin de la superstition, adorer—les premiers!—Noël sur la terre!
>
> When will we journey beyond the beaches and the mountains, to hail the birth of new work, new wisdom, the flight of tyrants and demons, the end of superstition; to adore—the first!—Christmas on earth!

Here "saluer" is unambiguous and the poem concludes with the anticipation of, the unmitigated yearning for the birth of new social relations figured in properly spatial terms: the as yet to emerge revolutionary space of "Noël sur la terre." The various geographical synonyms to "Noël sur la terre" which spring up at the end of the poem, the "splendides villes," the "plages sans fin," are all situated in a future time which suggests that "Noël sur la terre" is not to be construed as the founding of a new "proper place," but rather that which, in its instability, in its displacement or deferment, exists as the breakdown of the notion of proper place: be it heaven or hell, Orient or Occident, winter or summer. The dizzying religious or vertical topography of the poem, with its meteoric descents and ascensions ("I believe myself to be in hell, so I am"; "hell is certainly *below*—and heaven above"; "Ah! to climb back up into life"; "It's the flames which rise up with their damned one") is resolved in the narrative's final sections by a horizontal and social topography ("I, who called myself magus or angel, exempt from all morality, I am given back to the earth, with a task to pursue"), a kind of lateral vision, which is not so much a vision as a movement ("The song of the heavens, the march of peoples!"), and not so much a movement as a future movement: "Let us receive all the influx of vigor and real tenderness. And, at dawn, armed with an ardent patience, we will enter into splendid cities."

To the extent that the particular revolutionary realization of the Commune can be seen in its political understanding of social space, we can speak here of an analogous breakdown of the notion of "proper place." Class division is also the division of the city into active and passive zones, into privileged places where decisions are made in secret, and places where these decisions are executed afterwards. The rise of the bourgeoisie throughout the nineteenth century was inscribed on the city of Paris in the form of the Baron Haussman's architectural and social reorganization which gradually removed workers from the center of the city to its northeast peripheries, Belleville and Ménilmontant. An examination of the voting records in the municipal elections organized by the Commune shows this social division clearly: less than twenty-five percent of the inhabitants of the bourgeois *quartiers*, the seventh and eighth, voted in the election; only the tenth, eleventh, twelfth and eighteenth workers' *quartiers*, and the fifth, the university district, voted at more than half.[11] The workers' redescent into the center of Paris follows in part from the political significance of the city center within a tradition of popular insurgency, and in part from their desire to reclaim the public space from which they had been expelled, to occupy streets which were no longer their own.

If workers are those who are not allowed to transform the space/time allotted them, then the lesson of the Commune can be found in its recognition that revolution does not consist in changing the juridical form which allots space/time (for example, allowing a party to appropriate bureaucratic organization) but rather by completely transforming the nature of space/time. It is here that Marx's "transform the world" and Rimbaud's "changer la vie" become, as the Surrealists proclaimed, the same slogan. The working existence of the Commune constituted a critique pronounced against geographical zoning whereby diverse forms of socioeconomic power are installed: a breakdown of a privileged place or places in favor of a permanent exchange between distinct places—thus, the importance of the *quartier*. Lefebvre's work is especially important in emphasizing the disintegration of the practical, material foundations and habits which organized daily life during the hardships of the Siege of Paris in the fall and winter of 1870. In the midst of this disintegration sprang up new networks and systems of communication solidifying small groups: local neighborhood associations, women's clubs, legions of the National Guard, and, above all, the social life of the *quartier:* new ambiances, new manners of looking at one another or of meeting which are both the product and instrument of transformed behavior.[12]

11. Pierre Gascar, *Rimbaud et la Commune* (Paris: Gallimard, 1971), 66.
12. Manuel Castells, a student of Lefebvre, has substantially developed Lefebvre's hypothesis of the Commune as a specifically urban revolution in his chapter on the Commune in *City and the Grassroots* (Berkeley: University of California Press, 1983), 15–26. The Communards, while primarily manual workers, were not the industrialized proletariat evoked by Marx. Their self-definition, if not their origins, was decidedly Parisian, and their immediate concerns had less to do with gaining control over the means of production than with avoiding eviction. Thus the enemy and obvious target of the Communards was not the industrial capitalist, but rather those three nightmare figures known for their policing of everyday life: the *curé*, the *gendarme*, and the *concierge*.

The breakdown of spatial hierarchy in the Commune, one aspect of which was the establishment of places of political deliberation and decision making which were no longer secret but open and accessible, brought about a breakdown in temporal division as well. The publicity of political life, the immediate publication of all the Commune's decisions and proclamations, largely in the form of *affiches*, resulted in a "spontaneous" temporality whereby citizens were no longer informed of their history after the fact but were in fact occupying the moment of its realization. Writing in his journal, E. de Goncourt complains about this on 17 April 1871: "Des affiches, toujours des affiches et encore des affiches!" On the same day Rimbaud writes a letter to Paul Demeny reporting on the proliferation of verbal and visual material in the streets of Paris; his tone is decidedly more celebratory than that of Goncourt:

> On s'arrêtait aux gravures de A. Marie, les *Vengeurs*, les *Faucheurs de la mort*; surtout aux dessins comiques de Draner et de Faustin. . . . Les choses du jour étaient le *Mot d'ordre* et les fantaisies, admirables, de Vallès et de Vermersch au *Cri du peuple*.
> Telle était la littérature—du 25 Février au 10 Mars.
>
> We stopped in front of engravings by A. Marie, *les Vengeurs, les Faucheurs de la mort*; and especially the cartoons by Draner and Faustin. . . . The items for the day were le *Mot d'Ordre* and the admirable fantasies by Vallès and Vermersch in the *Cri du peuple*.
> Such was literature—from 25 February to 10 March.[13]

The workers who occupied the Hôtel de Ville or who tore down the Vendôme Column were not "at home" in the center of Paris; they were occupying enemy territory, the circumscribed proper place of the dominant social order. Such an occupation, however brief, provides an example of what the Situationists have called a *détournement*—using the elements or terrain of the dominant social order to one's own ends, for a transformed purpose; integrating actual or past productions into a superior construction of milieu. *Détournement* has no other place but the place of the other; it plays on imposed terrain and its tactics are determined by the absence of a "proper place." Thus, the *détournement* of churches: using them to hold the meetings of women's clubs or other worker organizations. *Détournement* is no mere Surrealist or arbitrary juxtaposition of conflicting codes; its aim, at once serious and ludic, is to strip false meaning or value from the original. Such an aim is apparent in Rimbaud's "Ce qu'on dit au poète à propos de fleurs," where the literary code of Parnassian estheticism is *détourné* by a jarring influx of social, utilitarian vocabulary:

13. Rimbaud, *Oeuvres complètes*, 266. The *Mot d'ordre* was Rochefort's journal which appeared from 1 February to 20 May 1871.

> Ainsi, toujours vers l'azur noir
> Où tremble la mer des topazes,
> Fonctionneront dans ton soir
> Les Lys, ces clystères d'extases!

> Thus, continually towards the dark azure
> Where the sea of topazes shimmers,
> Will function in your evening
> Lilies, those enemas of ecstasy!

Here the echo to Lamartine at his most elegiac ("Ainsi toujours poussés vers de nouveaux rivages . . .") coexists with the most mechanistic and technical of jargons: "fonctionneront" and "clystères." Elsewhere in Rimbaud's work, a similar subversion is carried out by the trivial, commonplace nature of the represented object, the introduction of the detail which is neither distinguished nor abject, the detail which has no higher significance than itself: the clove of garlic in "Au Cabaret-vert."

Rimbaud's poetry constitutes a genuine "lieu mixte": a half real, half fantastic libidinal geography of class exchange. It assembles formal elements from the realm of high culture—the alexandrine, the sonnet form—with Ardennais slang, scatological invective, and political diatribe. Nevertheless, it would be difficult to call this verse "countercultural" in relation to the philosophy, art, or poetry of the dominant high culture of Rimbaud's time. Such a rigid system of cultural purification or hierarchy was characteristic *of* that high culture—of Leconte de Lisle and others of the most conservative representatives of the Parnassian school. Rimbaud's work resonates instead with all the anxieties of the real and imaginary displacements authorized by a cultural place which enables passages, meeting places, contagion *between* one class and another, or even between one species and another:

> Chinois, Hottentots, bohémiens, niais, hyènes, Molochs, vieilles démences, démons sinistres, ils mêlent les tours populaires, maternels, avec les poses et les tendresses bestiales. [Parade]

> Chinese, Hottentots, gypsies, simpletons, hyenas, Molochs, old insanities, sinister demons, they mingle popular, homespun turns with bestial poses and caresses.

> J'aimais les peintures idiotes, dessus de portes, décors, toiles de saltimbanques, enseignes, enluminures populaires; la littérature démodée, latin d'église, livres érotiques sans orthographe, romans de nos aïeules, contes de fées, petits livres d'enfance, opéras vieux, refrains niais, rhythmes naïfs. [Alchimie du verbe]

> I liked absurd paintings, pictures over doorways, stage sets, carnival backdrops, billboards, colored prints, old-fashioned literature, Church Latin, erotic books badly spelled, the kind of novels our grand-

mothers read, fairy tales, little children's books, old operas, silly refrains, naive rhythms.

The point to emphasize about this famous heap is not so much the collective or popular "authorship" of most of its elements, but rather the latent political effect of the juxtaposition of badly spelled erotic books with Church Latin—all under the affirmation ("J'aimais") which renders them at once specific and equivalent. In Rimbaud there is no isolation of the popular into a regional preserve, into some ritualized carnavalesque space of pure *dépense*.[14] He is not a regionalist—his interest, rather, lies in promoting the danger and utopian fantasy which, both, result from contagion. The disorder of his poetry, in other words, is less about his having created a savage, adolescent, or Communard culture, than it is about his having articulated a savage, adolescent, or Communard relationship *to* culture.

IV.

Accounts of the Commune and accounts of the "phenomenon" of Rimbaud rely on a shared vocabulary:

> Rimbaud erupts into literature, throws a few lightning bolts and disappears, abandoning us from then on to what looks like twilight. We had hardly time to see him. . . . This is enough for the legend to be born and develop. . . .[15]

> The seventy-two days from 18 March to 28 May 1871, the length of time Paris was able to hold out against the National Government at Versailles and its army, though too short to carry out any permanent measures of social reform, were long enough to create the myth, the legend of the Commune as the first great workers' revolt.[16]

Brevity, eruption, lightning flash, myth, legend—these are the words which recur.[17] Neither Rimbaud, "the first poet of a civilization that has not yet appeared" (Char), nor the Commune, that "unplanned, unguided, formless revolution" (Edwards), reached maturity, and their lingering in the liminal zone of adolescence—"a perverse and superb puberty" (Mallarmé)—tends to create anxiety. It is striking to see the way in which narratives of both subjects follow a traditional developmental model,

14. "There is a zoo of pleasures to Rabelais. To Rimbaud. . . . It would be wrong to say that the zoo was a jungle, but the animals did not seem to have cages." Jack Spicer, "A Fake Novel About the Life of Arthur Rimbaud" in *The Collected Books* (Los Angeles: Black Sparrow Press, 1975), 154.
15. Gascar, 9.
16. Stewart Edwards, ed., *The Communards of Paris, 1871* (Ithaca: Cornell University Press, 1973), 9–10.
17. Mallarmé, for instance, uses the metaphor of a meteor when speaking of Rimbaud; René Char writes of his "sudden evaporation."

concluding almost invariably with a consideration of the reasons for the failure of the Commune to become stabilized, of Rimbaud to remain loyal to literature, and ensuing motifs: the silence of Rimbaud, the demise of the Commune. Speculations abound as to what "fulfillment" or "adulthood" *might have* looked like: the poems Rimbaud would have written in Africa, the social reforms the Commune would have put through had it been given the time to stabilize.

But such an ominiscient theoretical viewpoint gives way to easy proofs that the Commune was objectively doomed to failure and could not have been fulfilled. This viewpoint, as the Situationists point out, forgets that for those who really lived it, the fulfillment was *already there*. And as Mallarmé said of Rimbaud, "I think that prolonging the hope for a work of maturity would harm, in this case, the exact interpretation of a unique adventure in the history of art."[18] It is in this sense that Marx should be understood when he says that the most important social measure of the Commune was its own working existence.

The Commune, wrote Marx, was to be a working, not a parliamentary body. Its destruction of hierarchic investiture involved the displacement (revocability) of authority along a chain or series of "places" without any sovereign term. Each representative, subject to immediate recall, becomes interchangeable with, and thus equal to, its represented.

The direct result of this kind of distributional and revocable authority is the withering away of the political function as a specialized function. Rimbaud's move beyond the idea of a specialized domain of poetic language or even of poetry—the fetishization of writing as a privileged practice—does not begin in 1875 with his "silence," but rather as early as 1871 with the "Lettres du voyant." In these letters writing poetry is acknowledged as one means of expression, action, and above all of *work* among others:

> I shall be a worker: that is the idea that holds me back when mad rage drives me towards the battle of Paris—where so many workers are dying as I write to you!

The *voyant*, as has been frequently pointed out, *"se fait* voyant": "I *work* at making myself a *voyant.*" The emphasis is on the work of self-transformation as opposed to predestination. The *voyant* project emerges in the letters as the will to combat not merely specific past or contemporary poetic practices, but the will to overcome eventually and supersede "poetry" altogether. Like the "abolition of the State," the process outlined by Rimbaud is a long and arduous revolutionary process which unfolds through diverse phases. The work is not solitary but social and collective: "other horrible workers will come: they will begin at the horizons where

---

18. Stéphane Mallarmé, *Oeuvres complètes,* ed. Mondor and Jean-Aubry (Paris: Gallimard, Pléiade, 1945), 518.

the first one has fallen!"; and its progress is to be measured, Rimbaud implies, by the degree to which "the infinite servitude of women" is broken: "When the unending servitude of woman is broken, when she lives by and for herself, when man—until now abominable—has given her her freedom, she too will be a poet!" An exclamation from the letters like "Ces poètes seront!" must be placed in the context of the emergence, particularly in Rimbaud's later work, of a collective subject: the "nous" of the concluding moments of *Une Saison* ("Quand irons-nous . . , of "A une Raison," of "Après le déluge." Masses in movement—the human geography of uprisings, migrations, and massive displacements—dominate the later prose works: "the song of the heavens, the march of peoples" (*"Une Saison"*); "migrations more enormous than the ancient invasions" ("Génie"); "the uprising of new men and their march forward" ("A une Raison"); "companies have sung out the joy of new work" ("Villes"). The utopian resonance of "travail nouveau"—"saluer la naissance du travail nouveau"—can be found even in the project of *voyance:* an enterprise of self and social transformation which implies that poets themselves accept their own uninterrupted transformation—even when this means ceasing to be a poet.

ADRIAN RIFKIN

# Musical Moments*

For Celia

PART I

In 1913 Lucien Descaves opens his Philemon, his novel-as-oral-history of the Communard Exiles in Switzerland, with a description of Paris, a sparse and bare description that offers up a city of traces, of a kind of history.

> At the boundary of the fourteenth *arrondissement* [ward] and on the edges of the thirteenth, the rue de la Santé crosses a suburb of Paris which could be the envy of a remote, pious, and quiet *sous-préfecture* . . .
>
> In the section contained between Boulevard Arago and the rue Humboldt particularly, no commerce other than that of a wine merchant with a shop sign, *La Bonne Santé*, across the street from the prison, breaks up a long series of walls behind which human suffering and poverty are relegated, as in contiguous lazarets . . . an archipelago of sorrows.
>
> People there are seized at birth and only abandoned at death, satiated with the illusion of having lived. Their destiny is inscribed in a triangle to which everything brings them back. At the top, the hospice of Assistance to children, at the center, the Cochin Hospital, the prison, the Sainte-Anne asylum; on one of the side streets, Ricord and Maternity; on the other the former site of capital executions. . . . There is a very short way to go, and no way of wandering—all the buildings communicate with each other.[1]

---

*My thanks to a number of friends and colleagues who have assisted in the writing of this piece. First, Alice Kaplan and Kristin Ross for convincing me that it was worth writing; Molly Nesbit, for many conversations about Paris; A. J. Dunn, for a fine critical reading of the manuscript; and my many French friends, for tolerating my ethnocentrism: Anet and Michel Melot, Claire Beauchamps, Denis Echard, et al.

1. Lucien Descaves, *Philémon, Vieux de la Vieille* (Paris: Paul Ollendorf, 1913), 1–2.

Such brevity performs a complicated trajectory. If the attenuation of physical description is so complete as to excite little in the imagination, it allows for a rapid shift from the observed to the moral. The lack of architectural detail becomes a metaphor of the human suffering and of its effacement, and it is the plan—not the elevation—of the faubourg that alone represents this suffering's circuit and the closure of its repetitive motion. But, also, this setting itself prepares for the narration that is to follow. The thirteenth arrondissement constitutes a well defined topos of popular militancy, as a historical site both of working class economic activity, in the tanneries of the Bièvre, and of political activity at the time of the Commune and before. In the suggestion of its past the political optimism of the revolution can be evoked as nostalgia, while the bitterness and other nostalgia of failure can be felt through the harshness of the present.

As he opens his story, the narrator (Descaves), has just rented a place to live in this faubourg. ". . . a little pavilion behind one of these six-story buildings which face the street on its right." Here he has a tree in his garden, "in Paris, a luxury in itself." However, it is in the building on the street that an old man lives who will turn out to be an ex-Communard, and who will unlock for Descaves the entire content of his own current research—into the life of the Swiss "proscription" of '71. So the *quartier* not only already contains the narrative that Descaves has undertaken to write, but it also contains him within it, alongside the object of his study. And it is he who lives in the older building, the pavilion, while it is his informant who inhabits the six-floor block, more utilitarian, specifically constructed for the cheap lodging of the "classes populaires," no doubt. Descaves gradually becomes aware of the peculiar character of the old man and his wife, especially upon hearing that they argue through singing popular songs of different political tendency. Increasingly conscious that they are bearers of the culture that preoccupies him, he listens, watches and collates signs of their lives with other "faits divers," until he knows that he is in the presence of the history that he seeks. Meeting the old man, he wins his confidence, which means that he must overcome the resentment of worker against intellectual, and becomes for him the bearer of his past. Through his narrative, and the services he performs for the old man, he assumes the role of executor of the revolution's heritage. In the special overlappings of Parisian social structures, it becomes possible for the intellectual both to confirm the fixity of a history in its site and to bear it out of that triangle of the prison, the hospital, and the place of execution that he himself has mapped out. One effect of this movement, in its social structure, is that historical meaning becomes inseparable from the evolution of a set of literary tropes.

The first photograph is one of these, and is an attempt to reinvent the classic *taudis* [hovel] of some time in the last century and somewhere in the thirteenth arrondissement (Fig. 1). That is, to take an old, working-

*Figure 1.* Doorway, rue Samson, Paris XIII<sup>e</sup>, 1980.

class dwelling still left in an area (in this case the Butte aux Cailles), to isolate it, and so to free it to illustrate a historical discourse on the city and the Commune. The nonapparent irony of the photograph is that it could only have been taken thanks to the legal restrictions on expulsion and building types that set some, temporary limit to the processes of gentrification. For the Butte aux Cailles, with its unplanned mixture of low houses and six-floor buildings is a desirable area; and the city government has endowed its central crossroad with those street blocking flowerpots made of thrown up cobble stones that turn a memory of barricades into a civic decor. Anyway, as I was focusing the camera an old woman approached me to ask what could be my interest in such a broken-down old place, in which she lived. My explanation—Paris, Paris history, Commune, architecture, students . . . left her nonplussed, but partially assuaged the fear that I was the representative of some developer, precisely trying to capture charm in the place. It is still the custom in France to buy apartments occupied by old people on the cheap—one only has to wait. For her, however, this dilapidation was better by far than expulsion to the suburbs, though she took a certain interest in improvements going on next door, a house already owned by young professionals.

These, of course, in coming to an area like this, destroy the charm they are looking for.[2] To tolerate their own role in this process of social recomposition, hygienization, expropriation, and revaluation they must, through their own social group, fantasize some other kind of worthwhile neighborliness. For instance, the naming of restaurants and cafés in terms that connote a revolutionary history and the emphasis of "co-operatives" in the supply of such services, these constitute an aspect of the way in which those with access to history can live out a history of the population they have replaced. In another site, of some of the most brutal expulsions, the Ilot St. Paul in the fourth arrondissement, the change in streetlife is characterized by an enormous number of antique shops. Like the cafés, restaurants, and bookshops of the Butte, they market history as a commodity where the actual historical fabric has fallen prey to the mortician's art of renovation, and where social diversity, which is an effect of the city's history, has been suppressed.

The photograph, then, which is intended to amplify a particular historical analysis, can do this only on condition that the analysis itself remain unconscious of its own fantasy. As it is, the image names a nostalgia that can only come into being through the elimination of its subject. Just as, with the diminution of their irony, Atget's photographs fade into great art, this attenuated Atget-like beauty alone can remain as justification for the image. Just as, in Francis Carco's sentimental song of dead love, "Chanson tendre" [Tender Song], in a "chambre abandonnée"

---

2. See Manuel Castells, *La Question urbaine* (Paris: Maspéro, 1981) for a mathematical formulation of this process.

[deserted room], everything remains in place except an original meaning. "On s'en fout" [The hell with it]. Yet memorialists of old Paris from Georges Cain to Richard Cobb, even if the signification of "old" and of "Paris" changes from one to another, have relied upon the identification of their individual nostalgia for what they feel to be lost with entire processes of historical change. Without this identification their works would appear simply irrational, and it would not be possible to let slip from view the way in which the nostalgia feeds off change and destruction almost to the point of being their reason. So, in Cobb the photographs themselves do violence to the city in their random selection of one or another dilapidated court or café. Abstracted from the actual fabric of the city within the relations of social life, they can only figure as phrases in a discourse of Old Paris. Also, depending upon what part of the city is looked at, and what memories of what histories are called up, the same streets and the same buildings can serve the elaboration of different meanings. Even in a single text—Hillairet's dictionary of Paris streets—a single area like the Marais has histories that function differently in its present use. If the use which is passing now, its history as an old Jewish area, is therefore the most apt for nostalgia, it is the more distant aristocratic history that values the restoration of old *Hôtels* [Mansions] for the use of a new, wealthy middle class. And these meanings must be blind to their difference from each other, and so, too, to their unity. Otherwise they must enter into a conflict where they will come to dominate, so that their politics will no longer be silent, and their interests openly articulated. In Hillairet they simply jostle with each other as architectural description and historical anecdote.[3]

This blindness and unspoken conflict is not unlike the daily use of the city for different purposes. Crossing the Tuileries in summer, from Rivoli to the quai; from the crowds of tourists and art lovers, to the childrens' entertainment of sideshows and boats; to the cruising and flesh display of the habitués of the terrasse and the river's edge; it is a crossing of open and mutual clandestinities, even if individuals make the move from one to another. In this way, then, the daily use of the city and historical/literary uses display a common structure, and it is also common to take these two as the same. In a book like Louis Chevalier's *Montmartre du plaisir et du crime*, or Francis Carco's *Du Montmartre au Quartier Latin*, this conflation coincides with the identification of personal experience with history in the production of nostalgia.[4] While Chevalier can easily pick out countless instances of the articulation of criminality as pleasure, or of death as entertainment, and their inver-

3. See Georges Cain, *Le Long des rues* (Paris: Flammarion, 1913); G. Hillairet, *Dictionnaire historique des rues de Paris* (Paris: Seuil, 1963). My conception of Old Paris is indebted to many conversations with Molly Nesbit.

4. Louis Chevalier, *Montmartre du plaisir et du crime* (Paris: R. Laffont, 1980); Francis Carco, *Du Montmartre au Quartier Latin* (Paris: Albin Michel, 1929).

sions, he reads them as attributes of his experience of place, and their complexity as attributes of the nuances of that place—some forms of violence at Blanche are not the same as at Barbès, and so on. In effect, social relations subjected to a connoisseurship of their representation, cease to be relations at all. They are only things to be named, like birdwatching without ecology. The processes implicit in the naming, that value and order it, stay out of sight and out of earshot. For all their apparent attachment to the specificity of historical moment, then, the namers can hardly give voice to historical change; expropriators themselves, they can at the most produce the formulas into which another experience, of dispossession for example, might be displaced, within the boundaries that they produce for culture. This is why "love," or its loss, which is one of the most common themes in song, might, at certain moments, voice something else as well. This possibility of standing in is the basis for the popularity, which is also the ambiguity, of a refrain like:

> Je n'attends plus rien
> Rien désormais ne m'appartient
> Je n'ai gardé que d'vieilles histoires
> Au fond de ma mémoire . . .

[Music Cazeaux, Guillermin, words Poterat, recorded by Fréhel]

> I expect nothing anymore / Nothing henceforth belongs to me / I've kept only old stories / Deep in my memory . . .*

*Moment 1*

It is a pity that only one journal, (as far as can be seen) a music magazine, referred to Carmen as "musique Communarde" in its review of the opening night. If many of the reviewers were professionally uninterested, curious or cautiously enthusiastic in their reception, a number latched onto signs of some kind of social disorder in the scene, and it seems to have been their views that placed the opera in French musical history for the short term at least, as a failure. Best summed up in a standard musical history of 1885:

> Were the music as interesting as it is uneven and hybrid in its composition, it could not redeem the shame of such a subject, which for two centuries had never dishonored a stage meant for the delicate pleasures and amusements of good society.[5]

True, if one were to take only the highest literary standards in judging Carmen, it fell far short of the finesse and subtlety of Mérimée's story, by

---

*All translations ae literal. They make no attempt to communicate tone. Editor's note.
5. Félix Clément, *Histoire de la musique* (Paris: Hachette, 1883).

then thirty years old and a classic of the naturalist genre. But the Opéra Comique was, very simply, a place for making marriage introductions among the children of the upper classes, where even the stock-in-trade of opera, death on stage, was already excessive. And there, on the scene, 3 March 1875, the mezzo Gallié-Marie sits on a table and entices a soldier to desertion and the exercise of sexual freedom. So there unfolds an unintended confrontation of the two polar opposites of bourgeois sexual life, the *"fille"* [prostitute] on stage and the *"jeune fille"* [young woman] in the loges, the inhabitant of the "bas-étage" [lower floor] and the inhabitant of the first. Any dumb policeman on vice duties knows, that, if he goes into a bistrot and the girls are sitting on the tables, or have their feet up on them, he is not dealing with the genre of the exotic, nor can the local color of Bizet's Spanish tunes induce this illusion in the Salle Favart. Any good bourgeois knows that the Communards of 1871 were drunks, that prostitutes like dancing because their nature is agitated, that it is because of their nature that they like men . . . too much! So perhaps the reason none of the critics, favorable or unfavorable, quoted the line, with which Carmen entices Jose, "La chose énivrante, la liberté, la liberté . . ." [The intoxicating thing, freedom, freedom . . .], was because it was too obvious that it should not be heard. Be that as it may, the presence of the fille in literary culture, unchastened by its moralizing fires, was remarked the same week in *Le Figaro* in an article questioning the literary status of *Manon Lescaut*. Speaking of "filles," and comparing Prévost to Balzac:

> . . . It is necessary to depict them, since they are everywhere, since they climb up to all levels of society in this rising tide of low morals. But he [Balzac] depicted them with the fire of his genius and this fire burns and purifies everything . . .

In Carmen, then, a "Manon Lescaut de plus bas étage" [lowest class] had crawled onto the stage, clicking her castanettes to the subversion of military order, in the privileged place of the middle-class marriage market.

A few critics ironized about this, but the more touching irony unfolded in their columns a week before, and not far away, in the Gaieté, where a lavish revival of Offenbach's "Geneviève de Brabant" had just opened. Here, to a man, they heap praises on the performance of Thérésa in the role of Biscotte. Yesterday's "fille," the raucous and stupidly bawdy heroine of the cafés-concerts of the late 1860s, and foundress of a music hall style for the entirety of the Third Republic, had moved from the "street" to the stage. In the process she became a great "artiste." The respected Gallié-Marie, on the other hand, tainted her reputation not because she sang Carmen badly, but because she sang her too well. Carmen was not performed again until 1883. Not that military insubordination had come into fashion. On the contrary, when Eugène Pottier's little-known poem, "L'Internationale," was set to music, in 1888, the authorities preferred that it should not be sung.

Here, then, a few marking points of a geopolitics of cultural meaning are in their place. A marking of space within histories and nostalgia, and two movements of a fille—one from literary "street" to operatic stage, one from street to operatic stage. At this point the fictionally "loose woman," Carmen, is rather more frightening than the penitent chanteuse.

## PART 2

*Moment 2*

January 1932, in the Boîte à Matelots, Lys Gauty is presenting a subtle and refined program of songs, much admired by her worldly clientèle. They sit at their tables and talk or listen, or, to a number of songs, they can dance as well. Like the audience for salon music of a century before—of Chopin, for example, they will miss little if they pay only partial attention, as one repetition or another will make itself heard, while the wider repertoire of phrases and images within which the songs are produced is already well known. It is not easy to imagine quite what went on in places like this. Reading contemporary accounts of clubs and bars, like Francis de Miomandre's *Dancings*, feels more like a tradition of description that descends from Delvau's *Cythères*[6] than sociological fact. The sexual codings that determine the tone of Miomandre's distinctions between one or another club excite a desire for distinction that precedes the objects distinguished, opening out into a voyeuristic imagination of city life. The author's act of revelation itself carries much of the charge. And if you were to speak to old nightlifers, there is no guarantee that what they remember doesn't come from the gramophone, and is no different from the memories of people who never set foot in such expensive spots. Going out to enjoy yourself for a night is not an activity usually subjected to much interrogation. (Other factors apart, "having a good time" docs not seem to be quite as worthy of theorization as "pleasure" or "jouissance.") So, it can be supposed only, that this audience has decided not to go to the Vikings, or the College Inn, or the Jungle, or even to the Bateau Ivre, where "the Baron of Repsfeld, proprietor of the 'Bateau-Ivre' assured me that he would need the *Gotha* to give the list of his patrons who were dancing the tango like vulgar scruffs."[7] On another evening they could

6. Francis de Miomandre, *Dancings* (Paris: E. Flammarion, 1932); Alfred Delvau, *Les Cythères parisiennes* (Paris: E. Dentu, 1864). For accounts of Parisian nightlife, see C. Brunschwig, L. J. Calvet and J. C. Klein, *Cent ans de chanson française* (Paris: Points Actuels, 1981), and a dictionary, G. Barbedette, M. Carassou, *Paris Gay 1925* (Paris: Renaissance, 1977).

7. Lucie Derain, *VU*, 31 December 1930.

have gone to a Bal Antillais, to learn to dance with real rhythm, but listening to a singer like Lys Gauty, they are not after nonstop noise of bands and loudspeakers, "for fear that all illusion of pleasure be engulfed in a note of silence."[8] Lys's songs, rather, will weave a special, literary kind of magic, in which different types of cultural referent will overlap and merge into each other. This evening she includes work of Nylson Fysher, her sometime *patron* of the expensive Boîte "Chez Fysher." There she made her debut to upper class audiences, as did many other singers of her generation like Lucienne Boyer. It was a place where wealthy and titled people would pay a fortune to hear the "chansons de la rue" [street songs], and, more important to rub shoulders with and "tutoyer" [say "tu"] the "filles du peuple" who sang them. Writing of "Chez Fysher" in his memoirs, Vincent Scotto described Fréhel in her youth:

> Sought after, wined and dined, witty, splendid, gavroche, she was the queen of the place. From her, everything was accepted. She could dare anything. . . . One night, addressing the queen of Rxxx who was wearing an enormous pearl necklace around her neck, she did not hesitate to say to her: "Well, old girl, don't you think that your necklace would suit my neck better than yours?" People were looking at each other, a little embarrassed even so.
> ——"When you are my age, you will perhaps have one."
> And Fréhel answered without losing her cool:
> ——"You are right, I am not yet ugly enough to own jewelry."[9]

The musician Georges van Parys, (who continued to compose for a later generation of artistes like Gréco or Mouloudji), accompanied the singers at Fysher in the late '20s, when he and Gauty recorded *Paradis de rêve* [*Dream Paradise*], a poem of Richepin set by Nylson Fysher. The text is an elaborately overstretched image of sexual pleasure as voyage, and the music recalls the salon delicacies of Reynaldo Hahn. Lys uses a rather tight sounding half-voice, plenty of rapid vibrato and she draws out and purifies vowels and "ou" sounds to the verge of the ridiculous. So the whole style of the piece signals its artistic character and points to a gulf between the demands of the nightclub public, and the public of the Casino de Paris, the Folies Bergères, or the Moulin Rouge. The crass orchestral ritournelles of Mistinguett singing *Mon Homme* [*My Man*] could hardly seem more distant. Yet that January, of 1932, alongside settings of Heine and Richepin, Lys's program included *Barbara's Song* and the *Pirate's Fiancée* from the *Threepenny Opera*, which she recorded the same year, and with which she won the Grand Prix du Disque. Here, the pointed precision of address and vocal technique construct a shamelessly coy

---

8. R. de Beauplan and G. de Belay in a late '20's magazine. These quotations are taken from the "recueils factices" of press cuttings in the section Ro/Théâtre of the Bibliothèque de l'Arsenal, as are all the later press comments on Damia, Fréhel, and Piaf.

9. Vincent Scotto, *Souvenirs de Paris* (Toulouse: Editions S.T.A.E.L., 1947).

pretence of sexual transgression, a merely tangential deviance in sleeping with the man whose collar was not white, even on Sundays . . . in the end the performance stands as close to conventional morality, as, say, does Mistinguett's gesture, on her return from the U.S. of hitching of her skirt, so her public can see her legs again.

Meanwhile the success of the Brecht/Weill songs was sufficient to induce Weill to do two settings especially for their singer in 1934. One, *La Complainte de la Seine* [*The Complaint of the Seine*], represents the detritus of the river bed as an emblem of Paris, "armes," "larmes" [arms, tears], and slime, the inverse of glamour and the intensification of sorrow. The musician is completely at ease in a fusion of cabaret style and modern methods of composition, so that the piece is coextensive with the political cabaret of Germany and the artistic cabaret of Paris, and sounds like serious entertainment. On the cover of the sheet music, however, in full-length silk amidst the art-deco typography, Lys stretches out her arms and smiles in the fantastic ecstasy of the artiste receiving her acclaim. It is, after all, through her professional activity that the constituent parts of music and verse, whatever their character or intent, are held together in this form of entertainment, through which Weill can make a living, as one meaning gets exchanged for another.

In September 1933 Gauty opens a new cabaret in the old Chat Noir in Montmartre, where she has the waiters got up as grooms and the orchestra in eighteenth-century costume. The site, the sometime home of the old Montmartrois avant-garde of the late nineteenth century, implied a certain continuity of origins. As critics remarked it was an appropriate point of transition in the movement of a career that extends from the street to the street, through the valorizing attentions of the rich, the famous, the chic. When Lys gives an interview to *Femme de France* in 1935, after she has started singing in the really big music halls, she is proud to recount that her debut, in her youth, was in singing opera arias in "Je ne sais plus quelle boîte d'un quartier populeux" [In a forgotten dive of a crowded neighborhood]. So if she started out singing opera to the people, she was not long in singing popular songs to the rich. Her most famous hit of the '30s, *Le Chaland qui passe* [The passing Barge], is a fantasy of fugitive love, love that embarks on the barge that slides by in the night. It is full of the imagery of *bals musettes* and *auberges* [country balls and inns] that most love songs of this kind have to include, but Gauty remarked that she was moved to ask for something about barges after she had seen a large number in a dock, immobilized by a strike. If the approach of some critics to these songs is right, then she was guilty of irresponsibility in turning that scene into a romance like the *Chaland*.[10]

---

10. Claude Fléouter and Robert Manthoulis, *La France des années trente*, seen in videotape at the Bibliothèque Publique d'Information, Paris; G. Coulanges, *La Chanson et son temps; de Béranger au juke-box* (Paris: EFR, 1969).

But the relation of this kind of entertainment to political events is really very indistinct. Its meanings are produced within its industry and its habits, its modes of consumption and distribution, its available stock of signs and their polyvalence. The workings of entertainment are so routine as to be almost invisible. And it is with this that we are concerned, not with the economic crisis, even in the recording industry. As Jean Sablon, Mireille and Lucienne Boyer all remark, they just sang on and on.[11] The presence of the mutual aid societies of intellectual workers, musicians, and entertainers organised to assist the unemployed had no impact on this, and to pretend that they did would prevent us from seeing something of how things did work. (Equally, political music is a different social formation, not an alternative form of music.) In October 1936 *Voilà* magazine ran an article on freshwater sailors, with a full cover illustration and a full page spread inside (Fig. 2). It was inspired by the *Chaland*, and the reporter went for a meal with a family of bargees. This barge is not the site of a murder by Simenon, but of domestic bliss. After lunch the wife sings, *Le Chaland*, of course. The old bargee remarks:

> . . . A beautiful song, said the old man. A beautiful song, but the one who wrote it didn't know that one never sails on a river between sunset and dawn. But a beautiful song anyway!

Well, he seems to have understood that in this case, at least, realism is only a relation.

*Moment 3*

> Entre Saint-Ouen et Clignancourt
> Je suis rev'nue hier faire un tour
> Sur la zone
> Quel changement alors j'ai trouvé
> On démolit de tous côtés
> Quel Cyclone
> Plus d'bosquets, plus d'baraq's en bois
> Plus d'ces chansons qu'étaient pour moi
> Une aumône
> Et devant mes souv'nirs détruits
> Tout'seul'j'ai pleuré dans la nuit
> Sur la zone
>                     [Aubret/Sablon, Salabert, 1933][12]

Between Saint-Ouen and Clignancourt / I came back yesterday for a little stroll / On the zone / What changes I found then! / Things are torn

11. In Fléouter and Manthoulis, op. cit.
12. Cited from the original 1933 text, published in the sleeve of Edith Piaf, *C'était un jour de fête* (Philips).

*Figure 2.* From *Voilà*, weekly pictorial magazine, October, 1936.

down on all sides / What a Cyclone! / No more shrubs, no more wooden shanties / No more songs which were for me / Alms / And in front of my destroyed memories / All alone I cried in the night / On the zone

Such a song is not intended to be addressed to the people of the zone. Rather, it is a message from the zone, frankly cynical and sentimental at the same time. Sentimental, because of the past that it regrets, cynical in that the performer who sings it is an escapee from the zone. The lure of the zone is its history. It came into being as the area around the fortifications of Paris on which nothing could be built. But just because nothing official could be built, everything unofficial was. To come from the zone was to come literally and metaphorically from the periphery.

> j'ai vendu des fleurs aux terrasses
> Quand j'avais dix-sept ans,
> Mais la roue tourne, le temps passe
> j'ai du fric à présent

I sold flowers at the terraces / When I was seventeen, / But the wheel turns, time passes / and now I have money

It is the reality of demolition that permits the realities of the zone to be transmuted into nostalgia as the song offers the outer city slum as the object of un-nameable desires, as a geographical space that can be reached in a métro ride, but which is as far away as the past. A photograph of the late '30s, taken about the same time that the Môme Piaf recorded a rather softened version of this text, shows a young man kneeling to sort through a miserable display of second-hand books on the pavement of Saint-Ouen. He wears a large old coat, and has something of the look of a First World War poet, and his interest in the books sets him far apart from the old stall-holder slumped in front of him in a chair. The young man's fingers are pale and long, clean and work free, in the background there are other people, who might be businessmen or just men with briefcases. It is what we would expect of the zone at Saint-Ouen, not a confusion of social types, but certainly a mixture of different intentions, different needs and different uses, all in one way or another dependent on the detritus thrown up and out by the city. In another photo a young man in a double-breasted suit and a shabby borsalino pushes up to a stall to look at an eiderdown. About eight people seem to be watching him closely from the crowd, as if something important might take place, or as if there were nothing else to watch. In a rather different view of the market at the Porte de Montreuil, an old lady scrabbles through a heap of rubbish on the pavement; it is not possible to see what there is, except that it cannot be very desirable to us. To her right are the vast terrains of the zone, and behind her rises a dark wall of '20s "Habitations à bon marché" [Low income housing], built on the line of the old fortifications. She is curiously less defined than the rubble and the rubbish, but sifting through the scrapyards of the zone is an activity that defines a person and their relation to the city, to its past, and to its present. Perhaps, as slumming in the zone became more and more popular for the middle and upper middle classes in the '20s and '30s, as knowing "zonards" by character and by name became a kind of sign of social grace, these images are the kinds of histories that the slummers were looking for.[13] In the markets of the zone, you might find either the rubbish or the antiques that you threw out or sold only the day before, processed, repossessed, or you might consume someone else's shards. And, among these shards are the characters, the old, the dispossessed, the proprietors of the "guinguettes" or their dancers, the French fries and the lilacs. All these are part of the mythic history of the city, living in its present, the residual evidence for myths that arise out of the processes of economic and social changes, and recompositions of urban life.

So, over a number of years, the zone, as the stake at the center of different political and economic situations, remains important to the definition of Paris and its streets. Its representation draws on already existing stocks of imagery, reinforces and adds to them. For example, the "fille des fortifs*" [prostitute of the fortifications], who, by the '30s, is a dying phenomenon anyway, circulates as a trope alongside the fille of Sébastopol or of the Rue Pigalle, to merge into a single vertical and horizontal stratification of the city—a taxonomy of social relations that extends from the street to the seventh floor and from Saint Lazare to the suburbs.[14] Below society, or at its edges, this life must be spoken through the appearance of its own self-expressiveness, or through the mediation of some person who appears to have wandered through these social spaces, across their barriers and through their experiences, or some person who handles the signs of having accomplished such a movement—perhaps a singer. And what it is to be such a person, is also to have the real knowledge of the un-nameable desires.

In *Saint-Ouen et Clignancourt*, the singer also deals with sex on the zone.

> A mon avis les gens du monde
> Ne s'av'nt pas fair'l'amour
> Au moment critique ils abondent
> En bobards, en discours

---

13. See, for example, Lucien Aressy and Anto Parménie, *La Cité des épaves* (Paris: Editions Littéraires et artistiques, 1943); P. Lagache, engravings, and P. MacOrlan text, *Ambiances populaires de Paris* (Paris: Musy, 1948); S. H. Moreau, lithos, and André Warnod text, "Les Fortifs, Promenades sur les anciennes fortifications et la zone" (Paris: Editions de l'Epi, 1927).

*fortifs: diminutive for fortifications.

14. For the overall question of the "fille," the historical development of prostitution, see Alain Corbin, *Les Filles de noce* (Paris: Aubier, 1978). I have used the word "fille" in an ambiguous way, to denote both a professional prostitute and a woman who might just be seen as being close to that.

Alors cell's qui comm'moi connaissent
C'que c'est qu'un mâle, un vrai,
Cell's là s'dis'nt: un mec, en vitesse
Et je me rattraperai

In my opinion society people / Don't know how to make love / At the crucial moment they are glib / With tall tales, with speeches / So those who, like me, know / What a man is, a real one / Those say: a man quick / And I'll make it up

Here the address of the singer to the audience of the well-heeled club merges with a relation of the singer with the song, as the representative of its meaning as well as the messenger. In the case of a performer like the Môme Piaf, especially, the intrusion of the fille into the club is literally an instance of a social movement on the one hand, and the acquisition of its history by the audience on the other. To arrive in the Champs-Elysées, and to inform its public that they don't know what sex really is unless they've had it rough in the zone, is to flaunt an exotic sexuality as more than real, and, also, to fantasize a possible relationship with the boy, or the girl of the street. But if the insult to "les gens du monde" [society people] or "de la haute" is essential to the appeal of the song, it can also, with the singer's history, subtend a different articulation to a popular audience, who can read it as an insult made on their behalf, an expression of the relation of rich and poor, a widening of the gap in favor of the poor. In the music hall this must have been an element of Mistinguett's satin-covered vulgarity, that dressed up the "common" to banalize wealth, yet made just a spectacle of the often rather antibourgeois, slangy lyrics that were written for her. And, like Piaf, Mistinguett was a bird of Paris, "un moineau" [a sparrow], who struts the pavement and the stage, across and up and down the strata of urban civilisation.

LEGALITY, HEALTH, AND SONG

All those interested in the good repute, hygiene and beauty of Paris would like to see the disappearance of this seedy belt called the "Zone." Upon entering Paris, one's eyes are irresistibly drawn to this corner, disinherited above all others, and leaving an indelible impression upon many. One's heart contracts at the thought of these thousands of people who, close to so many commodities, live in slums without running water, without light, at the mercy of the elements and all ills.[15]

Brisset's thesis was not intended as anything other than an attempt to sort out the complex laws of exploitation affecting the zone after the

---

15. P. Brisset, *La Zone de Paris et la loi du 10 avril 1930*, doctoral thesis, Faculté du droit de l'université de Paris, 6 March 1933. The zone had been the subject of replanning for transport, garden cities, etc., for over thirty years. E.g. see Gustave Péreire, *Note sur l'utilisation des terrains des fortifications* (Paris: Imprimerie Dupont, 1901).

decision of 1919 to demolish the fortifications, and the general development plan of 1924. Nonetheless it seemed right to begin with a moving account of the terrible conditions of life that existed there. Mortality statistics for the Parisian region from 1901 to 1933, drawn up for the minister of public health in the Popular Front governments, Henri Sellier—himself a longstanding advocate of social housing—present a grim account of life outside the twenty arrondissements.[16] If the figures for almost all forms of mortality for all ages were already poor in the thirteenth, fourteenth, fifteenth, nineteenth, and twentieth arrondissements, the most working-class areas of the city, they shoot up as you move across into the zone and beyond. For the age group 20–39, for example, in the eighteenth, violent deaths run at 2.4 per 1000, as an annual average, while across the walls in Saint-Ouen it is 4. In the same movement, suicides go up from 1.7 to 2.2, and for the age group 40–59, cirrhosis rises from 5.4 to 11.2 and pulmonary tuberculosis from 30.4 to 46.5, this last 9 in excess of the rate for the same disease in the thirteenth. In comparison with a working-class suburb like Kremlin-Bicêtre, 220.8, it is low. We do not want to enter into a discussion on the way Dr. Ichok put these figures together, or how they entered into the urban politic of the Blum government, only to indicate that they form part of the representation of the city, and tell us something about those areas that were particularly preponderant in its mythology of place. Photographs of the zone sometimes show something more like the content of the songs. In a series by René Jacques of 1939, the streets of the flea-market of Saint-Ouen are empty but promising, while another series of the Seeberger Brothers, made this time as the German authorities were about to demolish the "barraques" in 1943, shows the gardens and trellises of what was, after all, the nearest open space to Paris. It is possible to imagine in these, at least a dream of poverty and freedom, of cheap shops and dance halls, lilacs and French fries. So, the alcoholism, the tuberculosis, the murders, and the trash are only a part of life there.

However, looking at the worst areas in Dr. Ichok's report, both inside and outside the city, the names of the areas read off like a list of the titles of Aristide Bruant's songs, in the period of his success at the Mirliton after 1885. *Belleville-Ménilmontant, A Montrouge, A la Roquette, A la Bastille,* and so on. It was from Montmartre that Bruant indulged his endlessly repetitive sentimentalisms of a wholly lumpen image of popular life, in which each sign of "deprivation" or "marginality," like illegitimacy or prostitution, is taken as a signifier of social class. And it was in his club that the bourgeois smarted under his supposed insults and rubbed shoulders with the fille. Yet there is more than a little irony in the double meaning of the "à" in his titles, for it is always possible to read it as "to" rather than "at," the indicator of an imaginary journey, not of a social

16. G. Ichok, *La Mortalité à Paris et dans le département de la Seine,* preface by Henri Sellier (Paris: Union des Caisses d'Assurances Sociales de la Région Parisienne, 1937).

position, in which the singer conveys a knowledge that he does not want, and, maybe, does not really have. In Bruant we can see already that ruthless classification by type and place that leads Louis Chevalier to those refined differentiations that repress the origins, production, and meaning of social difference. If the zone and the poor quartier are fetishes in the litany of entertainment and of a certain type of literary culture, it is not unrelated to an attitude toward the fate of the urban poor and working class, to their history and to their future. But, as we have suggested, with *Saint-Ouen et Clignancourt*, through the image of the singer, and a two-faced working of the song, the song can multiply its value as the account of an actual as well as a nostalgic loss. In some of those recorded by Fréhel in the '30s, "Où est il donc" [But where is he?], "Tout change dans la vie" [Everything in life changes], or "La Chanson des fortifs" [The Song of the fortifications], the memory of the city and the zone as popular are woven together. In "Où est-il donc," the saddened reminiscing of a Parisian emigrant to New York comes to stand in for the transformation of the city itself, his memory of the "bistrot du coin" the "bal musette," and the "frites" becomes a lament for the demolition of "nos vieilles maisons" and the building of banks on the wastelands of the Butte. "Tout change" written for the film "Gigolette," sings of the crumbling "barraque" on the zone overlooking the bleach factory, and of poverty and domestic misery. To console herself for the view, the singer sticks up postcards of the Côte d'Azur, while to forget her brutal man, she looks at one of Maurice Chevalier—"tout change dans la vie, avec un peu d'imagination" [everything changes in life with a little imagination]. Now, the misery of life on the zone is pictured in a comic version of Dr. Ichok's statistics, but if it can be changed by a simple act of imagination it is in reality imaginary, and can pass into nostalgia. In "La Chanson des fortifs," "bâtiments à six étages / ascenseur et chauffage" [six-story buildings / elevator and heat] replace the *fortifs,* and as they do, the characters of Bruant's songs are translated into respectability. Bruant himself has a street named for him, the *fortifs* disappear, and with them the old songs and their heroes. Julot is at the Institut and Nini has a château. But if these are gone, there will always be new songs, and this song's own conclusion is the opening up of an unending reproduction of the materials of entertainment in the industries of the music hall, the nightclub, the record, and the cinema. All these songs are written by adepts of the genre, steeped in literary culture, and successful in these industries. We will come back to this. For here the important issue is the biographical relation of the singer and the song and the way in which it holds together a number of the other relations with which we are concerned.

THE WOMEN WHO SING. In the case of the three principal "realist" singers of the '30s, Damia and Fréhel, whose careers began before the war, and Piaf, who met with her first success in 1935, their image as a "femme du peuple" was essential both to their representation and to the ways in which value was ascribed to their performance. That all three came from lower class or lumpen backgrounds is rather beside the point, as the way in which their origins is repeated and anecdotalized exceeds its factual content, and itself constitutes a fully developed discourse on the nature of the popular, and on the relation of this popular to society at large. As a discourse it also forms an important element in the representation of the star as the source of the material that she (or he) sings, and so allows us to think that their relation to the entertainment industry is a voluntary, willed, and individual relation. Indeed the attribution of the meaning of the song to the singer is one of the forces that effaces the industrial nature of cultural production, and faces the consumer with a set of choices and meanings that can be made out of their personal relation with the star. Of these three, Damia is rather exceptional, as she is the only one to be seen as strong or healthy, and as essentially in control of the meaning of her songs, rather than being of it. She also played the "Marseillaise" in Abel Gance's film *Napoleon,* which allowed some notion of a muscular, national glory to rub off on her, a notion reinforced by constant critical reference to the size of her arms. Writing in *Le Soir,* in September 1928, Renée Dunan had this to say of her, although it was well known that she lived near the Parc Monceau and had a fine country house: "Wrested from this feminine mouth, verbal values assume a piercing and dogmatic certainty. It is the people itself speaking out," while in an interview in *Vedettes,* (December 1940), Damia had this to say of herself:

> je suis une fille de Paris. Je suis née à Paris. La pioche des démolisseurs s'est acharnée sur ma maison natale. Elle n'était pas très belle. Elle était très vieille. . . . Si je vous dis que mon coeur se serre chaque fois qu'il m'est donné d'aller dans ce quartier, peut-être vous me croirez. Je le fais rarement. Mes souvenirs sont bien plus beaux dans ma mémoire comme dit le poète. . . . Le studio où j'enregistre mes disques est dans le quartier. A chaque enregistrement mon coeur se serre. C'est mon quartier, ma toute petite patrie.
>
> I am a daughter of Paris. I was born in Paris. The shovel of the demolishers attacked my native house. It was not very beautiful. It was very old. . . . If I tell you that each time I happen to go back to this neighborhood, my heart contracts, perhaps you will believe me. I do it rarely. My memories are much more beautiful in my remembrance as the poet says. . . . The studio where I do my recordings is in the neighborhood. At each recording, my heart contracts. It is my neighborhood, my little homeland.

Her words have all the hallmarks of a *plainte* on the city as they home in: "Paris quartier," "vieille maison," "démolie," "coeur qui se serre." One of the peculiar interests in Damia is the way in which she carries these values out of the previous century. When critics write about her, it is still possible to hail her as the singer who makes the '80s live, who recycles and renovates the great social songs, like "La Veuve" of Jules Jouy. But in an earlier interview (with André L. Daven, *Bonsoir*, April 1923), she refuses the exclusive label of "realist," which she specifically associates with the song of the "barrières" [gates].

> Je chante ce qui est beau et j'imagine que *Les Goelands*, par exemple, ne sentent ni la zone ni les fortifs.... Si la triste complainte d'une fille des faubourgs s'intitule réaliste, ça n'est pas moins une histoire d'amour où la beauté trouve sa place entre un bec de gaz et un ruisseau.
>
> I sing what is beautiful and I imagine that the *Seagulls*, for example, do not smell either of the zone nor of the fortifications.... If the sad complaint of a fille of the faubourgs is called realist, it is none the less a love story where beauty finds its place between a gas lamp and a gutter.

Her asserted freedom in relation to the genres of song reveals something of the way they are constructed and of the fixity of their attributes. If *Les Goelands* was literary and *Sur les fortifs* realist, the category of realism itself is composed of literary images, of city life, the "bec de gaz," the stream and love. A very early review of La Môme Piaf, in the *Petit Parisien* of November 1935, makes this quite explicit:

> Mais elle chante ... cette fille venue de la rue donne aux chansons de la rue la même poésie poignante, pénétrante et doucement vénéneuse que Carco à ses romans de la rue. On la sent mouillée, transie, glacée par cette bruine qui trempe l'asphalte où passent d'inquiétante silhouettes. Personne n'a exprimé l'affreuse et irrémédiable détresse de la pluie dans certains coins de Paris comme Carco.... Mais la Môme Piaf la chante aussi 'vraie' qu'elle l'a sentie ruisseler sur ses épaules maigres.
>
> But she sings ... this fille of the streets gives to street songs the same poignant, penetrating and sweetly venomous poetry that Carco does to her street romances. One feels her soaked, chilled, frozen by this mist which soaks the asphalt where disquieting figures pass by. No one has expressed the horrible and irremediable distress caused by rain in certain Paris corners as Carco.... But la Môme Piaf sings it as "true" as she felt it drip on her shoulders.

And, much later, in 1944, in *L'Echo de la France*, France Roche comments on the way in which Piaf (by now Edith, no longer la Môme) puts a tradition into the first person, singing not of, but from, "ces chambres, ces quais, ces ports, ces zincs sales, ces tonnelles rouillées" [these rooms, these riverbanks, these harbors, dirty sinks, rusty arbors], which make up the material of the realist song. The identification of the singer with the material could not be more precisely underlined, nor the way in which the literary construction of the bitter-sweet substance of city life is also the singer's history, as she stands in front of her chic audience at Chez Gerny's off the Champs-Elysées, or in the Salle Pleyel. We have only to open, quite randomly perhaps, a number of Paris novels from Sue or Zola to Carco or Simenon, and have only to read the first page to find ourselves faced with the wet, the foggy, the shiny, or the gleaming, the light and dark, the fine rain on the asphalt or the cobblestones and so forth. The warehouse of imagery forms an inexhaustible panorama for the bourgeois intellectual who looks out on, steps out into, but stands out of the city. The projection of the city back into the realities of cultural production, in one fantasized form or another, from Mistinguett to Damia, has all the urgency of his (sic) self-fullfillment.

These catastrophes of weather or place, out of which the writer can form a text, the "people" must bear as a different kind of reality, and the singers, "femmes du peuple," must at least appear to bear the marks of their subjection to them. When Fréhel returned to the stage in 1923, after years abroad and now fat and suffering from alcoholism and drug addiction, she sang not only as a representative of the material written for her, but, in another sense as its victim, as the object of a middle-class voyeurism that held her in the realm of the popular, but which also enabled her to be seen as having returned to the people. Her career had definitively moved from the small clubs to the big stages of Bobino, Scala, Eldorado, Européen, or Pépinière. In 1928 she speaks to Michel Perrin (*Rumeur*, 9 September): "As a little girl I sang in cafés, I sang in the streets, and my apron filled with coins, I would go home to my parents'..." and in 1932 Gustave Fréjaville wrote of her performance at the Européen:

> ... on rencontre parfois des traits d'une humanité si simple, si dépouillée de littérature, comme cet aveu d'une déchirante mélancholie: "On avait pu de notre amour / Fait autre chose." Fréhel dit cela d'une façon si sincère, si bouleversée, qu'elle a peur de s'être trop livrée et qu'aussitôt elle éprouve le besoin de nous faire rire par quelque grasse intonation de voyou. C'est sa manière ...

> ... One sometimes meets such simple human traits, so divested of literature, like this heartrending melancholy confession: "One could have made / Something else of our love." Fréhel says it with such upset sincerity that, afraid of having opened up too candidly, she immediately feels the need to make us laugh by a raucous bad boy intonation. It is her manner ...

It is not exactly like speaking of an actress who assumes a role, or a number of roles, but of one who has only one role, in the enactment of which an individual trait, like a good voice or a miserable childhood, function as accessories. The page of *Voilà* devoted to Fréhel (16 May 1936) confirms her place, her true position and her fullfillment of the people's history:

> Bonne grosse, Fréhel, poings aux hanches, image du peuple réduisant l'histoire au quotidien et le lyrisme épuisé à la truculence; le peuple, ce "donneur de sang" rouge comme le foulard de la blonde Fréhel.

Good Fat Fréhel, hands on her hips, an image of the people reducing history to the everyday, and spent lyricism to truculence; the people, this "blood donor" red as the scarf of blonde Fréhel.

But if her life really did end in ruins, as an alchoholic, as a vegetable seller in the Rue Lepic, for Louis Chevalier this signifies no more than the fullfillment of the nature of the place on the one hand and the identification of poverty with nostalgia on the other. "Voix de la Foire du Trône, voix de Paris, Voix de Fréhel . . . ," *Voilà* seems to agree with him.

This figure of the woman of Paris who sings, however, stands at the congruence of relations of class and social power, which make and control the values and distribution of this kind of musical culture. In "Comme un moineau" Fréhel sings the classic story of the *gamine* who becomes a prostitute: born in a gutter, or under a rooftop, pretty at fifteen—the first gigolo who opens his arms and "mon amour est tombé là comme dans un piège" [my love has fallen there as into a trap]; deserted, she takes up with a "p'tit gars désalé" [a little wise-guy], who, not wanting to work, "me vendit à d'autres" [sold me to others]. Then she sings her decline:— "mon seul bien / ce pauvre corps que je le sens bien / déjà se lasse" [my only possession / this poor body, I feel it / is already weary], falls on the "pavé brutal" [cruel pavement] to end up in the "lit d'hôpital" [hospital bed]. The rhymes are crude, but the utterly deadpan rendition of their banal and inevitable sequence is rendered the more touching by their callous implication of their fatality for herself. What is touching is precisely this undefined boundary between the social destruction and self-destruction of the woman through the relations of urban life. Self-sacrifice to sex, to alcohol and to cocaine, to the limits of pleasure that break the body are the commonplace of songs like this, like *Quand Même,* and *La Coco,* all recorded by Fréhel and Piaf in the '30s. All offer the body as a victim of pleasure. Alternatively *"L'Obsédé,"* by two of the most famous songwriters of the period, Daniderff and Fleurigny, vents the frustration of a man at his enslavement by a woman in a sadistic fantasy that becomes one of self-destruction when it is sung by a woman. Hence their appearance in the nightclubs of the rich is, in a literal sense, a use of the working-class body for voyeuristic pleasure, and a stage in the financial valorization of the songs that sifts them for success or failure and prepares them for the radio or for the recording industry,—for another audience.[17] It was from the Chez Gerny's that Jacques Canetti took Piaf onto the radio and into the studios of Polydor, not from the street. At the same time, it is worth noting that, if a number of the singers themselves come from a lower class or lumpen background, the men who write their songs rarely do so.

THE MEN. Leave aside the interventions in the song market of men like Sartre, Prévert, Kosma, Weill, Aragon. Jean Nohain, who, with

---

17. For an important, if brief, discussion of the gramophone, see Jacques Rancière, "Le Bon Temps ou la barrière des plaisirs," *Révoltes Logiques* 7/8 (1978), 21–66.

Mireille, wrote one of the great '30s successes, "Couchés dans le foin," was a lawyer, as were Van Parys and Xanrof; Daniderff was an orchestral conductor and Willemetz, who wrote "Mon Homme" for Mistinguett, was a civil servant in the Ministry of the Interior. Vaucaire, producer of *Sans lendemain* for Fréhel and *Non je ne regrette rien* for Piaf was a journalist, radio producer and antique bookseller while Vandair, who wrote for Fréhel and Tino Rossi among others, started out as an engineer. This list is endless, though clearly many "paroliers" and musicians also came from professional music hall backgrounds, or from "below," like Mouloudji. But it suggests a certain mingling of a stratum of amateur literati in a culture that only in some cases became their profession, and which as an activity, left their class status intact. Though they could and did become well known, achieving, like Daniderff, a success of eccentricity or scandal, their relative occlusion behind the singers is not so much an expropriation of their role as its essence, which is to make others speak, as if in their own name. Nor, if we can take a professional literary producer, Parisian mythologizer and songwriter like Carco as symptomatic, were their views on class and sex anything other than ethnocentric. In a song, like *C'est déguelasse,* where a fille describes the messed-up face of her boxer boyfriend, Carco shows himself no stranger to the sadistic side of song culture and its cornering of women in a man's world. And his 1927 memoirs, *Du Montmartre au Quartier Latin*, are probably a useful representation of the intellectual world in which such values could be lived out.

The function of the memoirs is precisely to turn the past into literature, and, through this process, to reconcile the movement of the title, which is a movement from obscurity to fame, with the integrity of the author's own personality. The living out of a mythic avant-garde of Montmartre at the turn of the century (drink, women, Utrillo), can't call its bluff without undermining the author's status. So while he changes everything else must remain fixed, and therefore anecdotal and never analysed. What we get is an image of a social group made up largely of overexcited young men and their heroes, in which women are valued as models or as prostitutes, or, in some cases, in terms of their selfless devotion to a great artist. If Carco can recall every last word of this or that poet friend, an independent woman, like Marie Laurencin, disturbs his narrative, which makes this principal distinction between Montmartre and the Latin Quarter:

> Here certainly, there was a change from Montmartre where our friends were sitters and models rather than humble girls devoid of intelligence or imagination. These were a rest for us from the others. They were less intrusive, less tyrannical, and since they never lived more than fifteen or twenty days in the same place, never tried to impose. To see them regularly yielding their place to newcomers, we never had

time to get to know them too well. They preserved their mystery and the life that they led away from the place where we met each other was sometimes so difficult to imagine that in spite of our blasé poses, we would feel an odd and disappointing curiosity.[18]

The way in which Carco and his friends consume the life of the city is first and foremost an expression of their own freedom, to look, to choose, to impose: and if their gaze in one direction turns the filles and the voyous into images and anecdotes, in another it is turned longingly on the editors and patrons who will recognize them. This is not so surprising, but it does mean that they have a large investment in the fixing of the social distances across which they pretend to move with such ease. That is to say that they are already anchored within an already established literary tradition where endless lists of rain, "pavés," glistening lights, and fog delimit the possible meanings of popular life. In songs by Carco and others, then, a common theme is the imagining of the prostitute's life and memories, those details which could only have been known at the cost of social distance and the price of sexual equality. Here too is the basis for the constant repetition of the fantasy of the golden heart, the essential equipment of the long-suffering fille. "Les filles qui la nuit / S'offrent au coin des rues / connaissent de belles histoires / qu'elles disent parfois / mais aux phrases crues / . . . et elles croient toujours à l'amour." (*Les Filles qui la nuit*, recorded by Fréhel in 1936). [The girls who at night / offer their services on street corners / know beautiful stories / that they sometimes tell / but in crude words / . . . and they still believe in love.] And here too, the fetishistic differentiation of left and right bank, of one faubourg, quartier, street or another is produced out of the abstract professionalism of the writer's gaze as he moves across the city. The differences are the content of their own freedom of movement, not, certainly, of Dr. Ichok's statistics.

PIAF. In the second part of the early stage of her career, still a chanteuse of poetic texts set to the piano, their refined diction directed at small audiences, Piaf sang *Elle fréquentait la rue Pigalle*. It was written for her by Raymond Asso, and though his interests in prostitution might seem rather different from Carco's, the essential elements remain:

> Ell'fréquentait la rue Pigalle,
> Ell'sentait l'vice à bon marché,
> Elle était tout'noir'de péchés
> Avec un pauv'visag tout pâle.
> Pourtant y'avait dans l'fond d'ses yeux,
> Comm' que'qu'chos' de miraculeux
> Qui semblait mettre un peu d'ciel bleu
> Dans celui, tout sal', de Pigalle.

18. Carco, op. cit., 127.

144  *Yale French Studies*

> Il lui avait dit: "vous et's belle!"
> Et d'habitud', dans c'quartier-là,
> On dit jamais les chos's comm'ça
> Aux fill's qui font l'mêm' métier qu'elle

> She hung out on rue Pigalle, / She smelled of cheap vice / She was black with sin / With a poor pale face. / Yet there was something in her eyes / Like a miracle / That seemed to put a little blue in the sky / In the very sooty sky of Pigalle. / He had said to her: "You are beautiful!" / And usually in that neighborhood / One doesn't say things like that / To girls who ply her trade.

And so she confesses herself to him, and they try to live a life together that cannot flower on the scenes of her old sins, "Alors, ell'lui d'manda d'partir. / Et il l'emm'na vers Montparnasse." [So she asked him to leave. And he took her to Montparnasse.] We are not told on which floor they lived there, but it could hardly have been the basement or the seventh, for the movement to Montparnasse is one upward through the strata of society, in literature, and in the life of cafés, bars, and clubs. All we know is that, once there, he no longer finds her as pretty, and they go their own ways again, She "là-haut" [up there] to her dirty pavement, there to weep, whenever a joyous pair passes by. The tone is more tearful, more social than Carco's version of the same journey, but it is clear who may or may not make it, and who should stay in their place. Yet it is the singer herself who proves the exception to the rule, and it is her escape that renews the authenticity of the imagery of the zone, the faubourg, the street, the seventh floor, where, like the zone, sex is truer than on the bourgeois first, and of the broken-down prostitutes of the "purée,"—the banks of Canal St. Martin and the Boulevard de Sébastopol. Critics who acclaimed Piaf's renewal of the repertory of French Song were hearing a new voice rather than new themes, a reidentification of the singer and the words. It is one of the ironies of this culture, so built on the idea of evocation, that its effect is exactly opposite. It names only its own parts, time and time and time again.

Writing of a different question, that is the inadequacy of the connotative value of old systems of landscape representation to new subjects, Griselda Pollock describes a breakdown of connotation into denotation, and the parallel is useful.[19] The system of imaging that concerns us is also threatened with a collapse of its adequacy—that is, in relation to the viability of a store of tropes whose compositional elements may be vanishing or changing too fast or too radically for them to survive with anything like a general cultural value. But it is here, that, within limits,

---

19. ". . . But how could one arrive at an equivalently potent (to words) evocation by means of graphic signs of denotation that were being stripped of their traditional connotations by current social processes?" Griselda Pollock, "Stark Encounters," *Art History*, September 1983.

nostalgia can hold together voyeurism, pity, or a sense of loss within some common limits. And, an intensification in the vagueness of the images, that we find in some wartime and postwar songs of Piaf, their universalization into the most general notions of love and city, helps to perpetuate viability, if at the loss of literary precision. It is the extreme development of such a process in present-day Parisian nostalgia, of the old Halles in the new pavilions, for instance, that renders it eclectic and ridiculous. The new scale of capital transformation can only contain the petit-bourgeois ideal as kitsch. Be that as it may, in 1935, the renewal of the social movement of the singer "fille" could quite specifically, freshen and vary the connotative charge of the imagery. So with Piaf, the particular conditions of her emergence as a star, and the events surrounding it, make it possible to see her as a phenomenon at the center of a variation of the relations sex, class, and crime, in which the gap between biography and representation is narrowed so as to render it interestingly dangerous. She sings, "son visage tourmenté par les belles douleurs des chansons de rues" [Her face ravaged by the sweet sorrows of street songs]. (*Paris qui chante*, October, 1938).

In her famous *Voilà* cover spread of 1939, only just over four years after her debut, Montmartre can barely contain her (Fig. 3). The huge outline of Sacré-Coeur is no more than a ghost, while the not so distant figure of another woman barely comes up to her knee. The *pavé* glistens and the walls peel. Her gaze projects the whole image over the viewer, but without meeting his or hers. She is the name for some otherwise (unnameable) tragedy of Paris. When, in 1935, the wealthy nightclub owner Louis Leplée took her from street singing to his boîte, she was, for what it was worth, already known as a singer of the streets. Naturally at Chez Gerny's she sang those songs of the "filles de la purée" already carefully fashioned by the professional songwriters, and the audience liked it. They liked her misery and unease, and her modern biographers like to comment on how her "real" talent won through. They also tell us how Leplée was shot dead in bed in April 1936, a year after he launched her; how the police suspected her for her contacts with the "titis" and small time crooks who were her lovers and her friends, and harrassed her until they could find no lead. This resulted in months of isolation and rejection, catcalling at her performances, so that only Raymond Asso, who wrote new songs for her and taught her to sing better, and Jacques Canetti, who put her on the radio, stood by and saved her to win through again. But looked at rather differently this affair was essential to her, for it was already predicated in the culture of the songs. Not, as Chevalier would argue, as their "real" meaning, but in the sense of their needing to appear that this life is what they are about. In one aspect, the fille can be crucified again, while, in another, she can be made to stand in for those realities of which everyday life entertainment acts as the unconscious. (This is normal in the handling of women's images in representations on the bor-

*Figure 3.* The cover of *Voilà*, 10 November 1939.

derline of scandal and amusement.) A song of Gauty's puns on place and fate in its story of the murder of a fille, "Boulevard des Filles du Calvaire, Calvaire des filles du boulevard. . . ." [Boulevard of the daughters of Calvary, Calvary of the streetwomen.]

In *Voilà*'s coverage of Piaf after the killing of Leplée her relation to Paris is more subordinate than it was to be in 1939, produced more within the specific context of the low life (Fig. 4). At the top, the sparrows for which Leplée had named her, and a vignette of her at his funeral. Below, the "titi" she loves at the moment—the "petit homme" she invites to breakfast with the reporter. Then below, the ever-present accordeon, which defines the music of the people, and her image as a street singer. To the left the Place du Tertre and the dome of Sacré-Coeur this time defined, as if she still has more need of it than it of her. In the text, Montarron explains how Leplée put her unchanged on the stage, "She sang her roaming life of môme of the bell, of street urchin. And Leplée, each evening would listen to her profoundly moved, his eyes wet with tears and would hug her in his arms when she had finished."—and this in front of his audience in their tuxedos and evening dresses. It is with ease that Montarron slips in the phrase "môme de la cloche" as if it were a sociological fact, when it was the title of a song composed by Scotto, and the first she sang at Gerny's. It was a hit of the day. The stories that surround this debut become the content of her life as they pass from one journalist or biographer to the others, and enter her own memoirs as the seal of their authenticity. Variations on them abound like talmudic readings, but their fundamental structure is not touched—the triumph of the street.

Yet the merest possibility of seeing Leplée's patronage of her as a source of his death opened up the possibility of Piaf connoting two other obsessions of bourgeois popular culture. First, and, especially after the Stavisky affair, the lurking criminality beneath the tuxedos and evening dresses illustrations of which *Détective* regularly preferred. And, second, was the lurking of men's bodies beneath the evening dresses (Fig. 5). For *Détective* Leplée's death was more a moment in its own shady "rapportages" [snitching] about homosexuality as the site of violence, exploitation and crime between classes than it was a moment in Piaf's career. Leplée's relation with her appears as one of sexual competition, and his death is seen as the inevitable consequence of his own lonely search for exotic and illicit pleasure. This is why, for *Détective*, she could not have been implicated. So, the great drag balls at the Magic City, quite open and well-known events, are fantasized as the context of the murder, and, just as Piaf's songs precede her, so does Leplée's death precede him, regardless of exactly how he lived his life. It exists in the narratives of deviance. At the same time another axis or trajectory of the city is revealed in which the tropes of gleaming darkness now play their part in another sexual story (Fig. 6). Reports on the apparent murder, or death through pleasure, of a young man, Léon Lijour (Figs. 7, 8) and on male prostitution not only

*Figure 4.* From *Voilà*, 18 April 1936.

*Figure 5.* From *Détective,* 16 April 1936.

*Figure 6.* From *Détective,* 16 April 1936.

*Figure 7.*
From *Détective*,
10 January 1935.

*Figure 8.*
From *Détective*,
10 May 1934.

illustrate this trajectory, but the construction of their pages shares something with the narrative forms of songs. Each object of the fantasy is named, placed, and catalogued. And, it is in magazines like these that writers of Carco's circles, such as MacOrlan, also find their outlets in producing the exoticism of the secret and the illicit. Or, as was the case with Carco's buddy André Warnod, in the seedier still pages of *Paris Sex Appeal*.

So we can suppose that the particularity of Piaf's biographical conjuncture with the French song was that it endowed its naming lists with some fresh, if unspoken, connotation. In the scriptural biographies it is usually assumed that the subject of the song *Mon Légionnaire*, written by Asso and Marguerite Monnot, first recorded by Marie Dubas, but made a hit by Piaf, is a part of Piaf's life. A youthful passion

> Il avait de grands yeux très clairs
> Où parfois passaient des éclairs
> Comme au ciel passent les orages.
> Il était plein de tatouages
> Que j'ai jamais très bien compris.
> Son cou portait: "Pas vu, pas pris."
> Sur son coeur on lisait: "Personne."
> Sur son bras droit, un mot: "Raisonne."
>
> J'sais pas son nom, je n' sais rien d'lui,
> Il m'a aimée toute la nuit
>    Mon Légionnaire.

He had big very light eyes / Where sometimes lightning would flare up / As in the sky storms sometimes flare up. / He was full of tatoos / Which I never understood very well. / On his neck was inscribed: "Not seen, not taken." / On his heart would be read: "Nobody." / On his right arm, one word: "Figure it out."

I don't know his name, I know nothing about him, / He loved me the whole long night / My Légionnaire.

In terms of contemporary texts there seems to be little reason to credit this memory of hers, and the reasons why the enormously famous Dubas should not have had a hit are hard to see. Yet looking at Asso's poems, which he published after the war as *Chansons sans musique* (1946), his desire to distance them from their performance by Piaf, whose grand orchestral style he had rejected, makes their meaning more evident. Some are addressed to legionnaires or colonial soldiers, dwelling on the beauties of scars, tatoos, and superior strength; one is a parody of gangster violence (*Browning*), another the account of a meeting with a stranger on a night train (*Paris-Méditerranée*). A good number celebrate that most inevitably fleeting of all lovers, the sailor, whose body and welfare at this point was as much the stake of the conflicting discourses of erotic fantasy and social reform as was the zone itself.[20] If Asso gives a specifically social meaning to the layout of his book, and concerns himself with issues of peace and justice, the main poems that formed the bulk of Piaf's early hits have all the current literary and urban codings of homosexual desire—codings that shift from the pages of *Détective* to the drawings of Cocteau or the memoirs of Daniel Guérin. Sung by the "fille des rues," whose voyou companions might have been her patron's lover/killers, this desire becomes their illicit meaning. What could be accepted, barely and with scandal, at the Bal Magic City, or in the semiclandestinity of the bals mixtes of the Rue de Lappe, acquires in these songs the perfect clandestinity that allows it to circulate with ease. It does not seem so strange that, coming from the lips of Marie Dubas, a "diseuse" [storyteller] much loved by children, they should resonate less richly than from the mouth of a woman who had just emerged at such an intersection of the fantasies and realities of crime and sex. In the plain, everyday normality of the worn-out imagery, through the daily repetitions of the entertainment industries, the song can still multiply its uses. This is what we mean when we say that the everyday acts as the unconscious of other realities, normalizing meanings of poverty, dispossession or sexuality outside the realm of scandal: for scandal calls on regulation or retribution. It is hard to know at what point this power to turn denoting and connoting the one into the other is a freedom and at what point a stranglehold. Carmen is avenged, not through the success of the opera, but through the gramophone. Her message becomes the commonplace of (polite) society.

## PART 3

It has not been my intention in this piece to replicate the highly conservative cultural pessimism of Adorno in his essay on fetishism and popular music. Nor, indeed, to approach its more current manifestation in the work of Baudrillard, who has seriously misunderstood his central thesis on the self-referentiality of signs by attaching it mainly to contemporary culture. The values of different "levels" of culture are not discontinuous even though, on the one hand their nature as a site of conflict over meaning is never fixed, and, on the other, the tools and methods for demonstrating their relation are by no means fully established. Kiki de Montparnasse seems to have had a rather good grasp of the problem. Researching into the nature of urban pleasure in *Les Amuseurs de Paris*, Maurice Verne, in his imagination at least, interviews many of those singers we have written about, and other figures of Parisian nightlife. (Kiki reminds us of Brassaï's secret Paris, which has been absent from our

20. The way in which urban culture consumes the sailor as a lover is analogous to the way it consumes the working-class woman as fille. As such, the sailor can be read as the equivalent male sign to the fille.

text, and it is well to recall his contribution to our conventions of representation at this point.) Kiki, chatting to him of her life as a model to all the Montparnasse artists of her day, Man Ray, Foujita, Kisling, and *tutti quanti*, has this to say: ". . . C'est pas donné à tout le monde, (blague Kiki), je s'rais une môme de musée, comme la joconde." [Not everyone can swing it (Kiki kids around), I'll be a museum gal, like the Mona Lisa.] The paintings are perhaps like the songs she sings in smoky dens:

> Encore un baiser veux tu bien
> Un baiser qui n'engage à rien
> Sans qu'on se touche.

Another kiss, are you game? / A kiss that leads nowhere / Without our touching.

That is, they do not engage in the conventionality of the social relations that produce them, and of which they are signs of affirmation. They are seen only as signs of their purely artistic intention. The museum turns the fille into the Mona Lisa.

*Moment 4*

Lucienne Boyer saw things less clearly. The most outstanding woman exponent of the "chanson de charme," her submission to the need for love is but rarely touched by the most attenuated irony. But at a meeting of women, a feminist meeting, in support of the Popular Front election campaign, she is reported as speaking like this: "Mme Lucienne Boyer who has succeeded in spreading French song throughout the world has seen almost everywhere women endowed with the same status as men. She wonders why French women are considered at home inferior to Turkish or Chinese women in *their* countries." (*Illustration*, 2 May 1936). The refusal of submission in social and political rights does not seem to pose a question about submission in the song.

The same question set for an exam might read like this: "Did Sartre's songs for Juliette Greco make it more or less necessary for Simone de Beauvoir to write the *Second Sex*, and what did this have to do with the evocation of city streets? Discuss in relation to Sartre's own comments on the hit parade in the *Critique of Dialectical Reason*."

POSTSCRIPT:

The last photo (Fig. 9) was a rather conscience-striken attempt to put the first to rights. The concept of the Bellevillois has been so inseparable from the history of the Parisian working class since the election campaign of 1869, when Gambetta won on the Belleville platform, that shooting these old shop signs seemed fair enough. The Rue de Ménilmontant is only

*Figure 9.* Old shop signs, rue de Ménilmontant, Paris XX$^e$, 1984. *André Marty hid here.*

waiting for Chirac to clean it up, to build new heated cabins for the police, and then to glorify it in that most right-wing of city magazines, *Ville de Paris*. (On its cover the "i" of Paris dotted by a little ship scheme with a red and blue sail.) So it seemed worthwhile to preserve this relic of a bygone era of popular consumerism. It's also only a stone's throw from the last barricades of the Commune, including the one where Jean Baptiste Clément saw the ambulance girl to whom he dedicated his song *Le Temps des cerises*, thus forging definitively the relation of the red blood of pleasure and revolution on the streets of working-class Paris. The whole area connotes. But this attempt also went wrong. Puffing up the hill with his shopping, a very old man asked me what I was trying to photograph. "The old signs." He seemed surprised, then sorry. "Mais il y avait quelque chose de plus important là, et on n'y mettra jamais une enseigne pour ça." [But there was something more important there, and a sign will never be put up for that.] The old man had known André Marty from his youth, and at the time he had mutinied his ship during the allied intervention against Bolshevik Russia. It was in this building that Marty had lived clandestinely, and for the old man it was a sign of all their struggles of the '20s and '30s. He did not know if this history had been written up. Certainly, he was not an habitué of the library at "Sciences Po." But he wanted it passed on.

ALICE YAEGER KAPLAN

# Taste Wars: American Professions of French Culture

I would like to capture in this article something of the spirit and self-consciousness that the Seeberger brothers must have had in the late 1920s when, commissioned by a group of American movie moguls, they set out through their own familiar Parisian streets to take photographs that the moguls could use to reconstruct France on Hollywood studio sets.[1] Only here I'm working in the other direction, sketching a series of tableaux that correspond not to any real streets but to the fantasy sets themselves; an imaginary space or psychogeography of a France made in the United States by students and real estate agents, literary critics and professors, mental patients and linguists, journalists, cooks, advertisers, a France invented and reinvented by the forces of cliché and the forces of history. The clichés of the setting precede its history: a place smelling at various times of perfumes and tonic lotions, peopled by soft-focus resistance heroes, or boulevard songsters, or women in turbans and men in chef hats. A place suitable for polishing American men and for "finishing" American women.

Before the Second World War, when education conformed more closely to European models and when French was tied more literally than it is today to the acquisition of culture by an elite, this imaginary France appeared to the American in "monumental" fashion. By this I mean that France was represented to students as a museum about which one learned. The study of French often had a specific function: preparation for the "Grand Tour" which was that elite's "reward" for a University diploma.

The Grand Tour is an essentially English institution. As far back as the seventeenth century, passage to the continent was a guarantee, in England, of a specific class distinction, outlined here by the nineteenth-century antiquarian Rev. Ebenez Cobham Brewer in his *Dictionary of Phrase and Fable:*

> Tour. The Grand Tour. In the 17th, 18th, and early 19th centuries it was the custom of families of rank and substance to finish their sons' education by sending them under the guardianship of a tutor or Bear-Leader on a tour through France, Switzerland, Italy, and home through western

1. The Seeberger Hollywood photographs can be seen at the Bibliothèque Historique de la Ville de Paris (Fonds Seeberger/Série K).

Germany. This was known as the Grand Tour and sometimes a couple of years or more were devoted to it. The young men were supposed to study the history, language, etc. of each country they visited and such travel was a distinguishing mark between the great landowners and the ordinary squire.[2]

To the extent that American models of intellectual elitism are inherited from the British, rather than the French, one might argue that Americans first came to love France as imaginary Britains—that American francophilia was, in its origins, a side effect of anglophilia.

The American Tour (substitute American industrialist for British landowner) involved a goodly supplement of American entrepreneurial energy and enthusiasm to the British aristocratic model. As Henry James's Christopher Newman declares in the opening pages of *The American:* "I have come to see Europe, to get the best out of it I can. I want to see all the great things, and do what the clever people do."[3] The American industrialist came to Europe with a sense of the spiritual limits of his economic conquests, but at the same time he came with a fervent optimism about what an industrialist spirit might accomplish in the realm of culture. In the words of James's Newman,

> I know the best can't be had for mere money, but I rather think money will do a good deal. . . . I want the biggest kind of entertainment a man can get. People, places, art, nature, everything! I want to see the tallest mountains, and the bluest lakes, and the finest pictures, and the handsomest churches, and the most celebrated men, and the most beautiful women. [25]

It should perhaps come as no surprise that in the 1920s, with British role-playing models still very much alive in the American Ivy League, the French major was the third most popular major at Harvard.[4] In the next two decades, Harvard students read Gifford's *La France à travers les siècles* in a course called "Introduction to France."[5] The book divided France into literary units—"Moyen Age," "Renaissance," "Le Grand Siècle," "Le Siècle des 'Lumières'," and "L'Age Moderne" (from Napoléon through Verlaine). "I have tried," writes Gifford in a preface, "to introduce the reader to works, personalities, and historical moments that are outstanding and representative." Gifford's text is punctuated by pho-

---

2. Ivor H. Evans, *Brewer's Dictionary of Phrase and Fable,* Centenary Edition, Revised [orig. publication, 1870] (New York: Harper and Row, 1981), 1129.

3. Henry James, The American (New York: New American Library/Signet, 1963 [original publication, 1877]), 22. A subsequent page reference will appear in parentheses in the body of the text.

4. According to Lawrence Wylie, "The Civilization Course" in *Contemporary French Culture and Society,* ed. Santoni (Albany, New York: SUNY Press, 1981), 22.

5. George H. Gifford, *La France à travers les siècles* (New York: Macmillan, 1936). The book was reedited in 1937, 1939, 1944, and 1948.

tographic illustrations, initially baffling, since they represent neither personalities nor histories, but rather paintings, churches, castles, and—with no relationship whatsoever to any passage from the text—the Arc de Triomphe. Not illustrations of the literary passages, but rather pictures of places where a student could eventually quote those passages. The Pont du Gard is pictured across from Rousseau's "Que ne suis-je né Romain!" (19) [Why was I not born a Roman!]; Watteau's delicate brushstrokes in a Louvre tableau across from the "comédies délicates et fantaisistes de Marivaux" (234) [delicate and fanciful comedies of Marivaux]; next to Notre Dame de Paris is Chateaubriand's "On ne pouvait entrer dans une église gothique sans éprouver une sorte de frissonnement et un sentiment vague de la Divinité" (73) [One could not enter a Gothic church without feeling a shiver and a vague sense of the Deity]. One can imagine the thirties francophile quoting Chateaubriand at the doorstep of Notre Dame, and making a grand speech with the help of Rousseau at the Roman ruin. Every text had a place of consecration, every citation a charted opportunity for use. The French course operated to establish a genealogy of monuments to culture, in advance of the actual trip. Pedagogical method, constructed around a tripart system of veneration, identification, and memorization, was tour-oriented—knowledge itself a prerequisite to the grand tourist's thrills of recognition and cultural self-esteem. James Tharp's 1935 test on French civilization, published in the *French Review*, consists of an extremely rarefied recognition test for proper names of authors and statesmen from centuries past.[6] He recommends that it be administered in French clubs! And on the *French Review's* back cover, one can find in each issue throughout the 1930s, either full page ads for the French Line cruise ships or informational ads for the French Line's Educational Department, whose headquarters were at the Maison Française at Rockefeller Center (Fig. 1). The menus on the S.S. France (even in second class) rewarded the good student with finely engraved verses from Ronsard and "bons mots" from Montaigne.

The best teachers produced by this marriage of French studies with the ideal tour represent a significant contrast to the older nineteenth-century model of French professor-as-philologist. Wallace Fowlie's description of his own dreamy adolescent acquisition of French in the Boston of the 1920s is one of the best accounts we have of the formation of a francophile in this grand tradition—one of the best and one of the most moving, for its utter sincerity and religious devotion. While still in high school, Fowlie started to substitute the names of metro stops for Boston street signs; when the fog blew through town, he abandoned Dickinson's weather verses for those of Charles d'Orléans. He was convinced, he writes, of the possibility of forming a purer relationship to French poetry

6. *French Review* vol. 8 no. 4 (March 1935): 283–87.

Figure 1. France This Summer.

than to his own native verse, because French sounds would always remain essentially "foreign" and undegraded.[7]

He practiced his learning by constructing French collages jammed with photos, maps, and proper names:

> I knew of Paris, before seeing it, the names of its streets, its railroad stations and cafés, its theaters, its museums, its churches. I had traced out on its map itineraries that would lead me through the Middle Ages and the Renaissance and the Age of Louis XIV. I had learned the peculiarities of each century by studying pictures of architectural modes and by memorizing poems. [40]

When he finally got to Paris, writes Fowlie, "every scene resembled a dream materialization."

These were the most dazzling results of the grand tradition: an amorous synecdochic identification of the most minor details of French geography with "La Belle France," and, more ubiquitous, a method of "declaiming" life in the style of France, rendering any experience translatable, and enchanting American daily life.

## WAR. FEMINIZATION. TOURISM.

America's knowledge of France as an actor in two successive world wars, and the combined presence of two generations of GIs on French soil were bound to alter both the American idea of French life and the teaching of French in American schools. The imaginary museum would become a barracks, or a bar. Those who visited it were poorer, and less "prepared" in cultural and textual terms.

The most direct effect of the war on French studies came through one of the war effort bureaucracies. The Army Specialized Training Program in languages, a hurried effort by the government to supply the Armed Forces and the Military Intelligence Service with functioning bilinguals abroad, was structured around rigorous oral methods from whence come the military metaphors in our language teaching vocabulary today: drills, question and answer sessions, and more advanced techniques of capsule memorization and improvisation of basic spoken dialogue. Descriptions of the training offered in this 1944 MLA report on the Army Program give a sure sense of its urgency: ". . . students were provided with words and phrases to be used in a vivid scene or skit, such as French workers being hounded by Nazi foremen in a French factory; or a popular radio program was caricatured; or, more seriously, a military board questioned prisoners."[8]

---

7. Wallace Fowlie, *Journal of Rehearsals* (Durham, North Carolina: Duke University Press, 1977).

8. The Commission on Trends in Education of The Modern Language Association of America, *A Survey of Language Classes in the Army Specialized Training Program* [pamphlet] (New Haven: The Tuttle, Morehouse and Taylor Company, 1944), 15.

Methods such as today's "culture assimilator," which prepares the student to act the right way in a series of cultural situations, were also developed by the army during these years and later adapted to a world in which the military presence in France had been replaced by a business presence. The fear of being "The Ugly American," the professionalization of International Relations in the American university, the democratization of tourism all contributed in the '50s and '60s to a pragmatic notion of language- and culture-learning: they were skills. The new methods meant better spoken French and less knowledge—and love—of French history or art. The American student was learning to communicate with the French.

Yet for all this new emphasis on communication, and for the increasing familiarity of the average American with France, the war had also produced suspicions. The occupation of postwar France by male American soldiers engendered male American fantasies about a reified "French woman," and an identification of womanhood with French culture as a whole. After all, "they were helpless. We've saved them twice." And if they didn't appreciate it, they were dirty, low-down—or frigid and stuck-up. This ambivalence can be read succinctly in *Life* magazines of the 1940s, where British females are consistently referred to as "women," hard working wartime heroines, while French females are painted as victimized "girls." A 1945 *Life* article on "the French Look" begins:

> War and hard times have enhanced, not diminished, the French girls' allure. Lack of gasoline has forced them into exercise, which they dislike intensely, and thus improved their looks. Scarcity of food has made them slimmer. Bare shelves and high prices have brought out the great French resourcefulness. If she cannot buy a good dress (for around $300), a Frenchwoman goes to a showing at one of the couturiers, sketches a dress and makes it herself at home. She wears handsome ersatz shoes of wood or straw. If she has a little chocolate or butter she swaps it for a blouse. The Frenchwoman's genius for looking smart is based on her good taste but is finally achieved only through the spending of an enormous amount of time and effort.[9]

Certainly the women of every occupied country—at least since Odysseus left Calypso—have been subject to similar rhetoric from the families of conquerors waiting at home. The force of this particular expression of misogyny is in its romantic reversal: the American "barbarian" GI maintains moral superiority over a foreign woman deemed decadent, his sadism and envy couched in naive demystifying description. The French girl is savage because she is *too* artificial, "more openly sexy, more consciously stylish, less 'natural.'" France is criticized, through its women, for having a barbarous surfeit of civilization, while the old dream of an

---

9. *Life*, 10 September, 1945, 91.

untouched, uncorrupted (and manly) American civilization is buoyed up in France's stead.

The *Life* writer is both relieved that GIs still prefer "the Great American Girl" and insistent that it is only by means of their "artificial aids" (heavy makeup, underwire brassieres, hair from the heads of nuns who've cropped theirs . . . ) that French women look "sexier" than their American counterparts. The usual confusion about a mythological object is also present. French girls are both energetic (" . . . the gay but artful beauties of France . . . they make it their prime purpose in life to please men. . . . French girls make the most of the many natural attributes they possess and the many artificial aids they devise") and lazy ("French girls prefer massage to exercise. . . . Lack of gasoline has forced them into exercise . . . "). The author considers wartime food shortages and lack of gasoline an appropriate punishment for girls who "scheme" for their beauty. The punishments cause them to suffer and to become even more beautiful.

The real proof of the "French Look," however, is in its illustrations. The disarming theatricality of the French woman presents itself to the American writer as a suspect foreign practice against which he must defend himself and the occupant GIs in whose names he writes, by taking off her all but her "natural" characteristics. And so there follows a guide and explanation of the French body in the form of studio photographs of body-parts (Fig. 2). American body parts are mentioned, by comparison, in the legends that accompany the French photos. "Legs are one of the prime assets of the French girl. They are shorter and slimmer than the typical American legs." "Small bust is characteristic of the French girl, who frequently does without a brassiere" . . . but not in *Life* magazine. Aiming to strip the French woman down to her constituent girl-parts, the American photographs reveal much of what is most American in their inspiration. Though the article speaks in the name of the occupant GIs and of their experience of French women, it is also addressed to the American woman, waiting, and reading, back home. She is shocked, perhaps, by the photos' resemblance to what may look to her very much like a GI pinup poster. And at the same time she is reassured by the legends and the layout, neatly categorizing all that she sees, in the manner of the all-familiar Sears mail-order catalog. Perhaps, the article implies—without ever stating so directly—the American woman should come home from her war effort job at the factory and start to work on her beauty instead. She needn't go as far as the French girl, but she ought to do *something:* wartime French brides, after all, were arriving in America in some quantity in the late 1940s. There is a backhanded welcome to them here, as well, perhaps, as some dim historic evocation of the prairie mail-order brides of the nineteenth century. However strong their resemblance to a crude form of pseudoanthropological race cataloguing, the photographs are finally more closely linked to catalog advertising and

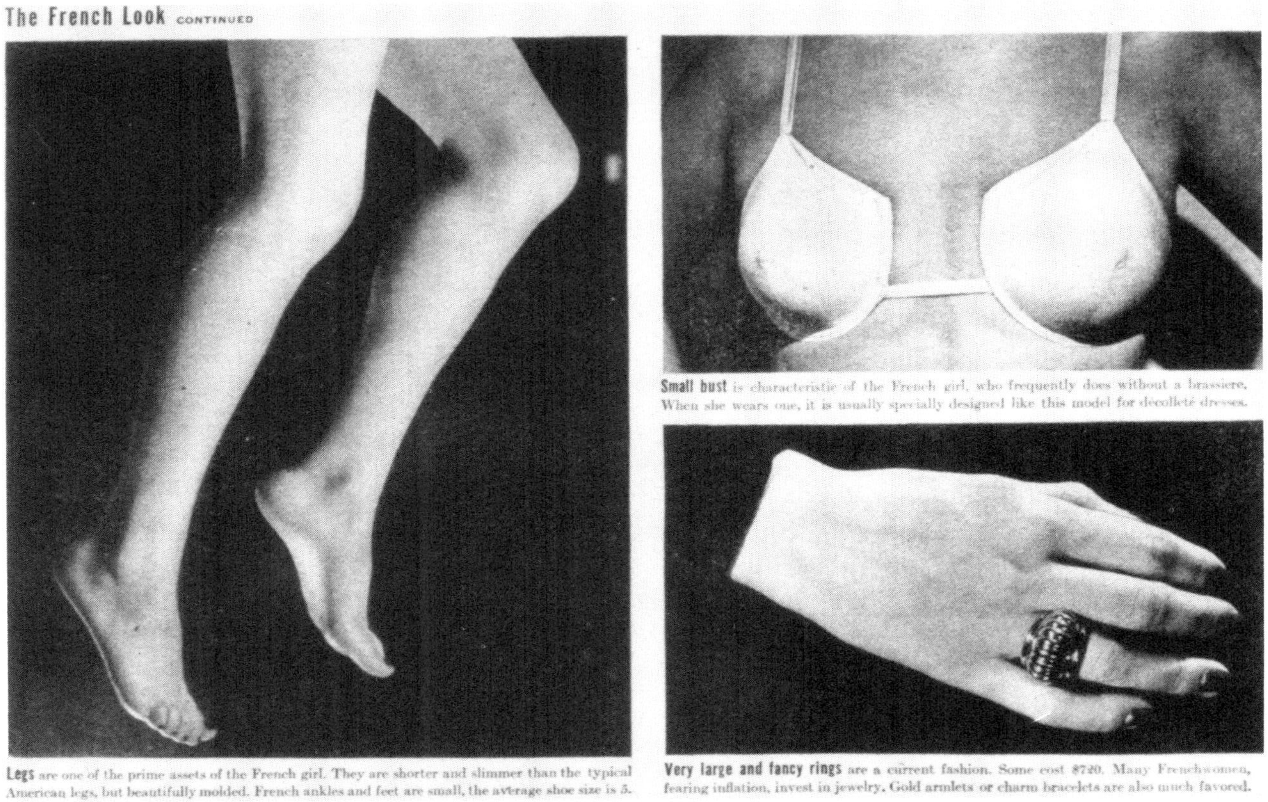

*Figure 2.* The French Look, with permission of *Life Magazine*.

coded in the visual language of fashion photography. They constitute an early example of industrialized surrealism or postwar "consumer cubism"; an indication that, by 1945, an effective esthetic formula using France to package women was already in place.

THEORY. FOOD. WORDS.

*Eating France*

The general message of the postwar marketing of France is that one no longer needs to be rich to live, in America, like the (imaginary) French. The message relies, of course, on the successful evocation of American access to an aristocratic France, and the gripping effect that this memory still has upon the upwardly mobile—or what trade magazines like *Advertising Age* call the "upscale"—imagination. Now, however, through food, access to aristocracy has been democratized, because unlike the grand tour, food is both accessible and interpretable by varying social milieux. Tracing the downwardly mobile marketing of the upwardly mobile "French Breakfast" from the menu at the Pierre to the strip mall Burger King, one could even speak of a "croissantization" of the French cultural icon.

The French food invasion started as an upper middle-class diversion, fueled by the elaborate volumes on classic French cooking by Beck, Bertholle and Child (1961), the televizing of Julia Child's cooking program on television, and the blossoming of food equipment boutiques. It's in the 1970s that snippets of French begin to be heard on American network television. In the genre, a late 70s commercial for yo-plait yoghurt is a veritable allegory of class mobility slogans in the French invasion. Jack Klugman, the most American of American character actors, ingests a spoon of yo-plait and suddenly comes forth with a torrent of fluent French, inviting viewers to get "la culture française." A country which has had so much trouble promoting the serious study of foreign languages, seems suddenly to promote French *as consumption*—or perhaps, consumption instead of French. The banner headline on an ad for Delacre cookies reads, "La Collection Delacre. Une Ligne de Biscuits Délicieux de l'Europe." A subtitle, underneath a silver plate of cookies, translates the French for the consumer: "Even if you don't speak a word of French, one bite will tell you these are no ordinary cookies." The ingestion subgenre spreads to other realms of advertising where, once again, the suggestion is that one can buy French instead of learning it: "Take a quick French lesson today and you may discover the fragrance that expresses you perfectly. . . . Choose Cabochard at Altman's Perfumerie."

In the print medium, an ad in the Raleigh, North Carolina *News and Observer* (1984) announces "single family homes starting in the

$60,000s" in a real estate development called Sans Famille (Fig. 3).[10] One suspects a paradox inherent somewhere in this display of the words "single family" under the rubric "sans famille"; the paradox proves groundless. "Single family homes" means, in the language specific to real estate, "detached dwellings." These are units with the advantages of a house, built on lots that are one third the size of typically zoned residential lots (technically, a "zero lot line project"), and that therefore don't entail major snow removal and landscaping responsibilities. Although in accordance with federal law there can be no deliberate exclusion of nuclear families from a subdevelopment, the buyers at *Sans Famille,* according to a source at the Adams-Bilt Company, seem to have gotten the (French) message. Most people in the development are childless, and many of them are what the real estate industry calls "empty nesters": adult couples whose children have moved out of the house, and who are looking for a smaller retirement home without foregoing the privacy and prestige of a single family dwelling. The "Sans Famille Development" offers both: its French name and deliberately winding streets, named "Rue Sans Famille" and "Cul de Sac," are meant, according to the company, to be reminiscent of "a little town in the Alps." The Development's name—automatically appealing to the cultural pride of those who are able to read it—restricts the village environment to the childless, without making them feel deprived.

The body of the "Sans Famille" ad pictures a stop sign whose letters have been rendered in a French bistro-style graphics. Under it is written "Even our signs are different." The meaning of French in this American ad, unlike the French in the ads for French products, is markedly untranslatable outside its American phantasmagoric context. "Sans Famille" may or may not have some phonetic relationship for the house buyer to the more familiar Americanized French phrase "Sans Souci," which could signify a call to carefree continental living; "Stop" in café graphics may be meant to command "Buy France! Be Different!" or it may be simply an attempt to transform "neighborhood" into a series of style-labels with status similar to those on French-designed purses and scarves.

In general, the use of French in ads has progressed steadily toward more and more use of French words in an authentic Frenc⁻ language situation, to the point where several ads with entirely French language sound tracks currently appear on American television (in the fall of 1985). Foreign product affiliation has come a long way from the early 1960s, when the name of that Maurice Chevalier look-alike, Chef Boy-Ar-Dee, had to be phonetically "managed" in American letter groups in order to

10. I thank Hal Blondeau of the Adams-Bilt Company for his helpful explanations concerning real estate practices. Michael and Hermine Riffaterre reminded me that *Sans Famille* is instantly meaningful to anyone schooled in France as the title of Hector Malot's tale of a virtuous orphan.

## FOR THOSE WHO VALUE THE QUIET, COZY, SECURE LIFESTYLE OF A PRIVATE COMMUNITY.

*Even our signs are different.*

The drive from Crabtree to Sans Famille takes only three minutes, yet the contrast is startling.

For here you'll find a special place, unique in all of Raleigh, designed for special people.

Sans Famille is a *private* place because traffic is reduced almost exclusively to homeowners and guests.

One entrance and exit helps insure that privacy.

Sans Famille is a *cozy* place because all the single family homes are built by the same builder, using architecture that is compatible with the landscape. And each home is thoughtfully positioned to take best advantage of the surroundings.

To say that Sans Famille is ideally located in one of Raleigh's most sought-after areas is an understatement.

This weekend, take a leisurely ride through Sans Famille and see for yourself; and if you should meet any of the residents, ask them how they like living there. But be prepared to have your ear bent for awhile.

*How's this for a prime location?*

### SINGLE FAMILY HOMES STARTING IN THE $60,000's.

**For information call Semi Mintz at 781-3368.
Models open from 12-5 daily.**

Another Adams-Bilt Community. ® Sales by Fonville-Morisey REALTORS.

*Figure 3.* Sans Famille. Courtesy the Adams-Bilt Company.

sell the company's canned spaghetti and meatballs. This is not simply a move in the direction of authenticity—that is, towards replicas of advertisements which would be shown in France. A case in point is an '80s advertisement composed of the slow recitation of individual French words for clothing items. The camera focuses on the body of a woman touching "la jupe, le tailleur, le corsage," etc., teaching the French names for clothes in the manner conventional to American language classrooms: with closed eyes, the sound track of the ad becomes indistinquishable from the laboratory tape for the standard chapter on clothing which appears in all first year French texts. The final words in the string of clothing substantives is a proper noun, "Pierre Cardin." It blends in with the actual names of objects in such a way as to abandon its fleeting status as brand name. The ad teaches that the brand name is, beyond the normally targeted "household word," a basic vocabulary word—a minimal unit of linguistic competency expected of a schoolchild. Contributing to its dissemination are many of the elements we have seen in other Americanized French episodes: the fragmented body of the woman—here in a reverse striptease; the citation of the Gallic word; the isolated luxury item on display.

*Letters.*

Whether or not one understands the meaning or translations of the individual French words used in advertisements is not always crucial, for the specific unit of French prestige in the bulk of the ads—the minimal mark of their difference and distinction—is not the substantive but the article that accompanies it. The substantive itself can even be very American, so that no real change in pronunciation is required: "La Taste" (a clothes boutique in San Francisco); "Le Car" (the American name for the Renault 5); "La Machine" (a food processor). Sometimes a French ending to an American word will suffice (La Perfumerie, La Baggagerie). Sometimes the French words insist on the French origins of a kind of service or product (charcuterie, coiffure, couture); sometimes the French is applied to the most American of products in an effort at Gallic pick-me-up ("Bonjour" blue jeans; "Sans Famille" homes).

The number of French article + noun clusters inserted in the consumer sector alone is vastly out of proportion to the number of people in the United States who actually speak French at home, dwarfing the number of Spanish or Italian words in similar use—words from languages which are spoken *on the streets* of many American cities. It is important to remember that the use of French in America is *not ethnic*, as is the use of Spanish or Chinese—the existence of ethnic French working class communities in Maine and Louisiana has not made a significant dent in American constructions of an imaginary France. Removed from a working neighborhood or community, French is reconstructed as a monument to purchasing power. The advertising media, which have as their goal to strip the American consumer of misery, of struggle, of bad memories, make available as a substitution for these impediments the possibility of purchasing a second, fake identity, which is French.

There exists in New York City a living emblem—or perhaps a critic—of that "second identity"; an American man named Louis Wolfson, an author and occasional mental hospital patient whose writings were discovered in the late 1960s by Gilles Deleuze.[11] Wolfson is not simply obsessed with French words. He writes entirely in French, the language of a place to which he has never been. The story he writes is one of an inability to tolerate his mother, and consequently, his mother's tongue—English. He describes a complex linguistic system for survival, which consists in deforming words from his mother tongue, translating them through systematic phonetic alterations, first into French, and eventually into a purely fictional language involving French, German, Hebrew, and Yiddish. Direct translation into a foreign language is not enough for him–he needs the sense of actually destroying the maternal word. The process of transformation calms him, and gives him a sense of mastery in the world. He writes his story in the third person.

Few things offer as great a challenge to Wolfson's system of defense as the ingestion of food. He is as incapable of eating food with English labels as he is of hearing the English language. His mother, with an uncanny sense of how to pierce his defenses, is constantly bombarding him with food—not with raw food products so much as with food that is also text—processed, labelled food: "packages, cartons, jars, boxes, and bottles" (49). When he gives in to temptation and ingests, he becomes heavy and dumb, losing his concentration and his ability to learn languages. Learning, in his mind, is the only act constitutive of his fragile self. He refers to himself ambivalently as "l'étudiant de langages schizophrènes" and "l'étudiant de langages schizophrène"—the student of schizophrenic languages and the schizophrenic student of languages at once.

Wolfson does not pursue French culture, either in the time-honored elite manner or in the degraded Madison Avenue sense. He arms himself against his impoverished daily life, against the empty world of consumer labels, with his own cultural vehicles: the headphone, with which he can listen to foreign voices in the subway or on the bus, with dictionaries, and with obscure scientific texts he consults in the 42nd Street New York Public Library. He chants slogans in French to keep the American voices away. He is aware of the traditional world of New York francophiles, content merely to skirt it. Reading about a picnic organized by the *Jeunesse Israélite de Langue Française* in their weekly French news-

11. Louis Wolfson, *Le Schizo et les langues*, intr. Gilles Deleuze (Paris: Gallimard/nrf, 1970). Translations from the French are my own.

paper, he skulks their rendez-vous station at Riverside Park, disguised as a picnicker, in search of pretty girls. He enters an essay contest for the Montreal Expo on the theme "Terre des Hommes"; his own entry is a marvelous American parody of the Cartesian "dissertation." And he even attempts to transform his French into something resembling a textbook sample dialogue when several French immigrants install themselves in his neighborhood to do repair work. His mother challenges him to say something to them in French, to see, he supposes, if all his studying has amounted to anything, or, perhaps, to invade his private linguistic world. But speaking "real" French to "real people" he discovers, does nothing for his knowledge of the language: "on the contrary, their presence created conflicts for his pathological state of mind" (193).

Wolfson, in other words, is passionate over a process of translation into French, but relatively indifferent to French people and themes. The foreign words that he manipulates do not free him from anxiety because of their "significance" or their "designation" (these are the terms of irrelevance cited by Deleuze in his introduction to Wolfson's book), but rather because of their role in a *process* of translation, in which he strips the American word of its original sounds and letters. This rejection of the referent or the "deep meaning" of words in favor of their surface values made Wolfson's text something of a manifesto of linguistic poststructuralism in France. Wolfson offered a spontaneous American confirmation, in schizophrenic practice, of continental high culture experimental thinking. He combined every French intellectual interest of his cultural moment: he turned his illness to "text," his symptoms were self-consciously linguistic, and he was a French "discovery" unrelated to any school of American literature or American thought. In an American context, the book was scarcely noticed by people outside French departments; after all, the ground rule of its composition was that it be untranslatable into American English.

Were more American readers able to read Wolfson's text, they might ask questions about it that come closer to the specific conditions of its production. Could France have produced an American-speaking Wolfson, or is there something about the bulemic consumptiveness of American society that makes Wolfson's a-contextual use of French uniquely American? Does his assumption of French as a particular escape-code link him, through parody, or perhaps merely through intensification, to a more generally American capacity for imaginary language worlds? And finally, what is the connection between Wolfson's French, and the French words packaged on Madison Avenue?

As I write, the academic marketplace has begun to reevaluate the focus of French in light of a stronger notion of French-as-commodity. Ph.D. job lists advertise positions for applied linguists to teach business French.

Many departments are divided into "literature" and "civilization" programs—the former for dated esthetes, the latter for the flourishing bachelors of business administration. Even on the more insulated level of literary critical exchange, a 1980 polemic in the *New York Review of Books* questioned the usefulness of deconstructive criticism and called, in one instance, for poetry to be read out loud in the classroom and savored like a fine wine. The loss of cultural aura is perceived as coming from the realms of technique. One critic derides "a suggestion of scientific method in Deconstruction which appeals to graduate students who have begun to doubt that the Humanities constitute a discipline." In the words of another: "We are shirking our responsibility if we look the other way while self-styled 'literary' critics deliver literature into the hands of one or another branch of the social sciences."[12] The attacks should be taken seriously, inasmuch as they represent real anxiety about the role that literature has in the constitution of a national culture. They refer to science or "social science," that is to some indefatigable superstructural force, which can steal from literature all its charm and its ineffable humanity in the interest of method and technique. And they speak an ethical language, a language reminiscent of that last breath of commitment through art in the existentialist modernism of the 50s and 60s. What may be at stake, however, are the losses suffered by high culture on the mass marketplace. In the metaphor of poetry-as-wine there is at issue not the sanctity of taste in itself but the fear of loss of a constituency "proper" to poetry, and to literature. The threat comes at two levels: from structuralist and poststructuralist "theory" which, since Roland Barthes's *Mythologies* directed our attention to the weekly magazine and the daily meal has de-sacrilized for many working critics the traditional hierarchy of cultural signs; from the cannibalization of high French culture by American mass-marketing, and from surprising combinations of both, exemplified here in the Wolfson text.

Both Louis Wolfson—that American icon of French linguistic structuralism, and the advertising community—those French iconographers of the American commodity—participate in a "surface culture," a world where signs are invested with transformative power, and where power is purposefully yanked from meaning. "Sign," of course, is a relatively new word on the American cultural scene—disseminated with this simple diagram from Saussure's *Course on General Linguistics:*[13]

---

12. Denis Donoghue, "Deconstruction and Criticism," *New York Review of Books,* 12 June 1980, 37–41; Roger Shattuck, "How to Rescue Literature," *New York Review of Books,* 17 April, 1980, 29–35.
13. See Marc Angenot, "Structuralism as Syncretism: Institutional Distortions of Saussure" in *The Structural Allegory: Reconstructive Encounters with the New French Thought* ed. John Fekete (Minneapolis: University of Minnesota Press, 1984), 150–163, for a study of the use of Saussure as an imprecise, but fetishistic "key word" in structuralist writings.

# ARBRE

The advent of a "linguistic sign" as a prestigious surface commodity of French origin was an important moment in American intellectual history; as important, perhaps, for native cultural awareness as the prewar myths of the ultimate Grand Tour (of the recourse to a fully signifying Europe) once were for the pursuit of high culture studies. Graduate students of the late '60s and '70s proclaimed the arbitrary relation between word and thing with an explosive sense of the importance of *all* language production—rather than of specific literary masterpieces. Arbre/tree was a canon—the starting point of every introduction to critical theory. It was subsequently on the heels of the French "sciences humaines" that nonofficial everyday culture entered the American intellectual arena, through the doors of the French department. Structuralism in America had a (French?) intellectual marketability that academic Marxism had never been able to obtain, and was thus far more successful than the latter had been in questioning a purely canonical history of literary masterpieces in favor of more complex conjunctions between literary texts and social experience.

The structuralist import had another effect of material importance: it granted great intellectual prestige to the act of reading, for *students whose studies had nothing to do with real travel.* The pilgrimage to France became a residual factor in French studies—as, to some extent, did "the perfect accent." A student who went to France was more likely to "pursue theory" in a seminar given by a critic or philosopher than to locate manuscripts or visit poets in their authentic milieu. There was an economy involved in this new French reading as well as a particular focus on culture, for one could respectably pursue French entirely on home ground. The element of fascination with France of course remained, with a difference. Wolfson, madly constructing new French translations of New York City street life, was a ready-made cultural hero for this new band of critics, unaware of—or uninterested in—simple referential contexts.

In a current economic climate, where student loans are threatened, where we face the prospect of nonvocational studies effectively reserved for wealthier students, and where, at the same time, the general public is being encouraged to return to the "basics," and "the cultural classics," one might anticipate a further retreat from such criticism into a conservative cultivation of French cultural monuments. At the same time, the use of the French substantive as the code language of facile gentrification seems likely to continue flourishing. In the distance between the two reconstructed Frances there will develop a rift—a perceived tension. Our understanding of the rift will be affected by the way French is taught in language courses, in literature courses, and in the standard "civilization" curriculum. But it will also be affected by the way these two "opposites"—French theory and the French commodity-marker in American mass culture—are themselves theorized and represented to students in American studies, anthropology, art history, and any other field which presumes to speak of significant "national experience."

*III. Signifying Practices*

JOAN DEJEAN

# No Man's Land: The Novel's First Geography

In the 1660s and 1670s, Louis XIV's chief military engineer, Sébastien Le Prestre de Vauban, began to plan and construct a complex of fortifications for the global protection of the territory of France. The building of "fortress France" had a decisive impact on the history of modern France, for it was the keystone of the Great Louis's project of military expansionism. Furthermore, in a movement of implosive cataclysm familiar to our nuclear age, inner geographies were created in the wake of the militarization of the French territory, "psychogeographies" whose mimicry of the fortress's structures reveals their creators' understanding of an architecture that simultaneously confined and excluded.

In the shadow of the rising French national fortress, prose fiction took on the form of what we now recognize as the first modern novel. The two writers most influential in this literary transmutation, Scudéry and Lafayette, were also those whose understanding of the dynamics of territorial security was most acute. Recent historians of the French novel delimit its formative trajectory as though that evolution paralleled *avant la lettre* what Ian Watt termed the "rise" of the English novel. The history of the early French novel has therefore been charted as a progression towards an ever more perfect representation of everyday life, as a steady rise to the model of fictional perfection, nineteenth-century realism.[1] Accordingly, some of the crucial links in the shaping of the French novel, such as Scudéry's *Clélie* and Lafayette's *Zayde*, have been undervalued, because their authors show no concern with the representation of the detail that commentators from Diderot to Barthes have seen as the cornerstone of realism. Today's literary historians follow the lead of such

---

1. Watt, *The Rise of the Novel* (Berkeley and Los Angeles: University of California Press, 1965). Subsequent references will be given in the text in parentheses, a practice I follow with all works from which I quote several times. Translations are mine, unless otherwise indicated.

early critics as Valincour and Grimm, who dismissed these women's fictions as *invraisemblable* (implausible or unrealistic). Their judgment reveals a blindness to the undermining and the redefinition of the mimetic function that is central to Lafayette's project in *Zayde*. This storming of the fortress of realism, at the very inception of its construction, has important implications not only for feminist criticism but for any critical model concerned with the hysteria and violence accompanying the philosophical and political foundations of all Great Walls.

In 1678, Louis XIV bestowed on Vauban the title Commissioner of Fortifications. The honorific commemorated the fact that the servant had become indispensable to his master both as practitioner and as theoretician. France's chief military engineer had already laid the groundwork for the complex of fortifications that is the visible sign of his influence on the French nation. He encircled France with the fortified places he designed or redesigned, fortifications that realized a theoretical dream. Vauban was the first to consider the global defense of the French kingdom, to define France as a territorial unit to be protected, and to mark off the limits of that territory according to their defensive potential. What have been referred to as France's "natural" frontiers are almost exactly the borders Vauban thought could be perfectly defended against invasion. Vauban made the kingdom of France coextensive with the fortress.

Vauban's writings reveal that this individual referred to as a modern "republican," as a "patriot," as "the best of citizens" (by Fontenelle, Saint-Simon, and Voltaire respectively) devoted his career to the transformation of France into a fortified place, because he saw "fortress France" as the perfect nation-state, as a nationalistic utopia.[2] Vauban recognized the power that would result from the realization of his goal of impenetrable frontiers. This becomes evident in his definition of the concept he invented as a representation of his system of fortifications, the *pré carré*. In the early 1670s, Vauban began to warn his monarch that he should stop dreaming of more conquests— "if we want to hold out for a long time against so many enemies, we must think of retrenching"[3] —and consider France a completed entity: "The King should think of making his *pré carré*. It's a fine and good thing to be able to grasp one's achievement within one's own hands" (89). The expression Vauban invented to characterize the outcome of territorial expansion, "faire son pré carré," trans-

2. I coin the expression "fortress France" to evoke the use of "fortress Europe" by Nazi propagandists in World War II. On the subject of "fortress Europe," see Paul Virilio's *Bunker archéologie* (Paris: Centre Pompidou, 1975). In the following pages, I present a theory of Vauban's and Louis XIV's use of fortification that I have developed at greater length and with more extensive documentation in *Literary Fortifications: Rousseau, Laclos, Sade* (Princeton, N.J.: Princeton University Press, 1984).

3. I quote from Rochas D'Aiglun's edition of Vauban's correspondence in volume 2 of his *Vauban, sa famille et ses écrits* (Paris: Berger-Levrault, 1910). This letter of 1675 is on 131–32.

lated his conviction that his feats of engineering could find the perfect shape for Louis's kingdom, could square it off.

Speaking of the fall of Charleroi, Vauban proclaimed that this conquest "completed for [the King] the most perfect frontier that France has had in a thousand years" (398). In his definitions of the *pré carré*, Vauban revitalized the commonplace of the monarch as figure for his country by representing King and country as sharing predestined territorial limits and by portraying the King as coextensive with his kingdom's frontier. These definitions reflected Vauban's conviction that the fortress, if properly exploited, could become an advantageous metaphor for a king seeking ever more absolute control over his domain. On the one hand, the impregnable fortress suggested that all those inside its invincible barriers would be safe from all enemies. On the other, the image served to refine the concept of enmity. All those inside the Vaubanian complex were Louis's loyal subjects, French, civilized, and therefore Same. Those outside the walls of fortress France and positioned beyond the no man's land they generated were potential enemies, barbarian, Other.

Since Louis did not share Vauban's vision, he took an action not unlike that of his imperial predecessor, the first emperor of China Shih Huang Ti, who, after completing his Great Wall, decreed that all books should be burned. Vauban's *Projet d'une dîme royale* was the culmination of his politicoeconomic philosophy. He began the work in 1697 and published it just weeks before his death in 1707. The book was immediately seized—and burned—by royal decree. In the *Dîme,* Vauban had provided his monarch with the statistical evidence necessary to use territorial security to bring about cultural and political security. The book would later make him a hero for the progressive economists of the Enlightenment.

The Sun King, however, had learned a different lesson for France's internal affairs from Vauban's military strategy. He assimilated Vauban's teaching so thoroughly that Saint-Simon, commenting on a ceremony in 1703 to honor the commissioner of fortification's achievements, declared that "the King . . . believed that he was making himself field-marshal (*maréchal de France*) and that he was rewarding his own successes" (Rochas d'Aiglun, 2:518). By this advanced point in Louis XIV's reign, he had followed Vauban's advice so literally that he had long since transformed himself into the fortified limit of the royal *pré carré*, becoming himself a Vaubanian fortress. Already in his 1667 memoirs, the King admonished his son that "a prince's heart is attacked like a fortified place. His first concern must be to take control over all the outposts by which one can gain access to it."[4] To protect his princely "heart," Louis

---

4. Louis XIV, *Mémoires*, ed. J. Longnon (Paris: Tallendier, 1978), 259. The paternity of these memoirs has been questioned, but even if the text was ghostwritten by a seventeenth-century author, it remains a valid confirmation of the royal self-transformation.

walled himself in behind a series of dazzling facades. Recent works like Nicole Ferrier-Cavevivière's *L'Image de Louis XIV dans la littérature française de 1660 à 1715* and Louis Marin's *Le Portrait du roi* chart the monarch's systematic mechanization of all aspects of royal "magnificence" and "glory." In the history of the Sun King's systematization of power, Vauban's dream for a French utopia plays a central role. The monarch always celebrated the cessation of hostilities as though a Golden Age of peace and prosperity were to follow for the French people—witness the account of the much-heralded peace of Nymegen in 1678 that Racine prepared for public consumption.[5] Yet Louis's memoirs reveal that he made peace the better to continue to make war: "Peace would give me the time to fortify myself each day with financial resources, with ships, with [military] intelligence" (276). The glory of France's most successful monarch was founded on a continuous proliferation of self-protective structures so that the King alone would know true territorial security.

The King's expansion of Vaubanian strategy provoked a radical redefinition of the concept of representation. The appearance of the word "representation" in the sense of ostentation or ostentatious performance can be traced to the period when the Sun King was altering the meaning of peace. The Littré cites a letter of Sévigné as the earliest example of a usage of the word not yet noted in seventeenth-century dictionaries: "Way of life appropriate for a person distinguished by his rank . . . , his fortune, and also way of life when one behaves as if in a theatrical performance, [as if] under public scrutiny." The representation that aristocrats were, in Sévigné's words, "obliged to carry out" was invented to camouflage a new reality: "rank" and "fortune" were no longer marks of distinction because only one individual, the King, still fully possessed the power they had formerly signified, and, furthermore, fortunes, dissipated to finance the royal thirst for conquest, could in most cases no longer sustain such magnificent ostentation. Representation had become a fallacious image, a facade created to hide the nonfunctioning of the definitional code that the Littré had as its raison d'être. In the words of a commentator on the Ancien Régime, A.-L. Thomas, habitué of the salon of Staël's mother, Suzanne Necker: "Under Louis XIV everything changed. The members of the court had only titles without power, and [were] reduced to a grandeur of representation instead of a real grandeur."[6] By the 1670s, "representation" had come to designate the dissolution of individual estates, inherited *pré carrés*, in favor of the Monarch's newly conquered fortress na-

---

5. "Since [the King] sees his glory at a point where it cannot grow any more, his frontiers completely assured, his empire enlarged on all sides, he is thinking of the tranquillity and the happiness of his people" (Racine, *Des Campagnes de Louis XIV, Oeuvres complètes* [Paris: Bibliothèque de la Pléiade, 1966] 397.)

6. Thomas, *Essai sur le caractère, les moeurs, et l'esprit des femmes dans les différents siècles* (Paris: Moutard, 1772), 170.

tion. For a chance to function in this new semiotic system, nobles were obliged to exchange a legacy whose transmission they could control for a share in a less easily negotiable patrimony.

French dominated the language of classical fortification to such an extent that much of the key vocabulary in English was borrowed from it. French was nevertheless outdone by English in one important area. Classical French military parlance had no one term to designate the space just outside the fortress's outer limit. English, however, possessed perhaps the most evocative expression in a highly colorful lexicon: in the early fourteenth century, legal documents attest the use of "no man's land" to designate the plot of ground lying immediately outside the wall of the city of London (OED). The expression thus stood for a spatial paradox, a territory defined by its lack of definition. The original no man's land was just beyond the containing wall, and was therefore theoretically unowned and under no one's jurisdiction. It was, however, used for a specific purpose by the rulers within the wall: they reserved it for the executions that would have bloodied the space within.

Early usage of the term demonstrates that the border's name was not derived, as dictionaries contend, from its ownerless, or outlaw, status— "a piece of waste, or unowned, land," [according to the OED]—but from its particular function within the law as a place of execution for the outlaw, the no(n)-man. This function, the city, like the dictionary, banished outside its limits. The first two usages of "no man's land" cited by the OED are accounts of the executions of "quaedam Juliana" (in 1320) and "quidam Arnoldus" (in 1326), names that are the onomastic equivalent of "no man's land" because they signify the absence of onomastic completion, "a certain Juliana," "somebody named Arnoldus." The indefinite pronoun "quidam"—to borrow the definition Tony Tanner adopts for the most celebrated "quidam" in early French literature, Rousseau's Saint-Preux—refers to a "person (name unknown)."[7] A "quidam" —as Julie's father demonstrates when he insults his daughter's suitor by thus referring to him—is someone without a family name, a Name-of-the-Father to act as a dual spatial indicator—indicator of place in a genealogy and indication of the ownership of land. The original no man's land was the space in which those who built Great Walls against the nameless barbarians executed those twice outlawed, first because they had violated legal sanctions and second because they played no role in the hierarchies that supported the law. No man's land, land of the nameless non-men or barbarians: the place where the law authorizes the builder of the wall to eliminate those who represent a threat to the system that guarantees his power.

7. Tanner, *Adultery in the Novel* (Baltimore: The Johns Hopkins Press, 1979), 138. "Saint-Preux" is the name Julie and Claire adopt to refer to their former teacher; the character's "real" name is never revealed.

"No man's land" finally entered French at the beginning of this century (at the inception of the most recent conflict alleged by its leaders, in a mode once favored by the Sun King, to be a prelude to world peace), by which time the evolution of military strategy had assigned it a new meaning: "zone between the front lines of two enemy armies" (Robert). In one of the first implantations cited by the Robert, Charles Muller comments that "the word is not in the dictionaries, but it will be necessary to let it in someday, because . . . French can't counter it with any creation of its own." Indeed, his statement holds true throughout the history of "no man's land," in which all the spaces thus designated in English acquired names only much later, if at all, in French. The space outside the wall of the city of Paris, today known as "la zone," as long as it was of strategic importance was designated through description rather than by a precise name. And yet this linguistic blank did not signify neglect, for a series of edicts dating at least as far back as the midsixteenth century prohibited construction on this strip.[8] Similarly, while a number of nearly synonymous terms served to indicate the land immediately beyond the wall of a Vaubanian fortress, none of them revealed the special nature of that territory. Words like "berme" and "esplanade," signifying a green strip, camouflaged the threatening aspect of this border; whereas "glacis," [ramp] "contrescarpe," [counterscarp] and "talus," [embankment] designating the slope that joins, as it were, fortress to ground, point only to the frontier's "oblique function"—what Virilio, speaking of subsequent military achitecture, referred to as its "scandal," its successful merging with the surrounding landscape (*Bunker archéologie*, 10).

Vauban himself was more concerned with defining the function of the scandalous strip, to which he referred with deceptive simplicity as "the outside" or "the outskirts."[9] The two functions Vauban reserved for this zone made it the equivalent of the original English no man's land. It was first of all the place to which those were banished who had no function within the system that guaranteed the authority of the builder of the wall, in this case, those presumed too weak to maintain the discipline of a state of siege. At the first sign of an impending siege, the governor of a fortified place was to "drive out of the fortress those who are useless in a siege, like women, old people, and children" (196). In addition, Vauban saw to it that, in the territory to which the powerless were displaced, the harshest edicts of the defensive code took effect. He warned commanding officers that they would be accused of "inhumanity," of "gratuitous persecution," but nevertheless ordered them to "lay waste" to the land within cannon fire of their fortress, to "burn" all structures, "slaughter" all animals, and "flatten" any heights (195–96,

    8. P.-G. Lorris, *La Fronde* (Paris: A. Michel, 1961), 32–33.
    9. "Les dehors," "les environs." *Traité de la défense des places* (Paris: Magimel, 1795), 195, 198.

198). In classical French military strategy, no man's land was understood as a nameless place where no rival prominence threatened the domination of the Great Wall and as the inhospitable outside to which the newly powerless could be banished.

The effects of defensive architecture on literature are most conspicuously displayed at the origin of a genre, the novel, most frequently defined, like a no man's land, on the basis of its undefinability, its formal anarchy. The expression "no man's land" enters English literature in the work often referred to as its first modern novel, *Robinson Crusoe*, when Defoe's hero speaks of "a kind of Border, that might be called no Man's Land" (OED). Its appearance there was perhaps inevitable, for in his narrative of man's struggle against nature Defoe assigned a central role to an activity never mentioned in the actual accounts of shipwreck victims that served as model for Robinson's other activities, namely the construction of fortifications.[10] A reader who shared Robinson's fascination with bookkeeping could undoubtedly demonstrate through calculation that the castaway devotes more time to this enterprise than to any other. Crusoe actually builds several fortresses; never satisfied with any of his efforts, moreover, he constantly details his attempts to perfect their outworks.

Robinson becomes increasingly aware that he builds fortifications not to protect himself from any actual danger, but because his miniature Great Wall provides the basis for the knowledge of the demarcation between inside and outside, Self and Other, civilized and cannibal that is in turn the foundation of his self-definition. "[A] Man perfectly confus'd and out of my Self"—thus Robinson characterizes the panic that follows his discovery of the lone footprint in the sand (121). He can only calm this panic by coming "Home to my Fortification" (121). His formulation indicates that he can exist as "[his] Self" exclusively within these walls, that the trace of the fortress marks the limits of Crusoe's self. But Defoe's novel also reveals an awareness of the limitations of this Vaubanian vision of the enclosed self as the self intact. When Robinson has a dream that a man with an "inexpressibly dreadful Countenance" is about to kill him, he imagines the scene as taking place while he "was sitting on the Ground on the Outside of my Wall" (70), as if to reveal his understanding that every fortress inevitably creates its no man's land. All his fortifications, no matter how perfect, will never eradicate violence. Furthermore, the physical barriers he erects cannot repress his own attraction to danger, the "fluttering Thoughts" (121) that never cease to betray his imperfect mastery of the self he seeks to enclose.

The work literary history has designated as the origin of the modern English novel reveals that the original space of that novel, the space at the

10. I cite Michael Shinagel's edition (New York: Norton, 1975). In *Great Shipwrecks and Castaways: Authentic Accounts of Adventures at Sea* (New York: Harper, 1952), Charles Neider reprints some of the early narratives that inspired Defoe's novel.

novel's origin, is the fortress. "Robin Crusoe, Where are you? Where have you been?" (112): the first words the castaway teaches his parrot show that his personal geography, once established, will protect him from *quidamity*, from the dreadful namelessness of those permanently expelled from the fortress of civilization. Completely isolated from fortress Europe but, much like Tristram's Uncle Toby in his kitchen garden, still keeping Louis's dream of perfect self-enclosure alive, Robinson's transplantation of a militaristic utopia translates that enterprise into novelistic terms. Defoe's hero represents the first novelist, perfecting the trace of his territory, so that his land will guarantee his being, his name, and his place in literary genealogy.

In France, figures from defensive military architecture also mark the original space of the modern novel. Like their contemporary, Vauban, early French novelists unable to name the space into which the nameless were driven, gave a more elusive portrayal than Defoe of the consequences of exclusionary architecture. At issue in their writing was the unreliability the system(s) of resemblance used to justify the fortress's existence. As a result of the Sun King's politics, "representation" was being redefined at the time of the novel's definition. Deception rather than mimesis was the goal of Classical self-fashioning. Unlike, however, the more aggressive transformations Steven Greenblatt has described in *Renaissance Self-Fashioning*, the "representation" devised by seventeenth-century French aristocrats was defensive, an attempt to prevent others from realizing that they were no longer able to guarantee the names that justified their place inside the fortress. Rather than simply echoing the literary commonplace that appearances are deceiving—what French critics traditionally refer to as the distinction between *paraître* and *être*—the first modern French novels proved that representation could malfunction.

The fact that Defoe's French counterpart, Lafayette, was a woman may explain her still more intricate construction of protective enclosures. We might remember that the text in which "no man's land" entered English was a record of the 1320 execution of "quaedam Juliana." Women, those most useless or threatening to the security of the fortified place, were those first expelled from it. Women would continue to be marked as the original nameless ones, assigned to the land beyond property. Their exclusion was just as absolute, even if no longer life-threatening, at the time when the Sun King warned his son that "a prince's heart is attacked like a fortified place." The monarch decreed that the princely heart must be fortified against the attacks of the "adroit" or "crafty" women who alone were able to render him "vulnerable" (*Mémoires*, 259). The most skillful women of Louis XIV's reign prudently demonstrated their mastery of emotional siegecraft only in the pages of their fictions. The first novel now called modern, *La Princesse de Clèves*, was published by a woman in 1678, the year when the peace of Nymegen was signed and when the king adopted the sun as his royal emblem. This was neither the first nor the only time that a relationship could be detected between the novel, Louis's repartition of territory and an ensuing definition of "representation." The initial volume of Madeleine de Scudéry's *Clélie*, for example, was published immediately after the Fronde (1654). The King had just returned to Paris from his exile to the no man's land outside his capital; upon his return he banished all politically adept women.[11]

In *Clélie*'s first volume, the heroine draws up the *carte de tendre*, an allegorical representation of the ways not to "a prince's heart," but to that of a woman. When Port-Royal logicians Arnauld and Nicole proposed the map as the most perfect representation, they undoubtedly had in mind the ever more perfect maps of actual topography that had been necessitated by their century's military advances, and not novelistic renditions like Scudéry's.[12] In Scudéry's presentation of her map of fondness or inclination, she initially stresses its representational qualities,[13] a claim that may have helped camouflage the subversive nature of the project. The suitor who follows the paths of Scudéry's psychological map arrives at one of three cities of affection, but the map continues past this alleged goal and shows the "dangerous sea" and finally a country beyond both description and access, the "unknown lands." Scudéry notes that her heroine is unable to explain how one arrives at this place or even to give it a name to reveal its role in her affective geography because Clélie has never been in love (405). For her tender utopia, Scudéry chooses a name that, like the term "no man's land," defines only its undefinability. The journey through Scudéry's affective geography culminates in the rejection of the possibility of representation.

In a later work, Scudéry demonstrated a comprehension of the Sun King's strategic ostentation that helps explain her earlier mimetic negation. In one of the *Conversations nouvelles* entitled appropriately "De la magnificence," she has a character explain to a newly arrived noble curious about the latest diversion at Versailles, that "since all that we could say about it would not equal it, let's leave tomorrow to take Philemon to 'l'Appartement,' so that he can see with his own eyes that it is beyond expression, that it can never be properly represented."[14] The price of Louis's magnificence in sociocultural terms was the redefinition of "representation" for aristocrats as fallacious ostentation. Men and women of

11. Accounts of several key confrontations of the Fronde, such as the victory won by the rebel princes after the Grande Mademoiselle ordered the canon of the Bastille to fire on the royal troops, stress the young King's position outside the walls of his city, gazing at his own fortress from its no man's land.

12. *La Logique ou l'art de penser*, ed. L. Marin (Paris: Flammarion, 1970), 80.

13. "A map . . . that closely resembles a real map." *Clélie, histoire romaine* (Geneva: Slatkine Reprints, 1973), vol. 1: 396. My description of the map is based on the illustration included in this volume.

14. Scudéry, *Conversations nouvelles sur divers sujets* (Amsterdam: Wetstein and Desbordes, 1685), 52.

letters, as Scudéry was one of the rare writers to note, paid a similar price: to provide what she terms "a proper representation" of the royal artistry would be to declare one's work the equivalent of the King's. But the King alone is his own equal—"the King has surpassed all his predecessors . . . but he will never surpass himself" (52)—and even his chosen emblem is not a true mirror of his glory, for "painting . . . has never successfully imitated . . . the brilliancy of the sun" (7). Scudéry used the dazzling royal model as testimony of the power won when the representational bond was severed.

In his parody of the *carte de tendre*, the frontispiece to *La Nouvelle allégorique* (1658), Furetière (or his engraver, Chauveau, who also illustrated Scudéry's novels) suggests an insightful reading of Scudéry's sentimental geography: her map can be seen as an illustration of the siege of virtue, with the "unknown lands" as the fortress under siege. Clélie has not yet explored this territory, but she does control both access to it and its potential representation. Scudéry's "Terres Inconnues" would therefore be a utopian no *man*'s land, a non-place, or a place in fiction, where women can protect the female heart by controlling representations of it and by denying men access to the language that expresses it.

This vision of seventeenth-century women's writing is confirmed by the most authoritative early treatise on the novel, Huet's *Traité de l'origine des romans* (1670). Huet's most evident purpose is the creation of a long, unbroken genealogy for a genre in fact characterized by a lack of formal coherence.[15] Huet's early "history" of the novel culminates in a eulogy of the prose fiction currently being developed in France, which he maintains has brought the novel form to its most perfect state. The superiority of the seventeenth-century French novel, Huet argues, was the result of the greater "freedom" that characterized the commerce among men and women in France. Elsewhere, men were obliged to concentrate on "overcoming" the physical "obstacles"—from duennas to locked doors—that separated them from the opposite sex. In France, however, defense and offense alike had become purely verbal: "Women having no defense but their own heart, they made it into a stronger rampart than . . . all the vigilance of duennas. Men were therefore obliged to besiege this rampart in proper fashion [*par les formes*]" (91–92). The "formal" art in which they learned to excel was the language of "politeness" and "gallantry," "an art almost unknown" to those who "rarely speak to women" and are therefore ignorant of "the art of cajoling them in a pleasurable manner" (91–92).

Initially, Huet's scenario reconfirms the situation *Clélie* prescribes. Women have fortified their hearts by inventing the terms of a new siege-

---

15. Thus in his descriptions of the "novels" from antiquity that he sees as precursors of the modern French novel Huet consistently maintains that works that might appear to be composed of "detached fragments" are in reality "perfect bodies." *Traité de l'origine des romans* (Paris: Claude Barbin, 1670), 44–45, 63.

craft, by building, like the Sun King, metaphorical fortifications, representations whose signifying code they control. Yet his treatise seems to suggest that women gave away the keys to the fortress by explaining all the terms of the tender geography (i.e. gallant language) to men, who, according to Huet, then used this mastery to carve out a new territory: the novel. Throughout his discussion of the French novel, Huet implies that its modern masters are male. His treatise was originally published as a preface to a novel, *Zayde*, that it praises as the latest masterpiece (98). It took the form of a public letter to the individual identified on the title page as that novel's author, "Monsieur de Segrais." Yet the homocentric origin thus assigned to the novel and the homocentric mastery discussed in Huet's theoretical epistle were illusory. At the conclusion of his treatise, Huet reveals that the novels he praises as the greatest prior to *Zayde*, while signed by a man, Georges de Scudéry, were actually written by his sister, Madeleine. Furthermore, as both Huet and Segrais later admitted in their memoirs, *Zayde*'s author was also a woman, Lafayette. Huet's decision publicly to resurrect one woman writer long invisible (officially at least, for Scudéry's authorship was an open secret) behind a male signature even as he effaced the woman writer who was her successor behind another male signature seems comprehensible only as a tactical gesture devised in concert with both Scudéry and Lafayette. "While she was working for the glory of our nation, she wanted to spare our sex this shame" (97)—thus Huet explains Scudéry's decision to keep her identity hidden. Scudéry's contribution to the most glorious achievement of contemporary French literature once completed, she could allow her name to be used as an official signature. While perfecting the outworks of the national literary fortress, however, Lafayette had to have her name covered up, so that she could spare male authors the "shame" of realizing that she controlled not only the language of emotional siegecraft but also its fictional representation. In an era of royal absolutism and enforced magnificence, a male signature served to distract attention from a rising alternate authority, the demarcation of a literary estate. This authorial namelessness realized an alternative to the constantly resembling language of "magnificance" described in the first pages of *La Princesse de Clèves*, where all those inside the royal *pré carré* are indistinguishable beneath their ostentatious facades. The first modern novelists offered instead a narrative impossibly poised beyond the ostentatious representation—the "inimitable example" offered by the newly fortified heart of Lafayette's princess.[16]

Lafayette's understanding of protective strategies led to the development in *Zayde* of a representation that questions the functioning and the politics of mimesis. In his preface to *Zayde* Huet places the origin of the novel, just as Defoe does, at the point of contact between Same (civilized)

[16]. In "Lafayette's Ellipses: the Privileges of Anonymity" (*PMLA*, October 1984), I discuss this authorial camouflage and the reading it suggests for *La Princesse de Clèves*.

and Other (barbarian), at the time when Arabs, the "inventors" of novelistic narrative, were "transplanted," taken inside the ur-fortress of civilization, Greece (he cites, among others, Heliodorus and Lucian, 11–12). This transformation, this making same, is recreated in *Zayde* itself. The Spanish army defeats the Moorish army in the conflict that serves as the backdrop for the characters' progress through Lafayette's version of the *carte de tendre*, just as Consalve, the novel's Christian hero, wins out over Alamir, his Arab double. This victory of the forces of Sameness is echoed in the person of Zayde, who, although the daughter of an Arab father and a Greek mother, speaks her mother tongue. At the novel's close, her father's conversion completes the process of her civilization. At the same time, however, as the novel appears to approve the flawless reinscription of national boundaries and the process of distinguishing Same from Other, the complexities of its plot belie the optimism of its happy end and cast suspicion on the practice of conversion.

The national fortress depends for its existence on the perfect functioning of a sense of resemblance and dissemblance, a situation, as John Lyons has convincingly demonstrated,[17] that *Zayde*'s protagonists confirm. Each of its heroes determines the course of his love affair allegedly because of a desperate need to find himself unique, that is, no one's rival. Each expresses the desire not to be compared by his beloved to anyone else, and thereby to avoid functioning in a system of resemblance—to forge an existence outside of the representation whose deceptiveness he believes he understands and can therefore control. Each hero claims to believe that to be so judged by a woman will somehow fix the limits of his "Self" and give him the tranquillity Robinson Crusoe believed he would find inside the impenetrable fortress. Yet these heroes find satisfaction only when they discover, not that they are unlike all others, but that they resemble others. Each consistently finds resemblances, real and imaginary, that produce fear. Consalve imagines that when the beloved looks at him she sees only his likeness to the Other she really loves. Alamir is afraid that when his lover looks at him, she sees only his "representation," his rank and fortune (Alamir's phobia).[18] Each obsessively seeks proof that the woman he loves has been deceived by the representational phallacy, thereby reducing him to the status of mere representation (see Lyons, 62).

*Zayde* ultimately undermines the system of similarity on which its heroes are so dependent by demonstrating that the most successful representations are also the most dangerously deceptive. Consalve believes that he resembles Zayde's dead lover. Zayde knows that he resembles the

---

17. Lyons, "The Dead Center: Desire and Mediation in Lafayette's *Zayde*," *L'Esprit créateur* 23, no. 2 (Summer 1983): 58–69. My reading of *Zayde* is influenced by Lyons's study, the most detailed and stimulating interpretation of the novel to date.

18. Thus Consalve shows Zayde the portrait of his imaginary dead rival he has commissioned, and Alamir orders his confidant to pretend to be him in order to test the origin of Elisbery's love. Lafayette, *Zayde*, ed. E. Magne (Paris: Garnier, 1961), 96, 197.

portrait of the man her father has destined her to marry. But, despite the fact that the portrait is an excellent likeness of Consalve, Zayde doesn't realize that Consalve and her intended are one and the same because in the portrait Consalve is costumed as an African. The story of the representation on which *Zayde's* happy end depends demonstrates that barbarianism is only an affair of clothing and that images, even, or especially, when accurate, are fallacious. More importantly, it shows that the source of all these deceptions is the failure of male authority figures to question the nature of representation. Zayde is fooled by the portrait because her father arranges her deception in the hope of tricking her into marrying the husband of his choice. But he himself has misunderstood both the portrait and its interpretation (235). Perhaps he does not question his reading of the painting because he is afraid, like the father of Rousseau's Julie, that, outside the fortress of representation, his own authority would no longer be recognized and his own virtual *quidamity* exposed (see Tanner, 138–39). Zayde's father's final conversion to Christianity is more than the parody of the easy dissolution of obstacles typical of romance fiction that it appears to be. It signifies the breakdown of all the systems of translation on which the national enclosure depends.

*Zayde* demonstrates that as actual geographies become more precise, as the frontiers of nation-states are more precisely delimited, nationalistic fictions proliferate in a process that is dangerous because their makers claim for them a share of the precision and clarity of the actual geographies. In England, the first novel known as modern reproduces the construction of a nationalistic fortress. In France, the first novels called by that name subversively indicate the need to withdraw to "unknown lands" and build private fortresses as a protection against the use of representation (in love and in war) by the makers of the nation-state. The frontispiece to the Amsterdam edition (1671) of *Zayde*—entitled "the origin of novels"—depicts a story unfolding on two levels. In the background, a play is being staged on an outdoor theater. In the foreground, several women are gathered around a central couple composed of two women, one of whom covers the other's mouth with her hand as if to prevent her from telling the story of the representation just beyond their space. Her enforced silence figures the central paradox of Lafayette's fiction: the creation of the modern novel originates in a desire to be outside representation, in the no man's land outside of fiction into which the Princesse de Clèves finally chooses to disappear.

The novels of Scudéry and Lafayette prefigure what Girard presents as the paradox of mimesis: "Mimesis is the primary source of what tears persons apart. It is the source of their desires, their rivalries, their tragic and bizarre misunderstandings and hence the source of all disorder. But it is likewise the source of an order brought about by scapegoats."[19] Seventeenth-century women writers may have rejected mimesis because they

19. Girard, "Generative Violence and the Extinction of Social Order," *Salmagundi* 63–64 (Spring–Summer 1984), 204.

understood that, in the literary community at least, the scapegoats chosen were likely to be women.

Boileau's dialogue "Des héros de roman" indicates that the most authoritative early French critic hoped to reserve for Scudéry a figurative reenactment of the fate known by *quaedam* Juliana. In the dialogue, the judges of the underworld, Pluto and Minos, condemn Scudéry's most successful heroes on a charge that her fictions are *invraisemblable*, not real-seeming, because her heroes do not resemble their models in antiquity. Boileau thereby turns against this woman novelist the language she had rejected and inaugurates an interpretive tradition in which critics privilege realism to destroy the credibility of women's fiction. Boileau's parody culminates in an elaborately staged ritual execution. The shades of Scudéry's ersatz heroes are "stripped," "whipped," and then plunged "head first" into "the deepest part of the river Lethe."[20] The fate chosen for these literary shades represents the authorial end the arbiter of classicism hoped to decree for Scudéry. He consigned her works to oblivion, effaced her *nom d'auteur* and reduced her to namelessness in the no man's land outside the canonic fortress. For Boileau, the *Pharmakos* whose fatal fall into water establishes the order of life inside the literary city was a woman writer.

Recently, a group of French architects and philosophers has attempted to revive this vision of the beneficial effects of defensive military architecture. Claude Parent, Paul Virilio, and the group of *Architecture Principe* call themselves Vauban's heirs in their efforts to construct and promote what they term an "oblique" architecture, structures able to revitalize living space in the nuclear age and thereby counteract the paralyzing effects of the architectural delimitations of territory that have been essential to military expansionism since the age of the classical Vaubanian fortress.[21] The revised image of the protective space inside the fortress they propose is contradicted, however, by contemporary literary portrayals of the psychogeography created in the wake of protective military architecture. It has recently been suggested that criticism should enter the nuclear age; following the model of Parent and Virilio, this nuclear criticism could explore the literature developed in the shadow of all military fortresses. The fortress and its no man's land do not disappear from the novel, the literary form most threatening to classical literary poetics, at the end of the age of the fortress (and the official end of literary classicism). Whenever the novel questions most subversively the dichotomies on which the nation-state and its militarism are founded, dichotomies that support the desire for total (nuclear) war, a poetics of

20. Boileau, *Oeuvres complètes* (Paris: Garnier-Flammarion, 1969), vol. 2:218.
21. Parent, *Vivre à l'oblique* (n.p., 1970), *Réflexions sur l'architecture* (Maison de la culture de Nevers, 1972); Virilio, *Bunker archéologie; Essai sur l'insécurité du territoire* (Paris: Stock, 1976); see also the contributions to the journal *Architecture Principe*.

fortification recurs. Among more recent examples, I think not only of Kafka but, to borrow Borges's terminology, of his "precursors" like John Coetzee and Nadine Gordimer, novelists who in our own day have disclosed the power for national unification of the concepts of the barbarian Other and of territorial security, and who dissect the mythic power achieved by geography become psychogeography.

LINDA ORR

# The Blind Spot of History: Logography

What attracted me to the little men called logographers taking notes during the Revolution? The situation of the logographers' box 10 August 1792, is one of those typically charged, symbolic moments in Romantic history of the Revolution. It has the advantage of not being too obviously symbolic, like the fact that Robespierre is shot in the mouth, or, at the other extreme, too small a detail, no matter how uncanny, like the King's flat wig or leaves falling already in August. When I was first drawn to this image, it was partly from a knee-jerk reaction common in those days to examine anything that focused on writing per se. But that interest corresponded to a theoretical motivation that steadily clarified itself: stenography is one of our major modern myths about writing history. Then the subject of my study took the lead and I became the willing victim of what Paul Veyne calls "pure curiosity for the specific,"[1] a motivation as strong if not stronger than the desire for truth. I felt that awe, coming upon the little copiers, as when you step into a quiet corner of rare books that everyone has noticed without going into. I added a self-righteous ideological justification of my own: historians had all abandoned the ungainly, monstrous, monumental histories of the nineteenth century implying that they were useless, if not silly. Some of these same contemporary historians were off writing social or labor history, even a version of the history of everyday life, as if they had found the place where a proper history would speak at last. They were still pursuing the stenographic myth of history: the coincidence of historical subject and object. Instead, I would go back, no less heroic myself . . . and find the magic they missed.

1. Paul Veyne, *Comment on écrit l'histoire* (Paris: Seuil, 1971), 63.

## 1. THE LOGOGRAPHER'S BOX: 10 AUGUST 1792

The Bastille had fallen (July 1789); the women had walked to Versailles, shouting for bread (October 1789); and the King had fled to Varennes (June 1791). The new Legislative Assembly (October 1791), elected after the National Assembly had set up the constitutional monarchy and bowed out, had an unsuccessful war effort on its hands: the "people" were afraid and wanted the King where he could no longer betray them so they marched to his palace, the Tuileries, on 10 August 1792. However it happened, some of the people fell dead after shots rang out; furious, their comrades invaded, destroying and preserving the furniture, rescuing and killing the Swiss Guard.

That morning just before the people arrive at his palace, the King finally agrees to leave and make his way across the Carrousel with his family to the Salle du Manège where the Legislative Assembly is in session. His flat wig, showing how well he has slept despite the danger, also reveals how much the King depends upon his coiffure as well as divine right. The leaves in the Carrousel (big yellow chestnuts?) are prematurely turning in August, thus fulfilling the prophecy of the revolutionary Manuel who said that the Royalty would not make it past the autumn leaves.

When the royal party enters the chamber of the Assembly, a sapper named Rocher (the names are always perfect) either props the Prince on the secretaries' desk to unanimous applause or (depending upon whom you read) snatches him away from his mother and displays him trembling there. The King says he has come to avoid a crime and seek security among the representatives. Vergniaud, President of the Assembly, says they have sworn to die for the people's rights and the constitution. The royal group occupies the spot where the ministers usually sit and then the King climbs up to take his place beside Vergniaud. This causes consternation because the constitution forbids the Assembly to deliberate in the presence of the King.

> And so King Louis sat him down, first here, then there; for a difficulty arose . . . finally he settles himself with his Family in the "*Loge* of the *Logographe*," in the Reporter's Box of a Journalist; which is beyond the enchanted Constitutional Circuit, separated from it by a rail. To such Lodge of the *Logographe*, measuring some ten feet square, with a small closet at the entrance of it behind, is the King of broad France now limited.[2]

When Louis XVI moves into this mysterious box, he transgresses perhaps more than when he enters the great hall, for all of a sudden a place appears

---

2. Thomas Carlyle, *The French Revolution: A History* (New York: The Colonial Press, 1900), 2: 95–96.

which we can well imagine having existed but which would ordinarily never come to light. The focalization of history follows Louis off the usual track where it discovers, as if by accident, the indigenous life that works there. It is like searching a photograph years later for someone who happened to be caught in the background and in whom you are now more interested than the characters in the center. The King is relegated to the marginal zone just outside the enchanted circle and separated from it by a railing: perhaps in fact that circle derives its power from this refusal to allow the (evil) presence in its midst. It is as if the King, for the first time and predicting the days to come, takes a step into real life. The *loge* could imply an old idea of prestige associated with the medieval church, for nobles reserved their elevated boxes just as they will later do at the opera. Instead of safety and prestige, Carlyle emphasizes the absurd contrast between this tiny room and the huge country Louis singly owned. The British historian does not mention the former inhabitants of the Reporter's-Box as will his contemporaries Michelet, Blanc, and especially Lamartine. Michelet mentions, though in passing, the name of the eyewitness from whom he got his information on the Queen:

> The Assembly designated, therefore, the *loge du logographe*, which was only separated from the room by an iron grating, and was located at the level of the upper rows of the Assembly. The King moved there with his family; he placed himself up front, indifferent, impassive; the Queen, slightly to the side, able to hide in this position the terrible anxiety in which the combat placed her. . . . The Queen did not say a word, her lips were closed tight, said an eyewitness (M. David, later consul and député); her eyes were blazing and dry, her cheeks burning, her hands gripped her knees.[3]

It is not clear from Michelet what David was doing there, if he was a logographer, guard, or whatever. Even if Michelet disliked history focused on royal individuals, he was not above the usual dramatic Romantic portrait of the Queen, that Fury, enemy of the people. Lamartine, who is more often drawn to the Queen, repeats, at times verbatim, the same information but takes time to notice the inconvenience caused by the King's arrival:

> This *loge*, ten feet square, behind the president, was level with the upper rows of the Assembly. It was only separated from the room by an iron grating sealed into the wall. The king was led there. The young secretaries who took down the speeches in order to reproduce literally the sessions, moved over [*se rangèrent*] a little to make room for the

---

3. Jules Michelet, ed. Gérard Walter, *Histoire de la Révolution française* (Paris: Gallimard, 1952), 2 vols., 1: 999. I have translated all texts from the French; hereafter references to this work will be given in the text.

family of Louis XVI. The king sat in the front of the *loge*; the queen, at an angle, in order to veil her face in the shadow of the alcove. . . .[4]

A little farther in the text, Lamartine gives more open recognition to M. David than Michelet did but uses David's description of the King, instead of the Queen:

> In this very *loge* of the logographer, a man, young at the time, recognized since then for his services, M. David, later consul-general, and deputy, respectfully noted for history the posture, physiognomy, gestures, tears, complexion, breathing and even the involuntary palpitations of the face muscles that the emotions of these long hours imprinted on the features of the royal family.
> The king was calm, serene . . . he ate, drank, tore apart his chicken with as much calm as if he had done so at a gathering after the hunt. . . . [3:188–89]

The logographers could get more of a close-up shot than they must have been used to, thus contributing not to the humanity of the King, but to his caricature.

Lamartine, as opposed to Carlyle and Michelet, explains the special nature of the secretaries or journalists who supposedly reproduced "literally" the Assembly sessions. Blanc, while suggesting that these are logotachygraphers instead of logographers, goes into more technical detail about these journalists or protoparliamentary stenographers:

> Behind the president's chair there was a recessed room [*un réduit*] twelve feet square by six feet high, where the journalists usually sat who claimed to have found the means of writing as fast as one speaks. This recess, that an iron grille which was sealed into the wall separated from the hall, is called the lodge of the *Logotachygrapher [la loge du Logotachygraphe]*. . . . The lodge of the Logotachygrapher was designated for the king and his family.[5]

Although for Blanc the journalists have vanished as if by magic, they are precisely associated with stenography since he uses the cliché found as the subtitle to almost every manual of the "art": the means of writing as fast as one speaks. Blanc's *loge* is two feet square larger than Carlyle's or Lamartine's but it realizes the metaphor Carlyle suggested in opposition to the enchanted circle. A corner or nook, the *réduit* can also refer to a humble—if not poor—dwelling, and the adjective leaves no doubt that

  4. Alphonse de Lamartine, *Histoire des Girondins* (Paris: Furne et Cie, 1847), 8 vols., 3: 187. Hereafter references to this work will be given in the text.
  5. Louis Blanc, *Histoire de la Révolution française* (Paris: Maurice Lachatre et Cie, n.d. [Popular, illustrated, quarto edition: the original 12 vol. edition was published by Pagnerre and Furne, 1847–62]) 2 vols., 1: 706.

the King like Alice in Wonderland must undergo a reduction in size to fit in.

An illustration from a popular edition of Blanc's history gives us the picture suggested by the text, focalized from the point of view of the logographer (David?). The spectator is inside the *loge* with the King, looking out on the turmoil of the Assembly from a kind of window. Inside it is quiet, though tense. A shadow is cast upon the door, slightly ajar, at the far left of the engraving. It is most certainly one of the many guards standing in the hallway but suggests as well that the angry crowd might penetrate at least that far. Although the royal family occupies the interest of the picture, everywhere there are signs of another absent presence, that of the logographer. Quill pens are left on the "sill," bookshelves line the wall next to the Queen (assuming it is Madame Elizabeth who comforts the Prince on the other side). Stacks of the newspaper *Le Logographe* lie in the bottom left corner with a copy open as if serving as the signature for the entire scene: in fact the engraver chooses this open page for his own signature. It is as if the contents of the page have been projected as the scene before our eyes. Has the logographer disappeared leaving metonymic signs in the hope of some remembrance? Or is his perspective so perfectly identified with ours, with that of the historian copying from him, with that of the narration itself, that he always remains invisible?[6] (See Fig. 1).

The mystery of this absence animated my research: like wanting to know who anon. is.

I hesitated (ashamed?) abandoning, first, the people storming the palace and, next, the heroes of the Assembly, who finally suspended the monarchy, in favor of the dubious logographer. After all, it was clear from the beginning that he [David] would end up as the bad-guy bourgeoisie: consul-general, deputy. But the impasse reigning in the larger event justifies my treating *it* as the digression, returning shortly to the story of logography. It is, however, important to go over once more the strategies that repress or deform popular expression, no matter how repetitive through history. This means looking at a history that is centered on the dominant symbolic institution of power. The new social, cultural, or labor histories have struggled to get out from under the monolithic and limited vision of political history so that it appears regressive to go back to those overemphasized events. The scene of the Assembly is not, then, a historical has-been because it fails to correspond to the fashionable

6. In *La Révolution*, (Paris: Réalité Hachette, 1965), 1: 226–27, François Furet and Denis Richet reproduce Gérard's drawing entitled "The Assembly invaded by the crowd which heaps invective on the royal family who has taken refuge in the *loge du logographe.*" The petitioners erupt into the space between the secretaries' table or president's desk and the *barre* (not shown); they gesticulate toward the royal family (especially the sneering Queen who alone faces them). The main light, eery, emanates from the cell (still with bars) in which the family is located.

*Figure 1.* Le Roi se réfugie au sein de l'Assemblée.

object of history. The parliament serves as a major modern metaphor of social discourse, whether it is studied firsthand in the Assemblies or in levels of displacement: the Clubs, Sections, secret societies, cafes, or the street. A researcher cannot get around it to an "outside," except as the one already coded as such in terms of that same pervasive institution. Although almost all of the nineteenth-century historians, especially the republicans, complained about the impotence of the Assembly, revolutionary history could not (then and now) be written otherwise than blocked through that mass, not necessarily corresponding to the other mass of popular unrest. As much work can be done reading with these structures as pretending that popular society can be isolated from them in a pure form of self-reflection.

The Assembly was the place or operation by which the act of the people, as insurrection, came into being in the act of its representatives, as legislation. We might define this founding, if not slippery, principle of the revolution as the speech act of democracy, its political performative. Like the two sides of the linguistic sign, each mutually constitutes the other. The tenth of August, one of the first and most archetypal of these legitimating instances, demonstrates the metaphorical quality of the perfect correspondance required by democracy. The event itself both celebrates and belies the unity of the people and its representation, the fragile discursive coherence of their society. (Romantic historiography makes in fact its mark by seizing upon this irony, in horror, analysis and confusion—which is why it unnerves us.)

The Legislative Assembly was implicitly restructuring society as fast as it was torn apart, through its form, as much as through its legislation, by its rules and procedures, even the floorplan of its hall. The raised tribune from where the *tribuns* or deputies spoke (for the benefit of the *tribunes* or galleries as much as toward their colleagues) was across from the president's desk (behind which sat, unseen, the King and logographers). Just under the tribune, at floor level, and across from the president's "secretaries" (where documents were deposed) was the *barre* to which the outside petitioners presented themselves. Their spokesman would then be recognized in the proper order. Although this "bar" referred to the idea of tribunal like the word "barrister," its other meaning, related to barrier, was not lost (see Fig. 2).

The tenth of August is structured by the repeated popular cry or petition for the King's removal to which the deputies, convinced that they have already removed him, turn a deaf ear so that the people, who also seem not to be listening, make ad nauseam the same demand as if it has not yet really been granted. The impasse is tricky, for who is right? (The revolutionary tribunal will insist that Vergniaud, intentionally or not, destroyed the monarchy with his right hand but restored it with his left by naming a tutor for the Prince.) The Romantic histories already read the contradiction of the event. Lamartine for instance: "Vergniaud had

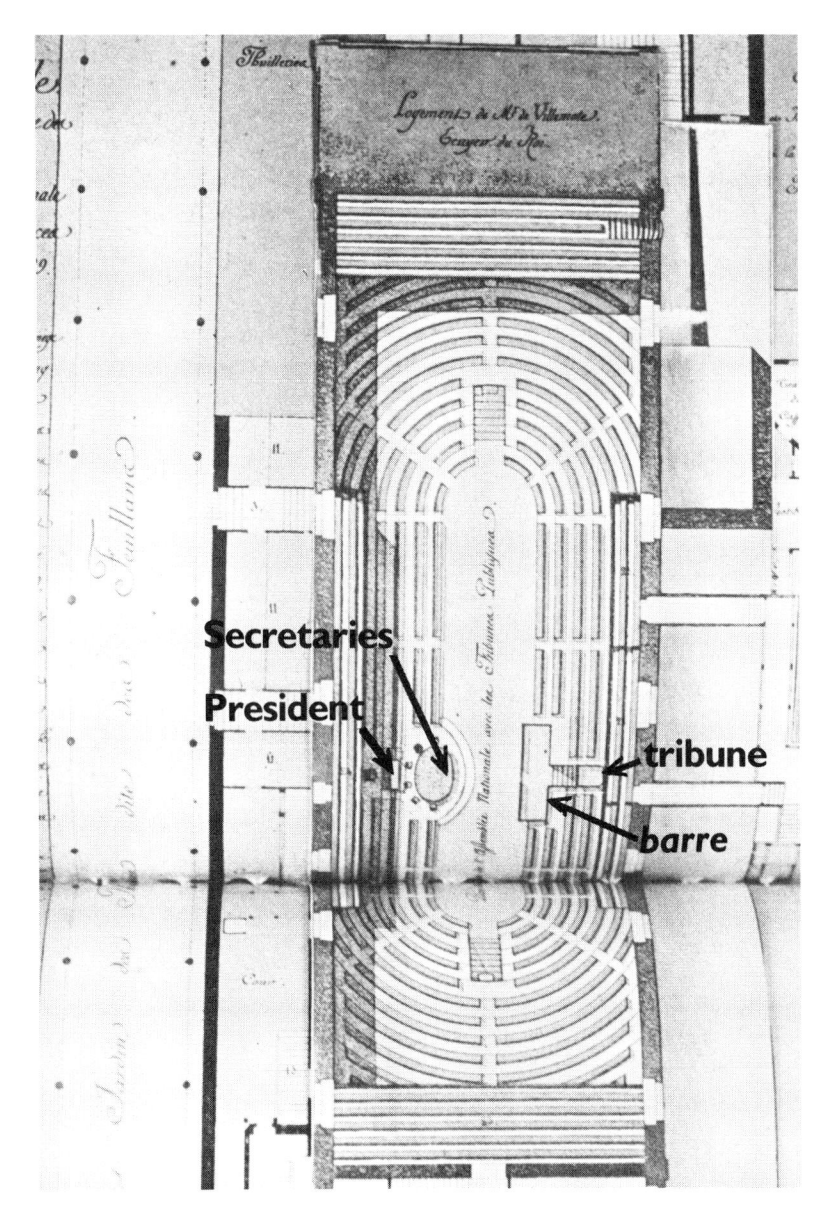

*Figure 2.* Floorplan of the *Salle du Manège*. (Shaded areas are second floor galleries.)

hardly finished reading, when more demanding petitioners presented themselves at the *barre* and called for the Assembly to pronounce the demise of the perfidious king . . ." (3: 240). Influenced by the Romantics' account and curious to compare it with an eyewitness record, I was even more struck by the pattern of repetition in the *procès-verbal* of 10 August 1792. Whereas Michelet writes that the petitioners "went away silent, but not satisfied," (1:1001) the *procès-verbal* paints a formal, almost ritualistic scene like ancient Japanese warriors dropping their anger in the sacred temple of freedom and leaving as lambs. All they want is their names in the public record:

> All the Citizens, satisfied at having been introduced to the Assembly, and at having faithfully returned the different objects that they found at the château, have the modesty of not doubting that the National Assembly would experience on its part a great satisfaction at knowing and publishing their names. . . .[7]

Was that promise of gaining a historical identity enough to make the petitioners forget why they had come? The petitioners appear in history in order to be politely turned away from it: they come, both to speak and to learn the lesson of the bar's revolving door.[8]

While the bar was repeatedly reinstated between the Assembly and the people (undermining the victory outside?), the bar between the logographer's box and the enchanted circle was removed. This information, of interest to these Romantic accounts,[9] provides the main focus in Thiers's version of the scene in the logographer's box: "The king . . . was removed to the office of the clerk of the journals, and the iron railing which separated it from the chamber was broken down, that, in case the

---

7. *Procès-verbal de l'Assemblée nationale* (Paris: Imprimerie nationale, 1792), 12: 20. When you compare the form of how the *Procès-verbal* and *Le Moniteur universel* record the same sessions, you notice immediately an important difference—which may have had an uncalculated effect on future history. The *Procès-verbal* notes the session in prose paragraphs, often using an indirect style to record the discussion, and refers to the deputy simply as a "member": e.g. "a Member asks the Assembly to pronounce the annulment of the nomination. . . . Another observes that . . ." (1). In contrast, *Le Moniteur*, on which most later historical narratives were based, uses a dramatic form, as if the occasion was a play, and identifies each deputy by name. Oddly enough one finds the list of petitioners' names in The *Procès Verbal* without the names of the deputies and (chiasmus) the names of the deputies in *Le Moniteur* where the people no longer appear by name. *Le Moniteur Universel* or *Gazette Nationale ou le Moniteur universel (réimpression de l'Ancien Moniteur depuis la réunion des Etats-Généraux jusqu'au Consulat)* (Paris: au bureau central, 1842), vol. 13.

8. For another semiotic interpretation of the (parliamentary) political system based on cybernetics, i.e. open channels of communication, see Pierre Avril, *Les Français et leur parlement* (Paris: Casterman, 1972), especially 37.

9. Along with Carlyle, Michelet, Lamartine, Blanc, and Thiers, Cabet includes the detail about the iron grillwork even in a very condensed version of the scene: "he [the king] arrives, with his family, through an almost impenetrable crowd, and is placed in the *loge du logographe*, from which the grille separating it from the Assembly is removed" (3: 55–56).

chamber should be attacked by the multitude, he could, with his family, take immediate refuge among the deputies."[10] An impassioned open appeal was, I assume, deemed to work better than leaving the King cringing in his dark lair. Carlyle interprets the gesture of tearing down that barrier as another sign of the Legislative's dependency on the Monarchy:

> Tear down the railing that divides it [the loge] from the enchanted Constitutional Circuit! Ushers tear and tug; his Majesty himself aiding from within: the railing gives way; Majesty and Legislative are united in place, unknown Destiny hovering over both. [2:96]

Michelet clarifies the irony that Carlyle alludes to: Louis XVI has a hand in his own unmaking for he practiced ironwork as a hobby: "Le roi s'y employa lui-même, avec . . . son bras de serrurier" (1: 1000) [the king was busy at it himself, with . . . his ironworker's arm].

One of the first in a long line of democratic misrepresentations, if not impasses, 10 August also dramatizes the social circulation set up in this backroom, as if the enormous pressure exerted by the popular insurrection on the institution had sprung a tiny leak in the *loge*. History is crossing paths in this small box: the artisan-king is descending and joining fates with the artisan-scribe. One enters into passivity, while the other waits to emerge from it. Whereas the petitioners could in theory participate in the official social discourse and the spectators in the tribunes gained power through their techniques of disruption, the logographers were socially and theoretically mute. They had no words of their own but silently copied those of others. Lamartine was the only historian (melodramatic enough, or open to the Symbolic) to exploit that mythic resonance of the potentially powerful scribe:

> For several hours now the silence of the tomb reigned in the lodge of the logographer. Only the noise was heard of the hurried pens of the clerks (*rédacteurs*) which ran along the paper, inscribing minute by minute the words, gestures, emotions of the hall. The lurid light of candles which shone on their table, showed the young prince in the lap of the queen and sleeping to the sound of the decrees which lifted both empire and life from him. [3:253]

The space of the box completes its transformation: the small step outside the magic circle leads in a slide from *loge* to hovel to tomb. The innocent bystanders, the logographers, assume a more threatening demeanor. The scratching pens make a tormenting noise, indicating what actually kills the Prince, death-by-quill, or at least what conspires with its own prediction of violence. Impassive, more than passive, the scribes take on an uncanny grandeur: *plumes* suggesting birds, Egyptian falcon-gods, other

---

10. Adolphe Thiers, *Histoire de la Révolution Française* (Paris: Furne et Cie, 1837), 10 vols., 2: 251.

worldly judges. If the people were not satisfied that the King had fallen once and for all, the pens already inscribed both his overthrow and death, along with the execution of many others who, unsuspecting, thought on 10 August that they had won the day (e.g., Vergniaud). Their words copied so diligently would be used against them.

## 2. A HISTORY WITHIN A HISTORY: THE MUTE EATS THE WORD, THE MUTE SPEAKS THE WORD.

My narrative now abandons centerstage to set up operation in the *loge*. But here we won't find a different history, rather the same history from another angle. The circulation released here takes on the same shape and flow of story (constantly threatened, as ever, by impasse). The history of stenography can fall into the usual organic plot of rise and fall or even a circle (or spiral) of a return-to-beginnings (with-a-difference). The stenographers move from muteness to possibilities of speech and back to silence, from the social ranks of the powerless to power and back again.

In our tradition, stenography culminates with the parallel growth of eighteenth- and nineteenth-century parliamentary institutions, although modes of abbreviation have existed as long as writing itself. Prerevolutionary stenographers in France, "tachygraphers," led a life reminiscent of the itinerant artisan but lacked the organization of a guild and knew hard times (the minibiographies of Coulon-Thévénot and his student Dupont will illustrate the case). Not until the July Monarchy did its practitioners profit from the new networks of power. The men who inaugurated this creative period of the practice were both wild innovators (Grosselin is a good example) and sober builders of the new democracy (e.g. Flocon, Lagache). Energy was to peak in 1848, the desired conjunction for so many hopes, but it too was shortlived. Already a leading steno (Prévost) had proposed that his colleagues become a part of the government bureaucracy, a proposal he realized during the Second Empire, when politics did not stand in the way of nascent professionalism. Today in France candidates undergo tough national competition, but the job in the Senate and Assembly carries still a kind of pre-Revolutionary artisanal pride and stays sometimes within the same family.

If that is the story, here again is the impasse pursuing it. The democratic speech act, impossible enough to achieve, is to no avail if no scribe is present to record it. All three elements are, therefore, mutually constituted to assure their common social existence: the representative (speaker), the represented (silent), and the historian (writer). History, like that fated tree falling in the deserted woods, might be happening off somewhere away from the nearest historian, and it would go unobserved, even unperceived. In fact the presence of a scribe defines the event, as well as vice versa. But often history and the historian are not together where they should be. One of the first stenographers to write about his profession, Delsart, complained in 1847 that "stenographers were lacking for Mirabeau, Barnave, Vergniaud, Danton . . ."[11] Stenography would have enabled that democratic coincidence of the people with its speech to be caught and preserved, converted intact from act to the writing material of history. Thanks to stenography, no gap would exist, nothing would be lost. At last history would be both significant and faithful, loyal to its objects. Later, during the Restoration and July Monarchy, the scribe was there with his new tool, stenography, but history would not show up—until 1848. That year the eighteenth-century revolution was finally supposed to realize itself and this time history would be there to record it. The twenty-fourth of February 1848, does come close to doubling 10 August since again the Chamber is invaded by the people, and the steno leaves an extraordinary testimony to the breakthrough, including his own which accompanies—coincides with—that of the "people." And for a short while, stenography too shares in the euphoria of possibility, but already the promises fall short—and that legitimating correspondence no more works in stenography and historiography than in the Assembly, politics, and history.

We'll put the impasse aside and enjoy the story.

Logographers were not yet stenographers—although already historians (the word also refers to the first Greek writers of history before Herodotus). The inhabitants of the box were probably not even Blanc's logotachygraphers. Thirty-eight members of the *Société logographique*, including M. David, had their own longhand method for getting out the newspaper *Le Logographe* from about April 1791 to 10 August 1792.[12] Few of the sessions were actually recorded *in extenso;* even so the task was arduous. Twelve to fourteen journalists sat at a round table in what the historian of stenography Breton calls a "vast room behind the chair of the president" (Navarre, 398) which we can only surmise is our *loge;* vast for the little person, small for the big . . . Each logographer scribbles quickly on a numbered strip of paper, then gives his neighbor a shove with knee or elbow and this one takes over from there, and so on around the table. The strips of papers are reassembled and recopied by other subscribes in yet another backroom. There was even some question about whether Maret—who knew stenography and has the reputation of

---

11. Albert Navarre, *Histoire Générale de la sténographie et de l'Ecriture à travers les âges* (Paris: Librairie Ch. Delagrave, n.d. [1905]), 398. Hereafter references to this work will be given in the text.

12. Blanc's confusion, it turns out, was legitimate, for it is not clear whether the King sat in the gallery reserved for the journalists of *Le Logographe* or their rivals *Le Logotachigraphe*. In *Histoire des édifices . . .* , Brette goes into details concerning the arguments for and against both propositions, concluding at last that we will never know exactly where the king sat (243–50). *Le Logographe* was accused of "truncating facts, distorting our meetings and distilling the poison of *incivisme* with a most perfidious art" (note 1, 246). It was closed shortly after 10 August. Armand Brette, *Histoire des édifices où ont siégé les Assemblées parlementaires de la révolution française et de la première république* (Paris: Imprimerie Nationale, 1902), vol. 2.

providing history (i.e. the future *Moniteur*) singled-handedly with most of our parliamentary documents—took down the sessions in shorthand. The stenohistorian Michelot (1959) (not Michelet) confesses that "Maret could only meet the task thanks to stenography. But History does not say what method he used."[13] Delsart says that Maret's notes were taken "in ordinary writing" (Navarre, 398). Once copied, the notes of the steno were destroyed so that if ever we had that text which comes closest to the event, it is now lost.

The Legislative Assembly (1792) did not act upon a proposal to use stenography, but Coulon de Thévénot finally persuaded the Convention at the end of its career to consider using his "tachygraphy." The deputies or Five Hundred actually took him up on his promise under the Directory but let the project languish since Coulon's issues did not live up to expectations.

Coulon-Thévénot (the *particule* was made up by him) is the best example of an unsung hero of the early prestenographic days. Although he started in the potentially elite prerevolutionary artisan class of Paris as a *maître d'ériture*, having attended the Royal Academy of Writing, he could not make a living at his chosen profession. Even the interest shown by d'Alembert at the Academy of Science did not help. Coulon had to make ends meet by traveling the provinces, where he made presentations to the local learned societies and gave private lessons like a music teacher. Records kept at Bordeaux show the difficult life both Coulon and one of his converts led: they seemed to hover, holding to their pride, between the working and unemployed (future "dangerous")[14] classes. When Coulon asked in Bordeaux for some more "lucrative occupation" than his beloved tachygraphy, unique "resource," the Musée de Bordeaux gave him archives to copy. The same fate awaited his student Dupont. Both returned to Paris where two was too much competition. Once they even performed a kind of public joust or duel to prove who was the fastest tachygrapher in town. The old man Coulon, now hard of hearing, managed ultimately to triumph by getting the younger upstart Dupont convicted of fraud. The master claimed that his student advertised as his own, new method one that was practically no different from the master's original. Dupont argued, in turn, that Coulon's method was no more original than his since the old man had only translated into French what he found already in English. (In this, Coulon was no different from his rival compatriots.) Just on the eve of the Revolution, Dupont like Coulon before him ended up in Bordeaux, reduced to seeking gainful employment

---

13. Marius Michelot, *Les systèmes sténographiques* (Paris: Presses Universitaires de France, 1959), 47.

14. See Louis Chevalier, *Classes laborieuses et classes dangereuses à Paris pendant la première moitié du XIXe siècle* (Paris: 1958). See also William H. Sewell, Jr., *Work and Revolution in France: The Language of Labor* (Cambridge: Cambridge University Press, 1980).

in business after living on the social fringe. He narrated his *curriculum vitae* ("précis de la vie") and job request, as was the polite custom, in the third person:

> The scorn that this moving around brings, ordinarily associated with charlatans, is one of the powerful and important reasons which finally today make the sieur Dupont ardently desire to see his errant institution at an end, and, perceiving no other means, that persuade him (stomping out all manner of self-respect) to announce publicly for the first time his wish to occupy a place in commerce, finance or any other position . . . however modest. . . .[15]

Dupont had formerly been a clerk or *commis* where he probably copied; after his dreams were dashed in Paris, maybe he began to copy again. If only Coulon and Dupont had resolved their squabbles, they might have anticipated the joys of Bouvard and Pécuchet.

It is easy to imagine the itinerant tachygrapher displaying on his tours the miraculous properties of his trade as in a traveling medicine show. His method could cure the ills of writing. Whole passages of books could be compressed into a few lines so the reader could retain all the volumes he read. And nothing would escape the listener. Writing, that poor laggard cousin dragging behind swift sound, was finally catching up and flew side by side with melodious words. As phono-graphy or tono-graphy, written language could achieve that ambition of being perfectly coupled with speech (i.e. phonetic). Such general improvement would naturally carry over from writing to the mind: people would think more clearly, express themselves better. Lawyers would correct their logic. Businessmen act more efficiently. Poets capture their precious burst of inspiration. Stenography offered no less than a victory over space (steno-narrow) and time (tachy-swift). A report filed after Coulon's presentation to the Musée de Bordeaux repeats the salesman's pitch:

> The goal of the tachygraphic art being especially one of serving to economise time, to multiply so to speak, the hours, to follow the rapidity of the imagination, . . . to come finally to the aid of men of letters and scholars, before whom time seems to fly . . . it is enough that this method be a mirror in which their genius again finds just in time and appropriately all the objects whose image he has once received. [*Deux sténographes*, 11–12]

Tachygraphy could not only save time, but gain it, make it, reproduce it. Everything received by the brain, if only subliminally, would be fixed there, fulfilling, in lieu of the computer, the dream of total recall. The

---

15. René Havette, *Deux Sténographes à Bordeaux en 1784 et 1789 (Coulon de Thévenot et Dupont, de la Rochelle): D'après les manuscrits de la Société littéraire du Musée de Bordeaux et les documents de l'Auteur* (Paris: Revue internationale de sténographie, 1903), 25. References to this work will henceforth be given in the text.

writing magician wowed his audience with his feats, for there was something awe-inspiring about what could also serve as cryptography as well as tachygraphy. However, it did not pay to emphasize that angle too much, for, as Dupont put it, many potential students "trembled at the mere view of the characters" (*Deux sténographes*, 27) and considered the art too hard to master. It paid rather to emphasize its simplicity: anyone could learn it, quickly. It's even easier than ordinary writing (because phonetic), uncontaminated by classical vestiges. Stenography could moreover answer to that dream of a common, universal language that intrigued the eighteenth century and modified itself to meet the aspirations of the revolution. The subtitle of a typical manual published in 1793 "chez le citoyen Charon" by a certain Armand confirms these values:

> *The Art of writing as quickly as one speaks, or tachygraphy applicable to all idioms and founded on such simple and easy principles to seize, that one can know in a day the elements of this art and put oneself in the position, in very little time, of following the speech of an orator.*[16]

Coulon-Thévénot saw the Revolution as his big chance, and he showed zeal taking notes at the Jacobin Club. But unfortunately a practitioner of a rival system brought his past as holder of the (empty) title "secrétaire-tachygraphe du roi" to the attention of a local committee, and Coulon had to lay low. He copied for the "administration" and later worked for the War Office. He had to eat the grandiose words of his promises and support himself on pedestrian fare, biding his time. I imagine him at this stage as one of those seedy but heroic copiers in Abel Gance's *Napoléon*, stoically chewing the convictions of prisoners.

But Coulon-Thévénot did not profit from the circulation opened up by the fall of the King. Both Michelet and Lamartine laud, on their part, the success of M. David (Lamartine sets up the echo with the better-known David, another painter of revolutionary scenes). Maret, steno with *Le Moniteur*, also made it big: Bonaparte noticed him and named him "secretary of the Consuls" and then "secretary of State." He will become a *pair* in the July Monarchy.

Although *Le Moniteur* hired three stenographers (Delsart, Lagache, Prévost) to cover the Chamber of Deputies during the Restoration, stenography came into its own during the July Monarchy and profited from the growing impulse toward democracy. In 1833 the Chambers first subsidized the service provided by *Le Moniteur* which hired eleven *réviseurs* and *rouleurs* who worked not unlike the present day parliamentary team. (Even today in France *rouleurs* stand at a desk so they can turn, look and listen while writing by hand, not using a stenotype machine. *Réviseurs* give a summary analysis which is then used to check the verbatim ac-

---

16. René Havette, *Bibliographie de la sténographie française* (Paris: Dorbon-Ainé, 1906).

count of the *rouleurs*.)[17] Two notable examples of this more fortunate generation of stenographers include Augustin Grosselin (1800–1870), who was swept up as much as anyone in the inventions that stenography stimulated at the time, and Célestin Lagache (1809—1895) for whom stenography became a political act in itself. The latter passed almost imperceptibly from silence into speech on 24 February 1848.

Grosselin had the advantage of being from a family of the legal profession. He started, as many a stenographer, by publishing his own manual at an early age and by taking down the courses of Guizot and Cousin at the Ecole Normale. From 1820 to 1851 he worked for *Le Moniteur* in the Chambers. But, like Victor Hugo, the coup d'état forced him to develop his more independent pursuits. Already in 1836 he had published a system of universal language in which fifteen hundred general ideas, organized into fifteen tableaux, each received a number. I assume you could then communicate with anyone in the world simply by a combination of these numbers. Besides producing what the historian Navarre called "curious atlases," Grosselin created in 1861 a "phonomimic" method for communication with the deaf. He also perfected a way of including, along with the words of a speaker, those all-important inflections of voice he called tonography. With three hundred variations possible on thirty basic signs, Grosselin could express "the least nuances of feeling." (Navarre, 217). (For instance, a heart with a point under it represented good will; an upside-down heart, hate; one with a grave accent: affection; with an acute accent: love.) Today's French parliamentary stenographers also choose from among a code of possibilities, a finite number of emotive formulae, what is called the *mouvements de séances*, for they have no time to linger over how they might personally express the various forms of disruption practiced by the legislators.[18]

The career of Célestin Lagache, who published his method at eighteen years old, represents the height of a certain kind of sociopolitical mobility. After working for *Le Moniteur* in both the Chamber of Deputies and *Pairs* for almost twenty years, he was first elected as a deputy to the Constituent Assembly of 1848, and then after a distance from public life during the Second Empire, returned to head the parliamentary stenographic service from 1861 to 1879 when he again made the transition to public life in the Senate until his retirement (1892). Before knowing that Lagache was its author, I had admired the *procés-verbal* of 24 February 1848, as one of the mythical texts which, along with 10 August 1792,

17. For an informative, entertaining, concise, illustrated story of the French parliament, see François Muselier (pseudonym for Bernard Pingaud), *Regards neufs sur le parlement* (Paris: Seuil, 1956). An illustration on page 23 shows (from behind) a *rouleur* at work in the almost empty room of the modern Assemblée Nationale, in the Palais Bourbon.

18. In addition to an interview with Pingaud, much of my information concerning contemporary French parliamentary stenography comes from an interview with the *Chef du service sténographique* of the Senate in the fall of 1976.

can pretend to have caught the word of the people in action. At that time I was aware of the odd, dramatic sense of that text, for the narrative voice is present when the eerie, empty Chamber first starts to fill up and stays until it seems that he is the very last person to lock up and go home after the crowd has left to follow the Peter-Piper of the day, Lamartine, to the Hôtel de Ville. It is an audacious narrator because he does not hesitate to enter illegal voices into the official record, to recognize not only the anonymous "voice from the gallery" or even the symbolic and real "voice of the people," but the name of those who speak after the President has fled and the Assembly is supposedly no longer in session. There is a moment in his text as uncanny as the one when the logographers shove over to make room for the King in 1792 and the reader catches a glimpse of them. It is as if the stenographers appeared in 1792 but waited to speak until 1848. As the Provisional Government is being named, the stenographers participate along with everyone else, the deputies and crowd they also give voice to:

> M. DUPONT (DE L'EURE).——We're proposing to you that we form the provisional government (Yes! yes!—Silence!) THE STENOGRAPHERS: Silence! We'll call out the names! M. DUPONT (DE L'EURE).——Here are the names! (Silence!) *Numerous voices.* Names! Names![19]

At this point, the stenographer enters his own voice into history.

When I was reading along in Navarre's voluminous history of stenography, there was Lagache, hero of the day, according to Navarre, along with Lamartine and the "people."

> On the 24th of February, 1848, Célestin Lagache, at the time *réviseur* of the stenographic service, was at his desk, when the House of Deputies was invaded by the riot, and everyone fled, preoccupied with the general every-man-for-himself. Concerned about duty and unconcerned about danger, remaining alone at his bench, he recorded, impassive and faithful witness, down to the least words pronounced, the least incidents taking place, at the first dramatic entrance of the Parisian people. It is thanks to his courageous composure (*sang-froid*) that the authentic proceedings of the first hours of the revolution have been conserved for history. [Navarre, 219]

For Navarre, Lagache is a brave, impassive soldier at his post, his desk. Lagache cannot, however, have been so disinterested if, when the Assembly reconvenes, he will find himself on the other side of the line he had already transgressed in his text.

Whereas the nineteenth century of French government is referred to

---

19. E. Laurent, ed. (L. Lataste and Pionnier, eds.), *Archives parlementaires* (Paris: Librairie administrative de P. Dupont, 1862–19—), 2nd series (1848), 501.

as the Republic of deputies,[20] 1848 might be especially called the Republic of secretaries (or even stenographers). Flocon, who began his journalistic career as a stenographer, was included, with Blanc, and Marrast on the list of the provisional government, but possessing only the status of secretary. After complaining, he is eventually promoted to full membership, along with the worker Albert. For Flocon, stenography was an inseparable part of the new Republican program. He believed that the Second Republic would not only educate all citizens but give them that means of universal, simple, and complete communication. One of his early speeches to the Assembly alluded to this expectation and must have struck his colleagues as a little strange. Or is that my interpretation of the ambiguous *mouvement*? The word indicates the basic *mouvement de séance* or some kind of general agitation. "I would like for stenography to be an integral part of the education of all French citizens. (*Movement*) A word: what I say can seem strange, but believe a man of experience . . . that there is no easier, simpler study, which puts more clarity and order in ideas . . ." (Navarre, 267). At last that message Coulon struggled so hard to deliver from the sidelines was close to being championed by the institutions of power itself. Like the Revolution, nothing could stop the inevitable spread and triumph of stenography. Victor Hugo, for one, prophesied that it "would be the popular writing of the twentieth century" (Navarre, 283: an apocryphal quote?).

Stenography was indeed eventually instituted in Europe and the United States and throughout the world. The practice was so familiar and universal that it served as a metaphor outside of the context of paraliament—while parliament too, and the political metaphors associated with it, functioned as a basic, if not the basic, cultural reference during the nineteenth century and even into the twentieth. Freud, for instance, wondered in *The Interpretation of Dreams* if the repeated dream symbols did not "occur with the permanently fixed meaning like the 'grammalogues' in shorthand (*wie die 'Siegel' der Stenographie*)."[21] (The psychoanalyst will reject this, albeit tempting, stenography of the unconscious in lieu of the concept of overdetermination. Even so, he is unable again to think this new concept without the help of another parliamentary metaphor, the *scrutin de liste*.) But, as stenography grew in popu-

20. For the rise and fall of speech-making and parliamentary prestige, see Roger Priouret's *La République des Députés* (Paris: Grasset, 1959).

21. Sigmund Freud, ed. and trans., James Strachey, *The Interpretation of Dreams* (New York: Basic Books, 1958), Eng., 351; Ger., 2–3: 356. Representation in dreams is no more "just" than parliamentary representation: "Thus a dream is not constructed by each individual dream-thought, or group of dream-thoughts, finding (in abbreviated form) separate representation in the content of the dream—in the kind of way in which an electorate chooses parliamentary representatives; a dream is constructed, rather, by the whole mass of dream-thoughts being submitted to a sort of manipulative process in which those elements which have the most numerous and strongest supports acquire the right of entry into the

larity and spread into certain educational institutions and bureaucracies, something paradoxical happened: it lost instead of gained prestige. The magic was gone. While being extended and diffused, it was, at the same time, cut off from the real centers of power. Although until relatively recently a lawyer might have been trained as a court stenographer (e.g. James Francis Byrnes, 1879–1972), the case is rare today. The women graduates of the once prominent secretarial schools (now technical colleges?) are today not likely to become Secretaries of State. The self-image of being a white-collar artisan, instead of a blue-collar worker, compensates sometimes for low pay and sometimes does not.

### 3. PETTY THEFT IN THE MONUMENTS

Stenography participated in the general disappointment when democratic history failed to realize its identity. Instead of closing that gap between word and act or between text and event, stenography continued to throw language back on itself. At such a point in time, one might elevate frustration to a poem or theory, or pick up again with fresh recruits in pursuit of a new insurrection, another political performative. As the forms of history evolve or revolve, the spin-off histories in its wake, that don't seem to fit anywhere, have their own energy: sometimes they end up explaining, even changing the direction of the rest, sometimes they never mean much to anyone beyond what they are, curious and specific.

One of the most (unintentionally?) humorous books that "deconstructs" stenography *avant la lettre* happens to have been published in 1849. Scott de Martinville writes a history of stenography which is really the chronological refutation of each method as it follows the other. Almost a litany, de Martinville's *Histoire de la sténographie . . .* shows how the perfection added to a system is just enough to undo it entirely:

> It appears, so I say, that signs provide the means of following without too much difficulty the orator who would speak a monosyllabic language. . . . In order to obtain speech and to facilitate reading, you soon saw that when a word was composed of several syllables, you had to combine the signs which constituted it in order to form a monogram; but that cannot happen, in most cases, except by means of parasitic

---

dream-content—in the manner analogous to election by *scrutin de liste*" (284). (Freud may have been referring to the controversial French elections of 1885 when the *scrutin de liste*, after short experiments in 1848 and 1871, was reinstated. On the second ballot, the republicans, who had won a majority of the votes but fewer seats than the conservatives (129 to 177) swept the seats, 240 to 25. *Scruta* are "old or broken stuff, trash, frippery, trumpery." O.E.D.)

Jacques Derrida picks up this metaphor of stenography in "Freud et la scène de l'écriture," *L'Ecriture et la différence* (Paris: Seuil, 1967), 312 and 321.

traits which necessarily augment the space covered, disfigure the signs some of the time but at the very least make them lose their first simplicity.[22]

In the beginning, you have no trouble, intimates de Martinville—and as anyone knows who has tried to teach herself shorthand or any foreign language—if you stick to one syllable words, i.e. baby talk. When you get to normal speech, you start to lose it. There was some kind of mythical understanding in the literature that writing had to be cut by a sixth to ready the speed or narrowness of sound. Although stenographic manuals may start out with alphabetic or syllabic equivalents for natural language, that first step saves no time or space because you only end up translating from one code to another. So abbreviation is the first essential principle: reducing a word not only to its phonetic components but to the minimum number of sounds necessary to be understood (vowels for instance can be dropped). Speedwriting stops at this stage whereas stenography only succeeds by trying to go further. The next strategy is the use of root signs to which "parasitical" marks are added to indicate, for example, prefixes, suffixes, or verb tenses. The paradox here is that our civilization which ethnocentrically prides itself on having a more efficient language than, for instance, the Chinese, ends up inventing a new business language[23] that looks strangely oriental. But even this important advancement of "parasitical traits" does not gain enough time: you can still only transcribe a drawl. The secret is found in the "monogram" or "brief phrases" as they are called in modern stenography: a single sign corresponds to certain clichés or frequently used combinations in the particular context, like business or law. Enough efficiency is finally gained when you can practice this art of pictograms, if not hieroglyphics. A secretary who doesn't use these phrases everyday may look at notes from the day before with the bewilderment of someone surveying a Babylonian tablet. And who can resist adding one's own twist to the system? So that if one secretary is out sick, no one else can decipher what the boss said.

From Condillac to Mallarmé, (i.e. during Romanticism) theoretical work on language (or anything?) is said to have undergone an eclipse: did it retreat into areas like de Martinville's history? Stenography was supposed to be the language that would overcome language, or at least pro-

22. Scott de Martinville or Edouard Léon Scott de Martinville, *Histoire de la sténographie depuis les temps anciens jusqu'à nos jours ou Précis historique et critique des divers moyens qui ont été proposés ou employés pour rendre l'écriture aussi rapide que la parole.* . . . (Paris: chez Charles Tondeur, 1849), 33.

23. Cf. the ideology of Michelot's *Les Systèmes sténographiques:* "In modern Times, the development of parliamentary life in England and then in France and the economic take-off resulting from the discovery of steam were necessary for the countries of western Europe to constitute, in the last century, the great stenographic systems securing a sufficient simultaneity between work and material notation" (8).

vide the mediation and conversion from nondiscursive reality into discourse. Instead of freeing itself from language, or even producing a new one, stenography kept reproducing the shadow of the old one in all of its complexity. It is no coincidence that such an ancient practice of abbreviation, which goes back most notably to the Romans, depends upon what are rhetorical devices: *apocope* (to cut endings: sigla or acronyms are radical examples) and *syncope* (to cut middles), forms of ellipsis—which only invite *augmentatio*. In essence, stenography rediscovered the figurativity of language, always double, or rather, shifting within itself. It is the uncanny representation of how we manipulate time like an accordion or how language manipulates our contradictory sense of time. It highlights the obsession we cultivate, convinced, at each age, of the geometric progression of our own speed, the unique acceleration of our particular lives. We talk like journalists, speaking a slang of modern abbreviations. But at the same time we get bogged down, invent long neologisms (like "figurativity") shaping concepts to embody our supposedly new complexities. The time we save, we waste. The time we gain, we kill. But everchanging language gives us a sense of movement.

Stenography also calls attention to the ironies implicit in our history that aspires to be scientific. The early "positivist" history (as it was called in the 1840s instead of "Romantic") hoped that stenography would insure its transition from the status of literature to science. Important documents, at the center of this new parliamentary, as opposed to royalist history, would be both complete and objective. Not that deputies could not, cannot, cheat in the official record, but stenography promised to give us the text that comes closest-to-reality—if we don't lose that text or if it is not always theoretically lost. We like to think of the reality toward which we direct our (asymtotic) approach as a kind of sound barrier (truth barrier) to break, instead of a barrier to be incorporated itself into our practice. Each time we appear to be getting closer, because of a new method or materials, the bar springs back again to reconfirm our distance. And perhaps we are approaching nothing more than the reaffirmation of that bar, so that it becomes, and not the historical object itself, the infinite or figurative limit against which history is produced.

As historians and literary critics continue to study the tricky relationships and confusions between text and real, we are reminded of the double imperative of the linguistic sign for which the bar between signifier and signified remains a crucial element. Although text and reality seem to advance and retreat in terms of each other, with one appearing at times to capture the other, so that the bar looks mobile, uncontrollable if not meaningless, it is also (arbitrarily) fixed so we (escape madness) continue to try to communicate with each other, make sense of ourselves, our society, and live our everyday lives.

Around the slippery yet stable bar between the angry masses and the Assembly, a new postrevolutionary society has to organize itself. Around the bar between the stenographer and the event, a history also seeks its narrative coherence. The "people" cannot cross that bar, although individuals may; they are by definition the represented, not the representatives. So, metaphorically, the stenographers too, although individuals may, cannot cross the bar from muteness to speech, writing to action, invisibility to the light. Roland Barthes speaks of that requirement in nineteenth-century history (succeeded by empirical-positivism and neo-realism) to suppress the signs of the *enunciation* (the "I," writing time and place). History depends theoretically on the silence of the steno—and it is convenient that it also depends practically on keeping the population in the Pandora's box quiet.

You might guess that about the time stenography became well ensconced in the institutions of society—as both the State and its ideological apparatuses, courts, schools, offices—history decided that those records, as meticulous and complete as they were, no longer held any interest. Aulard's *Histoire politique de la Révolution française* (1901) closes the circle begun with Buchez and Roux's *Histoire parlementaire* (1840). Social and labor history would precisely locate its object in the cracks and gaps of the stenographed monuments if these latter had not already crushed up to the very notion of (everyday) life. You would think that history defined itself, not by its ability to coincide with the object it sought, but by its very fickleness. Give it the answer and it will change the question. No archive stays in place; characters jostle back and forth from foreground to shadow. This makes the whole enterprise of history problematic: we know that what we carefully save for posterity won't interest them and that they will want what we overlooked and considered worthless. How can you run a museum under those conditions?

Baudelaire evokes an idea of history that tries to take into account that paradox and has recourse, not surprisingly, to the metaphor of stenography. The poet was preoccupied with how to record modern life, not in its traditions and institutions, but in its very evanescence. He detaches the most technically developed method of historical documentation, stenography, from its usual historical object, the Assembly and, so to speak, looses it in places one would least expect, in the street or park. His model, Constantin Guys, the painter of modern life, worked like a kind of stenographer; his rapid sketches of a moving carriage or boat, more of movement than the object itself, resembled the traces with which the stenographer transcribed the *mouvements de séance*. "No matter what position it is thrown into, with whatever speed it is launched, a carriage, like a boat, borrows from movement a complex and mysterious grace very difficult to stenograph. We can place a sure bet that, in a few years, the drawings of M. G. will become the precious archives of civilized life."[24] Baudelaire like an investor lays his money on the future of these

24. Charles Baudelaire, ed. Claude Pichois, *Oeuvres complètes* (Paris: Gallimard, 1961), 1191.

apparently frivolous sketches. He anticipates the change in a definition of history.

Or we can interpret Baudelaire's sentence more theoretically to mean that whatever does not last long, whatever passes from fashion composes history, and not what remains. A contradiction in terms, a history of modern life could perhaps not exist. Like Midas, history automatically converts its object, whether in movement or not, into a monument that is, by definition, never modern. Maybe this is why historians covet objects that are either fugitive or difficult to conceptualize (very difficult to stenograph) like *imaginaires, mentalités, longues durées*, even nonhistorical thought: most likely to escape the fate of monumentalization. But just as the people can become as frozen as the King, the King can also become as elusive as the people.

Instead of always missing its appointed rendez-vous with itself, perhaps history, on the contrary, can never go wrong no matter what it does or says. We talk as if whole populations have slipped through our nets, whole expanses of terrain lie undiscovered and virginal, or important details elude us as too subtle, but it is also true that history seems to hold within it exactly what we need—if never knowing we needed it until it is given. Whatever scrap survives suits our history best. Even the social history of modern or everyday life was always present if we knew how to read it. Whoever reports on Coulon's presentation to the Musée de Bordeaux (another secretary) thrills at the realization (as naive as M. Jourdan in Molière) that what we respect as hallowed by history is what happened to be left around. He marvels that the lowly slave Tiron knew tachygraphy and took down what Cicero said. These casual notes become our classics. "Our enjoyment today is the daily larceny (*larcins journaliers*) that they [the ancient tachygraphers] made in their modesty" (*Deux Stenographes*, 10). Like Guy's sketches transformed as if by magic into precious archives, the little larcenies of these servants are later revered as treasures. That means that our national archives are stolen booty. And one gets the idea that the copyist took the words out of the orator's mouth, to sell to posterity. There is still something *louche*, even illegitimate about the profession. One can see Coulon or Dupont, in his "modesty," i.e. poverty, committing a little petty theft at the table of the great. But their pilfering provides the luxury of our plenty.

Romantic history should, according to our tradition, be the most monumental and deadly of narratives, and yet even it could not help but transport the history we desire. The metaphorical and empirical sense of the historical object in Baudelaire that he calls modern life is preserved, to take a contemporary example, in the notion of everyday life. In his *Critique de la vie quotidienne*, Henri Lefebvre also insists on the dialectic of practice and theory in the study of everyday life. If he returns to issues now common to contemporary social history like work, leisure, and family, he never forgets the paradox of his uncanny object, so familiar as to be strange. The bizarre banal, it is everywhere the "ground" (sol) of history and nowhere, in no one privileged context. In the second volume of his *Critique*, Lefebvre erects a historian who raises "objections" to his program. This "historian" admits that the study of everyday life is interesting but frankly "don't you return, for better or for worse, to the anecdotal. . . . to the marginal"[25]? In other words, but the historian does not go this far: you are going backwards into Romantic historiography. In his defense Lefebvre comes close to making the implication explicit: "let's not fall into ethnographic romanticism." In fact he then proceeds to conceptualize one of the most elusive contributions of Romantic history. Going beyond "historicism" (to be avoided according to Lefebvre), in which everything becomes material for history, ethnography legitimately justifies its concentration on everyday life. Archaic societies fuse ordinary objects with culture itself, with the historicity of their culture—as opposed to western capitalist societies, except in times of revolution when the repressed daily life demands better representation. "The least usual object" is not "a product, even less a thing, but a work of culture and of art . . . always bearing symbols and multiple signification!"[26] While attracted to the ethnographic program, Lefebvre makes a case for the specificity of his own investigation: "for us, here, it is a question of the modern quotidian"—which only doubles the enigma.[27]

Romantic historiography was supposedly mesmerized by the sense-making event. That event, besides eventually calling into question the sense it ostensibly supports, is eroded, moreover, by the elements proliferating around it, the marginalia: portraits, flashbacks, subminihistories, digressions, and sidetracks like the visit to the *loge* of the logograph.[28] Like the structure of post-Revolutionary society itself, the event becomes a minimal narrative function holding together a constantly

---

25. Henri Lefebvre, *Critique de la vie quotidienne* (Paris: L'Arche, 1967), 3 vols., 2: 25.
26. Ibid., 26.
27. The conceptual connection between ethnography and everyday life is also useful for Michel de Certeau in "On the oppositional practices of everyday life": "This remnant left over by technological colonization acquires the value of purely private activity, becomes charged with the symbolic investments of daily life, . . . is in short made over into something like the active and legendary memory of everything still stirring in the margins or interstices of the dominant scientific or cultural norms." But this "remnant" requires the "explanatory discourse" of science and culture to be "known". Michel de Certeau, "On the Oppositional Practices of Everyday Life," *Social Text: Theory/Culture/Ideology* 1.3 (1980): 28 and 30.
28. Should we be surprised that especially Lamartine was a master of the *symbolic quotidian?* Maybe I should find an example of "popular" daily life instead of the oppressive royal daily life which Lamartine like Michelet pushed to its ludicrous extreme, thereby opting again for a critique within the system. But the details of Louis XVI's imprisonment are notable uncanny: how he and the Queen play chess with the King and Queen (4: 319), how the wallpaper of his cell depicts the interior of a prison (4: 310), how when separated, he and the queen communicate by hiding a pin-pricked paper in a ball of yarn (5:28, cf. Fabrice and Clélia, *La Chartreuse de Parme*).

overflowing coherence. Reading these nineteenth-century histories, in which our sameness is returned to us as curious, if not outlandish, best approximates the ethnographic experience whose pleasures, however, provokes less guilt in us than the analysis of our own commonplace romanticism.

TOM CONLEY

# Le Quotidien Météorologique

The institution of French literature has had strange fortunes in North America. The former model of refinement and impeccable taste for letters, the *French department* (and its vestal *maison française*) are not what they used to be. Anyone paging through *Dissertations Abstracts* or the *PMLA Bibliographies* of twenty years ago realizes that the ultimate product of extended training in French, either the Ph.D or an article in the yellow-jacketed issues of *Yale French Studies,* took the form of analysis praising a timeless moment in a frame of literary history. Certain themes were chosen to modify a practice that mastered biography, history, criticism and archival research. Begun in North America, the dissertation engaged its field work in the dark labyrinths of the Bibliothèque Nationale. The researcher learned the total social facts of archaic life among French families or in regional libraries before he returned, like a prodigal child, to the salvation of post-war America that knew different rhythms of cultural change.

The research was programmed and conditioned by an art of mediation. The fresh innocence of an American brand of existentialism took several generations of intellectuals overseas in the tracks of the Liberation. Commitment to things French was based on no reason other than a desire to study a mythic civilization and a literature without the democratic humanism of British or American writing, or perhaps on a need to examine the materiality of a foreign language instead of the moral themes of the familiar tongue that offered too little alterity to its user.

The French curriculum worked because of a time lag, as French was of a high and gracious order, and so simple and complex that the clarity of its ruling order (the orthogonality of *sujet-verbe-régime*) was heightened by the fascination of its many exceptions. Literature bubbled from the early classical font of Caesar in the green hills of Burgundy, and the mysteries of the dark ages were colored with the tan and yellow ochres of Lascaux.

216  *Yale French Studies*

Codes of research, whether in the line between Lanson and Peyre, Comte and Weinberg or Camus and Brée, were dominated by categories that produced order Americans had never known. Yet the aura of French arched back to times before the First and Second World Wars, at the very moment their effects were settling. There seemed to be at work a sort of grand-father effect, in which the student of French reached beyond the immediate, paternal generation of the American Army to the imaginary extension of a French heritage that recent soldiers had never known.[1] There are many other causes of American fervor for French that could be adduced, but a recension of them would take us beyond the aim of this article.

By now the fantasies that French culture offered to America seem to have waned. It may be that the media have levelled the sense of shared cultural difference that had been at the bottom of the Franco-American venture in the early post-war years. No matter what, some fallow areas remain to be cultivated; they may be located along the boundaries that make the teaching of everyday French innocuous for students who have known none of the aura of the longer traditions of our century. By innocuous this writer refers to the feeling of gratuity—which can be either preciously sublime or absolutely discouraging—prevailing in the classroom when a teacher wills to impart French studies to rural Americans born after 1960. In Minnesota the teacher faces youths who have known farming, taconite mining or a very limited urban experience in the horizontal sprawl of the Twin Cities. French is reduced to the names of downtown avenues inherited from the voyageurs Hennepin and Nicollet, to the names of hockey stars such as Lafleur or Potvin, or to the vocabulary of adventure in a last wilderness, along the portages canoeists make from the Embarass River to the origins of vermilion. The world of Henry the Fourth, the *grand siècle,* or the revolution of 1848 are requisite evils in language or distribution requirements leading to a B.A. degree.

The trick may involve adapting the great legacy of French literature and critical theory to the different cultural settings of North America. Here standard interpretations of classics have to be momentarily abandoned, as must the intoxicating subtleties of the reception of deconstruction. By using the heritage of literature as a stock of commonplaces whose historical variations inform scenes in the media, and by interrogating the effects of language that program our regions of daily experience, adaptation of French traditions of inquiry can yield practical—and even political—results. Theories derived from studies of discourse, anthropology, psychoanalysis, and philosophy can be fashioned to study daily life, which is to say, those areas most resistant to analysis of symbolic languages and behavior. The critique of everyday life has been cur-

1. The grandfather theory belongs to Walter Friedlander, in *Mannerism and Anti-Mannerism in Italian Painting* (New York: Schocken, 1966), 16–17.

rent but remains to be, as in the case of all daily life practice, relentlessly reinvented.[2]

In North America this need for reinvention may be especially acute at a moment when the ideology of experience—the stuff and substance of American literature, American Studies and quotidian life—is facing a fact that French theory has long been teaching: that language and symbolic process program experience; that an individual life has already been formed by discourses structuring the imagination and will; that individuals are products of institutions built over a long period of time, and mostly by agencies of information. The latter, we can suppose, have now all but conquered the last pockets of the unknown. In Minnesota these are, perhaps, the forbidding imagination of the North that has been associated with the cry of the timber wolf and the common loon, or the ferocious weather that gives a fresh and lusty beauty to daily endeavor. How, in effect, these can be incorporated into a study of the quotidian is crucial for localized praxis of French. The reinvention of everyday life must not veer to the stasis of a "social fact" informing behavior conditioned by discourses; rather, its analysis must produce extended morphogenesis, or continual,—if even microscopic—cultural change by virtue of active *play* with regional myths and the media.

Of immediate consequence for a shift in the tactics of French studies in North America is analysis of unconscious effects in the news—which may not just reflect, but may also produce broader dimensions of domestic and foreign policy.[3] These unconscious effects are situated—or, better, *anchored*—in the ways that the media tell us how to handle complex issues with radically efficient and often murderous simplicity. This is tantamount to saying that the institution of allegory has not at all disap-

2. An important avatar is Roland Barthes, *Mythologies* (Paris: Seuil, 1955), but which seems dated because the observer's role is almost omniscient in the alienating distance it establishes from the popular culture it studies in order to obtain an effect of perverse fascination. The book appears to be the French homologue to that of pop-art of the later 1950s in the United States. By now the quasi-Marxian perspective that the book has espoused seems romantic, for the attraction for petty-bourgeois effects has become integrated into rhythms of everyday life which incorporate the power of the gaze into speculation and greater sale. Much of contemporary advertising, for example, already accounts for the criticisms implicit in the distance between the observer and object in *Mythologies*. Some of the more recent studies in popular culture insist on contractual obligation requiring the consumer or viewer to have an active participation in the event produced and its sale. A lucid view is found in Jane Feuer on *Dallas* and *Dynasty* in "Melodrama, Serial Form and TV Today," Screen 25 (1984): 4–19.

3. Recourse to Michel de Certeau's notion of the difference between *tactic* and *strategy* is keynote. The latter involves calculated manipulation of relations of power when a subject (either a topic or an individual) can be isolated or localized. Thus a *strategy* "puts someone in his place" and generates a sense of exteriority and individuality—happy effects that one often uses to be self-mythified—by means of oppositional logic that de Certeau historicizes through the Cartesian tradition, in *L'Invention du quotidien* (Paris: Union générale d'éditions-10/18, 1980), 75.

peared from either literature or the structure of everyday life, but is more and more one of the most strongly constitutive forces that program the ways we live our lives. At this point it would be too ambitious to relate production of news to that of foreign policy—but nonetheless we can begin where these collusions are framed and sold through complex divisions of labor. Insofar as allegory does constitute a matrix of the everyday, the nightly weather report appears to be where psychomachia has a last and most persistent—if even innocuous—presence in the realm of high technology. The meteorological report brings us to a specificity and materiality lost in the headlines of events; it lends distance to them and both alleviates and intensifies the immensity of their dread. The real and lasting effects of cold air can palliate Beirut, the war between Iran and Iraq, the arms shipment scandal in Washington, the local accidents on the interstate highway, or even the loss of the tax base in the state appropriations to education. Here the battle of Nature and Man finds adequate configuration in isobars, colored maps and pulsed shots of our globe overseen by satellites. Fortune returns when the weatherman's voice calms the airwaves. We realize the planet has not yet exploded, and that the pathos of our own lives may count for little in face of the masses of low pressure and snow that are coming from the Dakota plains and the Red River Valley.

Since the weather is often sandwiched between increasingly equal allotments of time accorded to news and sports in televised reports, more and more we get a balanced sense of the identities of serious priority and immediate pleasure. Through identity of news with sports, micro- and macrocosm coincide; the public sphere can be grasped through a common experience that finds adequate representation in the self-affirming tracks of each discourse in their relation to each other. After all, what do we live for, if not to see clearly the honesty of combat and the spoils it reaps? Do not sports inflect the news more and more with issues of national economy? And in doing so, do they not tell us that the spectacle is a product of the media just as, analogously, are current events?

Here we can begin to theorize the immobilizing power of *le quotidien météorologique*. For indeed what is the cadre of the ten o'clock news, if not a tripartite division of hierarchy sanctifying areas of concern in their varied relations to each other? Acting out the effects of the first sentence of Marx's *18th Brumaire,* the newscast moves from a tragically stern report of events to their farcical underside in sports. "News, Weather and Sports:" the title and order tell us that even the first substantive signals the order of the whole, summarizing it in the *abîme* of its four graphemes *N, We* and *S*. That the emblem of the news is derived from its association with weathervanes is hardly fortuitous. Its rebus concretizes the identity of weather with history, and in such a way that the change is always registered by the shift in direction of its arrow in directions identical to the winds of events:

```
        E
   N       S
        W
```

Like the *girouette* that simply follows the winds of history, the allegory of news, weather and sports will, as the emblem implies, bring words back to the physical substance of the rhythms of the world.

Yet sports are, as recent studies insist, more directly concerned with the news: on the one hand, the collusion of the media with the production of dollars takes place in the broadcasting of professional struggle—"struggle" both on the football field and for the acquisition of adequate Nielson ratings to promote more advertising in order to secure more sustained viewership and returns. (Obvious proof can be found in the way the USFL had been reported in the sports pages. Its quality of spectacle or autonomy of game in no way plays a role in the news [Hershel Walker or Anthony Carter were promotions, not athletes], since the Nielson ratings and figures of attendance command more careful review and scrutiny. The latter threw the USFL into a battle with the NFL in such a way that the paradigm of the two politial parties or American-Soviet relations was reproduced—in effect, the ultimate victor or synthesizing winner is the network which has programmed the contest.) And on the other, collusion is manifest in the entire metaphorical panoply shared among politicians and reporters. We have witnessed how metaphors derived from American sports inflect the foreign policy of government. We will, they say, be able to "win" a nuclear war, make a "power play" in El Salvador, or "throw strikes" in Grenada, even "take command and win in the late innings" in longwinded debate over economic policy at summit meetings with tired European socialists. These are more than merely convenient representations, as the concept of endless play glosses the stakes, issues, and consequences of the policies.

That a number of networks have opted for supplementary news following the official program of N-E-W-S is sign of the fact that traditional coverage is used to minimize and, simultaneously, to protect the equivalence of major events and sports. An additional half-hour of opinion plays on the myth of news "in depth" but more effectively structures the oppositional frame that had just preceded it. In this way the Ted Koppel show has been intended exactly to guard the balance achieved in the regional reports that adhere to the strict division of news and sports flanking the weather report. Here meteorology mediates cataclysm and farce. If the news and sports are of the same stuff and texture, then the weather report plays a literally pivotal role in the inversion and return from tragical or serious impressions of everyday events to their comical or farcical identities.

There seems to be a long and unconscious tradition which informs this kind of mediation. On the one hand, the "weatherman" was an avatar of the specialist of the occult arts that a person—especially a king or queen—had to consult with reverence equal to that accorded to executive, religious and military advisors. The role that Nostradamus played in shaping Catherine de Medicis's policies is mythic; and so are reports of the daily behavior of Louis XIV, who met both with his priest and soothsayers with chronometric regularity. The wisdom of the horoscope, like that of the seasonal almanach or *calendrier des bergers,* stood strong as a reminder of Nature and Fortune playing a major part in producing the contingencies of history that leaders—from Louis to Ronald Reagan— could use in mediating folklore with the ongoing Christian conquest of the world. In this light there are powers, and then, too, it seems, there are *other* powers: these make up most of the marginal but central interest of syndicated newspapers. And, if we remember that the weatherman is a direct descendant of the respected counselor immersed in the arts of divination, occult powers are at the pivot of the evening broadcasts.

As such the weather report apposes a gay or eminently incorrect science to the surer ones based on scientific probabilities. Where the news commands serious attention and extended meditation, the weather allows almost always for levity and sighs of relief. News may promise disaster, but weather will affirm the presence of man. Catastrophe will come only when nuclear war will obliterate the unclear nature of weather. (The fear of nuclear strife seems in fact to hinge open the thought that with it will come the great night of weather.) Yet lately the history of weather seems to have taken a bizarre development, since more and more its appeal to advanced technology turns out to be a coded celebration of the media themselves.

The *weatherman* is an epithet which has disappeared from the lexicon of television since 1968. Once it described the happily bizarre, ineffectual, but always gentle soul of good will. Then, the interference of the name with that of the bourgeois guerillas engaged against leaders producing the War in Vietnam led to its eradication from the meteorological realm. After 1968 a change in orientation was needed: the media had to calm unrest and become definitively the power of order. With the advent of the meteorologist also came the newscaster as the president-to-be, whether Walter Cronkite, Ronald Reagan or, in another vein, Johnny Carson (who reports news in the standing one-liners inaugurating his show). Concomitantly, not only did the weatherman disappear, but his avatar became a scientized meteorologist sporting a license and emblem of the AMS in the lower corner of the screen. He (invariably *he*—there being few Cassandras in the trade—since the female is often awarded the role of the phallic anchor in such a way that sexual difference is maintained by a female at the center of the news (Fig. 1), at a virtual position around which the men must turn, *she* being a force of Truth) became privy to a panoply of transitional objects: screens that no longer slide up

*Figure 1.* The WCCO Newsteam: Skip Loescher, Pat Miles, Dave Moore, Mark Rosen and Mike Fairbourne (Meteorologist). Courtesy of WCCO News.

and down or left and right like Lacan's blackboards, but which flash one upon the other so quickly that the meteorologist's outstretched finger can point exactly to the critical mass of information without moving; computerized cyphers that in a single second can fill a regional map with dotted figures of temperature and its variations, recorded at regional outposts in the area covered by the network; scrolls of truth lending historical exactitude to highs, lows and predictable conditions adjacent to the meteorologist's stance and posture. In a word, the scientific apparatus and the computer have mythified further the role of the diviner by conferring upon him the agencies of veracity that he may formerly have spurned. Now that the meteorologist is certified and licensed to practice a surer science, and not a gay endeavor of divination or wager, he can *be* the News. Hence the projection of power and truth was directed more and more through areas whose nature he had to satirize gently in Horatian style.

The second paradox folded into the role of the meteorologist of course involves his own relation to technology. Where the latter is relegated to a secondary presence in the reporting of news—news bringing us quickly to the salient and crucial review of events by effacing their facticity in favor of their immediacy—it is now coded as all the more miraculous when the visible curvature of the globe can give an almost Pascalian aura to the fate of weather. So the weatherman must, at the same time that he embodies scientific pretension of objectivity, also be cast as a child who plays with the endlessly informative toys of technology. He must reproduce our amazement and disbelief at what the television screen and computer are ultimately "doing for us."

The wherewithall bringing us the microcosm of the weather is divested of the catastrophic implications that advanced technology had suggested in the news or economic policies in the preceding minutes. We see a happy regression to a dialogic condition when the childish scientist can effectively "play" with technology in the studio and embody all the pictogrammatical wonder of the intermediate area to which we would wish to return when we face the hard—and logocentric—news of international relations. Indeed, the intermediary position that the weather plays in the visible allegory of the ten P.M. report has incorporated the alluring psychogenesis of the individual subject that is acted out over and again in the sphere of daily activity.

If, as we should like to hypothesize, everyday life is legitimized by strategies in the media producing oppositional structures derived from allegory, the fabrication of the quotidian—either as experience or a concept—forces us to recreate psychogenesis at every moment of our lives. It pushes us toward an imaginary toss and stir of barely conscious activity with thoughts we use to produce and block off that activity. The everyday, like the weather, has us play with ourselves and our personal histories. We find the residue of this process in the proverbial wisdom of phrases like "Time will tell," or "If you think's it's cold right now, just wait five minutes." An apothegm always turns us to the world with brutalizing simplicity; it places us before a construct of life and language that are not exactly ours. When we confront the weather, we are positioning ourselves in an imaginary territory. And in proliferating scenes of ourselves in a climate of phantasy, we ask ourselves constantly to review and justify the productions of our lives and their vagaries before an absent jury. Often the latter is a panel of newscasters (for they are the cultural code, the ultimate judges of taste and calm decorum). Hence allegory seeps into the imagination. Before the television screen such repeated enactments of psychogenesis are the "scenes of writing" we play out, or that are acted upon us, whether in the way that we are shown how others approach problems or, more in proportion to quotidian behavior, in the model of the limited scope of activity we discern under the influence of televised meteorology. But in everyday life, which tells us to respect distinct and hierarchical orders between seeing and hearing or picturing and reading, regression to an anterior state of visibility—englobing their oppositions—constitutes the beginning of a model that can discern unconscious effects.

There are two historical edges of the weather: one aimed toward a production of its science, another toward its return to an intermediary zone by virtue of "play" with technology. This simultaneous forward motion and regress (tomorrow's weather is enveloped in a childish "scene" of enunciation) dictates, it seems, the very style and mode of exchange that *has to take place* in the transition from one announcer to another. The meteorologist must always be a laughing figure, of jolly voice or even, occasionally, of slightly self-parodying, caricatural shape.

A regional example is telling. In nineteenth-century Minnesota, Yankee speculators formed the Washburn-Crosby Corporation, what would later become a megalith of the Twin Cities. It quickly reaped huge profits and assumed a central economic role in the ways it took control of the technologies of milling and of the news media. Grain elevators, daily newspapers and television stations were to become grist for the same mill. Since its beginnings, the company has emblematized a network of television and radio that literally idealizes the lore of the state and produces its mythic physiognomy.

Until the middle 1970s, the most famous "weatherman" of the same network was named Bud Kraehling (fig. 2). He wore somewhat loud plaid suits but was always decked with a smile and a wise irony (no doubt appealing to "Scandanavian" wit of the type that has precipitated Garrison Keillor's regional persona onto the national scene). Most effectively, however, Kraehling's bald head reflected both the rotundity of the great globe of which he spoke and the glaring lights of the television studio. His waxed epiderm had shown both the technology of the medium and the natural course of time and nature. Prematurely of an "older"

*Figure 2.* The Grand Old Weatherman, Bud Kraehling of WCCO, Courtesy of WCCO News.

demeanor, he was young at heart, but reflective of the essence of weather, that is, of Father Time. Bud Kraehling also embodied that virtue of gentle laughter that could, like the mild *sagesse* of Rabelais or Bonaventure Des Périers, help us face the rigors of daily life.

A few paragraphs ago this brand of humor was aligned with Horatian satire, but it could also be a function of proverbial pioneer spirit on the great plains, where a grim smile and a keen sense of "grinning and bearing it" could be valorized as crucial elements for success in the wilderness where Winter is said, in lore, history, and wit, to determine those great courses and cycles, the fears and terrors, even the biology and psychology of our "pure and clean life in Minnesota." When Bud Kraehling could *ironize* a cold snap of thirty-five to fifty degrees below zero in the Arrowhead region from International Falls and the Iron Range (Eveleth, Mountain Iron, Hibbing, Virginia) to Duluth by saying that, 200 miles to the South, in "WCCOland" (i.e., Washburn Crosby Country), around the Twin Cities, the thermometer is pushing up to thirty to forty below, he was arguing for the great American will to endure. (Wind-chill factors were not yet invented; he simply had to appeal to the standard definition of *blizzard* and recall colder times "a few years back," since there were no historical records of wind chill on hand.) No doubt every weatherman of any given region could count on similar ploys to define a local character and impose its myth upon the viewer.

But even more, the irony used by the weatherman turns toward an embodiment of collective subjects—all gentle, warm, and crazy enough to live in the region not suited for ordinary human beings. But "all the same" there must be some everyday ordinariness in an exemplary figure. This kind of usual, everyday discourse attaches the anchor and sportscaster to the relation of humor that, above all, the weatherman has as his task to circulate through the news and sports. His is a mimicry of an archaic "joking relationship."[4] He also has a sort of mediated avuncular function. His laughing tone puts before the screen an imaginary family and a simplified idea of its complex structures of kinship. The laughing tone is based on inexactitude opposed to its contrary of fact in news, and is produced by the comedy of caricature of news held at a center within its medium. It may be that the increasingly scientific look of meteorology

    4. The joking relationship is close to that of an avoidance relationship (i.e., a man and his mother-in-law) insofar as there is an alliance and respect maintained by exchange continually marking distance in the terms of conjoinment. "The joking relationship is in some ways the exact opposite of a contractual relation. Instead of specific duties to be fulfilled there is privileged disrespect and freedom or even licence, and the only obligation is not to take offence at the disrespect so long as it is kept within certain bounds defined by custom, and not to go beyond those bounds. Any default in the relationship is like a breach of the rules of etiquette; the person concerned is regarded as not knowing how to behave himself," writes A. R. Radcliffe-Browne in *Structure and Function in Primitive Society* (Glencoe, Illinois: The Free Press, 1961), 103.

tends to force the comedy or attenuate its need to be based on chance or a space of play.

The area needed for the gentle humor might now be even more reduced. Because the stricture of reporting calls for expanding perimeters of screened views of the Twin Cities, the state, the Midwest and the United States, there is less room for improvisation. This observation suggests that there may have existed a freer and more autonomous frame for the weather man who could discourse with greater ease about his topic. Here a Marxian inflection could point to the fact that a mental space necessary for the gay science of meteorology and its uncanny intelligence has been eroded in a history of expanding technology.

An ironic proof of that erosion can be found by looking at the recent controversy surrounding the reporting of damages occasioned by severe weather. In mid-May of 1984, a series of tornadoes struck Northern Minneapolis and virtually razed a shopping center. Sirens warned the population of the impending danger only after the waterspouts had touched down. The meteorological stations were unable to detect the funnels in the immediate proximity. Local newspapers claimed that the experts were watching screens and not the world, or representations of things rather than the substance of life. Arbiters of truth, the newswriters accused the meteorologists of invidious faith in televised mirages. The latter responded by affirming that new and more sensitive instruments were on order and would eventually foresee catastrophe (future losses of shopping centers). Local Marxists sided with the newspapers, while the adepts of television showed renewed adhesion to the mediated visibility of high technology. At this moment weather became news, and the joking relationship turned to direct report.

These events underscored the fact that the joking relationship remains essential for the manufacture of everyday weather. It occurs when the meteorologist and anchor can turn to each other and utter, "Well, Bud, what's in store for tomorrow? What bad news do you bring us today?" Or: "Yes, Shirley, you saw those little flakes when you came to the studio this afternoon, and if you haven't had a chance to look outside the studio this evening, you'd better believe those little crystals are piling up with vengeance!" Mediated laughter always fills the conditions of the contract, allowing the society of newscasters to reconstitute their order— and the greater structure of a sensible world whose visibility they propose to be codes of reality—in the process of joking. Most often the anchor must make some evidence of the existence of news by carefully stacking into a neat pile the files of 8½ by 11 sheets of paper with three or four gentle raps on the desk to signal that the bell has sounded, that the show is ready for its parting shots. Here good luck must be in store (the ream of paper "knocks on wood," and the laughter neutralizes all remaining contradiction). At this and other programmed junctures the anchors and weatherman produce light amounts of *noise*, that is, echoes of meteorological disorder. The deliberate fabrication of gentle cacophony regulates the dynamics of the universe through the dialects of speech, laughter, sound and punctuation of silence.[5]

The sibylline and scientific duties of the forecaster do appear, ultimately, to play a role secondary to laughter. They moderate the effects of noise. Hence an unconscious dimension of meteorology may be glimpsed in the production of light interference reflecting the weather that has been rendered invisible through its translation into computorized images. The unconscious effects of the weather are, however, programmed to make the historical paradoxes of the métier, together with the soothing laughter they elicit in the staging of the report, its regulatory function—or better, its dose of daily ideology.[6]

It may be argued that the programmers appeal to the archaic side of the divining arts, as does advertising, in order to produce a timeless climate of myth. But a practical analysis of the theoretical dimension of the weather has yielded more. It shows that the myths which structure the manifold allegories also fabricate the news which frames the weather. In this fashion the meteorologist gives credence to catastrophe by forcing news to be subject to daily rhythms seemingly more timeless than the present currents of international event. He underscores their potentiality by folding them into patterns of the everyday, allowing us therefore to conclude that a balanced meditation on death (the news)[7] and life (the weather) will allow anything to pass through the interstice of history and myth.

The poles of this underlying binary opposition are so global and so

    5. These have been studied in Claude Lévi-Strauss, *Le Cru et le cuit* (Paris: Plon, 1964), 343–50.
    6. This is not quite the case that we recall from the European airwaves. If we think of M. Météo in *Libération*, the reporting of weather is occasion for expression of peripatetic philosophy. The weatherman strays from his métier to discourse on the state of the world, to affirm a corrective dialogue with its uncanny rhythms and to politicize his work in view of the permanancy of climatic change. Like the poet whose archaic task is to write verse inflecting seasonal change—at once reflecting and inducing, retarding or advancing it in the ambiguous cast of his words, in the poetry of their sound and shape or in his own brand of felicitous jargon—M. Météo embodies the timeless craft of the weatherman. He is not quite the media-scientist of WCCO or other stations offering gloss of truth to suburban lands and worlds of hobby-farmers of the regional cities of the Northern Midwest.
    7. To feel how the newspaper is a celebration of death we need only investigate the impression of time lost and *malaise* following the keen anticipation we sense before encountering, on lazy Sunday mornings, that great citadel of boredom, *The New York Sunday Times*. Or we can see verification of the same drive toward death in the way Godard films his characters reading papers. Michel Butor has theorized this effect in his iconography of the newspaper in painting of the twentieth century: "The quantity of writing which surrounds our daily life has considerably increased with the advent of printing. If the book has always been an essential element in the 'Still-Life', once 'Vanity' or meditation on death, it is the newspaper which will become indispensable in it when it will have become a celebration of intimate daily life in reaction to the increasing inadequacy of public festivals," in "Painting Words," *Triquarterly* 20 (Winter 1971): 106.

immediate that the individual subject cannot help being constituted—and cannot help periodically reconstituting himself—in the imaginary production of scenes that reproduce or combat their effects. A most extraordinary and most everyday production of *le quotidien*, then, is the weather. It establishes a split between news just passed and future events and allows the occasion, in the time of the climate,[8] for a fake presence to body forth through the report. That split does make for subjectivity and, too, for our need to analyze why and how it seems to be produced in the montage and rifts of words, speech, pictures and images.

---

8. Meticulously studied in literature by Arden Reed, *Romantic Weather: The Climates of Coleridge and Baudelaire* (Hanover and London: Brown University and the University Press of New England, 1983), 272 and 275. His sense of time arching back and forward determines much of what is projected in contemporary newscasting.

MOLLY NESBIT

# What Was an Author?

All Authors
What with the multiplication of reproductive processes, of the means of distribution, and the complexity of the techniques of creation, the identity of the author is more and more difficult to grasp and define. The paternity of a work, then, indefinable?
— *Les Immatériaux* (1985)

The French definition of the author has gone vague: the author is a general case, an orphan, some say corpse. It is a definition too diffuse to be useful; worse, it strips the author of distinction. As if in flight from such a fate, lately French authors have become authors by doing other things besides write; they may make music, psychoanalysis, Sartres, maps (Fig. 1). Whatever the result, it is diffused, scattered across an immense accumulation of spectacle, the "magazine covers, illustrations, ads, slick and pulp fiction, comics, Tin Pan Alley music, tap dancing, Hollywood movies, etc.," Greenberg's kitsch.[1] Those who go looking for authors must devise the means by which to recognize not only the worker but the work; at some point, perhaps by night, culture was camouflaged.

The situation of positive unclarity regarding the author has given rise to a growing body of criticism, full of dire pronouncements about the plight of culture, author death, and postmodern conditions; apocalypse weighs on the wind.[2] And yet, bourgeois culture has not changed all that much in the past two hundred years. Historically, bourgeois culture was always a little too crude to be believed. Where others cried vulgar, we rather lamely call vague. This crudeness so essential and so troubling is not difficult to find: we need only pose the question about what the author was.

  1. Clement Greenberg, "Avant-Garde and Kitsch", *Art and Culture* (Boston: Beacon, 1961), 9.
  2. Roland Barthes, "The Death of the Author," in *Image—Music—Text*, ed. and trans. by Stephen Heath (New York: Hill & Wang, 1977), 142–48. The French version was first published in *Mantéia*, v. 5 (1968). My thinking on this subject was initially stimulated by Michel Foucault's essay, "What is an Author?", in English in the collection *Language, Counter-Memory, Practice*, ed. Donald F. Bouchard, trans. Donald F. Bouchard and Sherry Simon (Ithaca: Cornell University Press, 1977), 113–38. The French version was first published in 1969 and should be read in conjunction with Foucault's book appearing the same year, *The Archaeology of Knowledge*, trans. A. M. Sheridan Smith (London: Tavistock,

Many have worked on an answer to the author question. They have usually been concerned with two kinds of evidence: the explicit statements written out by the authors themselves and the implicit, quiet assertions made in authorial practice. Like Mallarmé's explicit variation on the subject, written in 1895:

> The pure work involves the disappearance of the poet's voice, ceding the initiative to the words mobilized by the clash of their disparity; they illuminate one another in reciprocal reflections like a virtual trail of sparks on gem stones, replacing the breathing perceptible in the old lyric inspiration or the personal, enthusiastic direction of the phrase.[3]

Or, alternately, like this photograph of the cabaret *Au Tambour* (Fig. 2). In it, the photographer Atget took a picture of himself as something more than the man on the street: with a ripple effect in the glass, he worked out a dark, winter's day reflection on himself in which his body appears as a shadow attached to another man's head. The photograph is an answer of a sort, issued in 1908, to the question about what an author was. But it is partial and insufficient, full of insider's bias, just like Mallarmé's *pensée*. In order to gauge the full extent of authorship, it is necessary to move outside the author's house. A more reliable standard of measurement must be found. Fortunately such a standard exists: we find it in the law.

Authors of all kinds have for a long time been flatly equated in the law, though the equation is not made using the familiar terms like creativity, genius, and ancient lyric breath. It is instead an equation of rights. The legal definition of the author is windless, dry, and plain: the author is given rights to a cultural space over which he or she may range and work; all authors share the same cultural space; they are defined by their presence there as well as by their rights to it. Through the law, then, we can gauge the author and the work. But let us not look to the law for the easy answer: the same law that defines the author is responsible for much of the confusion about what authors were and are. French copyright law dates from the Revolution; the landmark law on author's rights was enacted in 1793; it governed *droits d'auteur* until 1957, when it was revised. In 1985 it was revised again.

> The law of 1793 gave authors privileges that ordinary men did not enjoy: The authors of every kind of writing, the composers of music, the painters and draughtsmen who have their paintings and drawings en-

---

1972). Brian O'Doherty and Barbara Novak showed me the relevance of *Aspen* 5+6 for this issue and to them I am grateful. My essay has also benefitted greatly from careful reading by André Rouillé, Adrian Rifkin, Leila Kinney, Carol Duncan, Kristin Ross, and Alice Kaplan; without them it would not have been the same.

3. Stéphane Mallarmé, "Variations sur un sujet," *La Revue blanche* (February–November 1895, September 1896), reprinted in his *Oeuvres complètes*, ed. Henri Mondor and G. Jean-Aubry (Paris: NRF, 1945), 366.

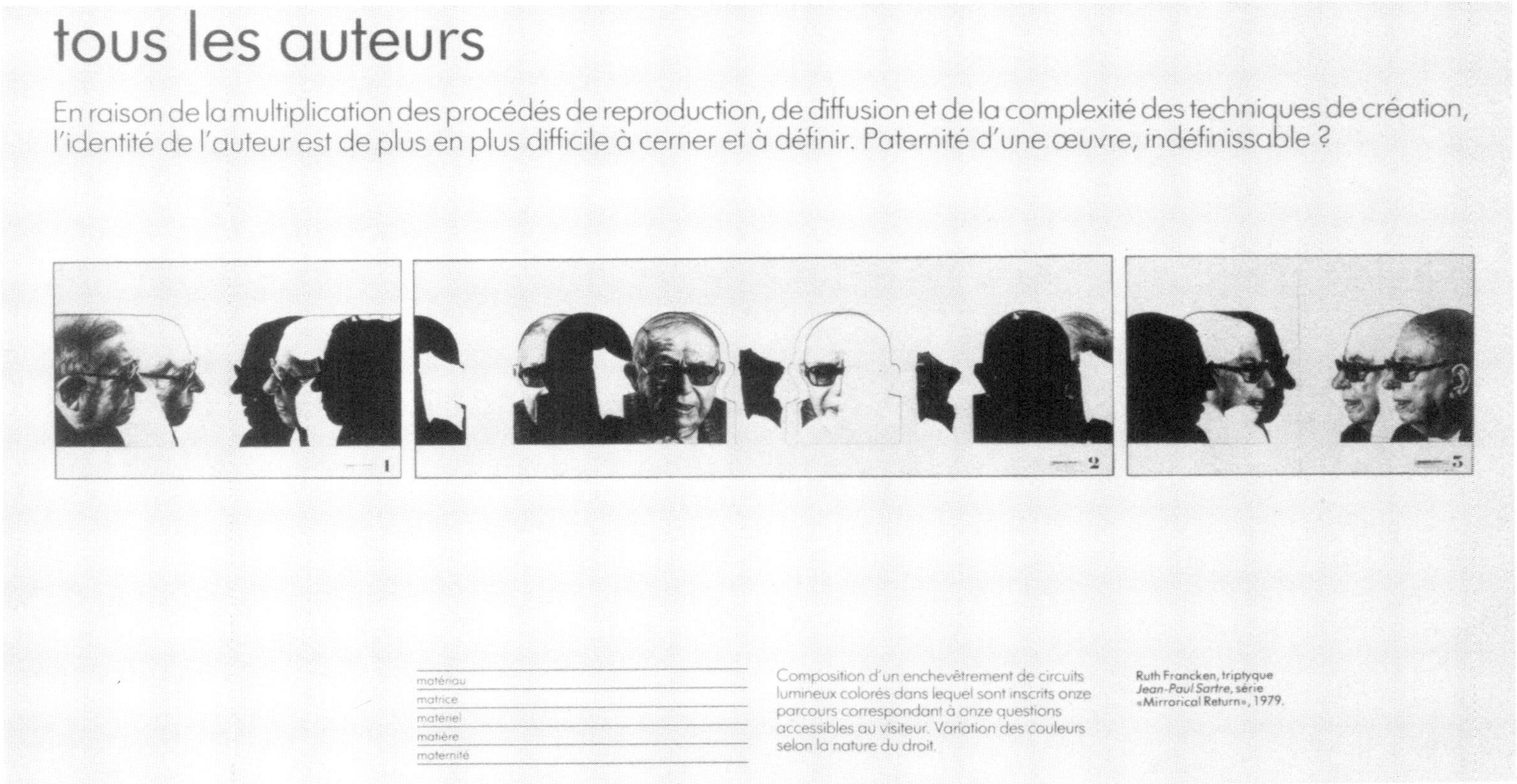

*Figure 1.* *All Authors*, text by Jean-Francois Lyotard, Jean-Paul Sartre triptych by Ruth Francken, lay-out by Alain Leboucher. *Les Immatériaux*, Centre National Georges Pompidou, Paris, 1985.

H. COUSIN

graved, will enjoy the exclusive and lifetime right to sell, to have sold and to distribute their work in the territory of the Republic and to cede the same in toto or in part.[4]

In other words, authors retained property rights over the fruits of their labor even after their work was sold to somebody else. That was the essence of the privilege. The rights themselves could be ceded or sold but this took a separate operation and was not assumed to be the natural part of any deal. The *droits d'auteur* were applied to any work done in the designated media, writing, music composition, painting, drawing, and engraving, basically those media that could be worked up into forms of high culture like poems, sonatinas, and red chalk sketches. The law did not even try to draw lines between good and bad work in these media and it did not presume to erect criteria for aesthetic quality. Slipshod failures and drawn reproductions were covered by the same rights as the masterpiece: a hack and a Mallarmé would both be called authors; an engraver of Salon paintings had just as much claim to the title as an Ingres.[5] The cultural field is broad, said the law. It covered kitsch, avant-garde, low, high, and middle brow work with equal justice. Authors were not necessarily artists.

The law did not divide culture into states. It set out a single field where standards were blurred and the different hierarchies of the arts eroded, irrelevant. Others in academies and newspaper columns and university lectures could and did quibble, insisting on other definitions of culture with genres, standards, traditions, and rules. The law let these storms erupt around it. It held like bedrock, content to make only basic distinctions. It entered the Napoleonic Code and as the nineteenth century progressed, it acquired more nuance in the courts. But historically the law of 1793 set a breathtaking precedent that was not to be undone. Its definitions of culture survived all the others: the collapse of the hierarchy of genres and the slow death of the Salon made no difference to it; neither did the rise of the mass-produced, printed forms of culture. The law had

---

4. Loi 19 July 1793, given in Georges Chabaud, *Le Droit d'auteur des artistes & des fabricants. Législation—Jurisprudence—Projets de réforme* (Paris: Librairie des Sciences politiques et sociales, Marcel Rivière, 1908), ii. Chaubaud's appendix gives the texts of the laws from 1777 to 1902 and his book gives a close reading of them.

5. Those interpreting the law would not mince words: See Eugène Pouillet, *Traité théorique et pratique de la propriété littéraire et artistique et du droit de représentation* (3rd ed.; Paris: Marchal et Billard, 1908), 97: "La loi récompense et protège toute composition due à un effort de l'esprit humain et se rapportant aux beaux-arts. Elle ne considère ni l'importance ni la beauté de l'oeuvre; elle n'envisage que le fait de la création; c'est pour cela qu'elle protège au même degré le tableau de Raphaël et l'image sortie des fabriques d'Epinal." [The law protects and rewards all work developing from an effort of the human mind and relating to the fine arts. It does not consider its importance nor does the beauty of the work matter, only the fact of creation. It is for this reason that it protects a painting by Raphael to the same extent as the images coming out of the factories of Epinal.] Unless otherwise indicated, all translations are my own.

*Figure 2. Au Tambour*, photograph by Eugène Atget, 1908. Collection of the Caisse Nationale des Monuments et des Sites, Paris.

already leveled the academic distinctions; in its very practical, authoritative terms, culture was flat.

In the law, the term author did not and does not carry with it a mark of supreme distinction, nor did it designate a particular profession, like poet. It was only meant to distinguish a particular kind of labor from another, the cultural from the industrial. This is the gist, the germ, the deep essential crudeness. According to the law, the privileged, cultural form of labor exhibited certain qualities. First, it took shape only in the certified media. Second, its privilege was justified by the presence of a human intelligence, imagination, and labor that were legible in the work, meaning that such work was seen, a little more crudely, to contain the reflection of the author's personality.[6] The cultural forms of labor could, conversely, be identified from the material used and by the imprint of the author's personality which would follow from working in this material. These two qualities of material and reflected personality were linked; they became inseparable. In the nineteenth century there was only one exception made to this marriage between matter and spirit; drawing, divided in two because technical drawing had been compromised. The compromises were produced by industry; they resulted in the technical drawing's fall from grace. The compromises also point to something clear in the broad and blurry cultural field: they are the black marks that show where the edge of culture lay.

The technical drawing fell from culture because it had participated in the manufacture of industrial objects. In this exceptional case, drawing, the material, was *not* felt to reflect the personality of the draughtsman. The bond between matter and spirit had been broken. In fact these sentiments were motivated by the basest instincts: industry did not want authors in its ranks; it wanted control over the property rights to every phase of production, from technical drawing to finished commodity. In 1806, the silk manufacturers of Lyon obtained this distinction in law from Napoleon: this had the effect of exiling the technical drawing from the cultural field and exempting its maker from *droits d'auteur*; its status was thereafter defined by another set of laws protecting industrial design.[7] Still, for our purposes, the episode is instructive. Clearly the authorial media were not naturally, as it were, cultural; one saw what one wanted in them; one refused to see a self-reflecting author in the technical drawing. Later in the century, in 1891, the courts refused to see the author in the poster; no matter if there was an established artist in-

  6. For a good summary of the evolution of this point of law, see *Dalloz. Encyclopédie juridique. Répertoire de droit civil,* dir. Pierre Raynard et Marguerite Vanel, v. 6 (Paris: Dalloz, 1975), "Propriété littéraire et artistique." Charles Aussy thought the point important enough to argue in his book, *Du droit moral de l'auteur sur les oeuvres de littérature et d'art* (Auxerre: Pigelet, 1911), 5.
  7. The law on design and patent is separated: the laws on design: loi 18 mars 1806, 14 juillet 1909, 12 mars 1952; the laws on patent: 5 juillet 1844 and 2 janvier 1968. See *Dalloz, Encyclopédie juridique. Répertoire de droit commercial* (Paris: Dalloz, 1986).

volved.[8] And so, in France manufactured goods, designs and objects alike, were not officially allowed to embody the personality of their makers or the signs of abstract human labor: they were not to display any evidence of the commodity's fetishism.[9] Manufactured goods were to be magically simple, not self-centered, not meant to serve the spiritual needs of the community the way books and pictures did. They served material needs. In essence the law of 1806 recorded the limits of a modern culture, limits which were inscribed in the economy.

Modern culture existed as an economic distinction, in effect a protected market that functioned within the regular economy. Authored work was always understood to be circulating in the market, generally in printed form. This had already been an element of the 1793 law, which had been necessary in the first place because the market for culture needed to be policed. Yet after 1793 authors were unlike other laborers: the law had given them some rights to their work; even as it moved through the economy, their work remained their property. The law played a critical, though largely unrecognized, role in the definition of modern culture. Daily the law stood by to arbitrate, to provide a practical definition of what an author was and where cultural work was to be done. It conceived of the cultural field as a marketplace and it was precisely in this place where culture (modernism too) would perforce develop. Time strengthened the law. For the duration of the nineteenth century, its terms remained sacrosanct; in a series of modifications in 1844, 1854, and 1866, the author's heirs won the rights to the work for fifty years after the author's death but the rights and regulations for authors themselves did not, in the essentials, change.[10] In theory and in practice, in all sectors of daily life, the cultural was always being distinguished from its other, the industrial; culture's basic identity was always being derived from this distinction, which was always exceptional and always economic.

The copyright law regulated the market economy for culture at the same time that it set it apart from the regular economy. The law did nothing more than negotiate the dialectical movement between the two economies with a maximum of simplicity and efficiency; it was functional but servile, something of a butler. Though it furnished the apparatus so that culture could work, it had drawbacks: for example, it could not be expected to accommodate uninvited guests. These began to arrive over the course of the same nineteenth century, new technologies and new materials for word, sound, and image; it was not long before the pho-

8. Pataille, *Annales de la propriété industrielle, artistique et littéraire* (1894), 48–55.
9. Bernard Edelman, *Ownership of the Image. Elements for a Marxist Theory of Law*, trans. Elizabeth Kingdom (London: RKP, 1979), *passim*. Edelman does not distinguish between the privileged, special nature of this market and the regular market but his book remains a fine discussion of how the laws for photography and cinema reveal the property relations between people.
10. Lois 3 août 1844, 8–19 avril 1854, and 14 juillet 1866.

tograph, the phonograph, and the cinematograph all became candidates for copyright. They tested the limits of the law in yet another way. To give these producers the status of authors involved granting the new technologies (the technologies we have come to associate with mass culture) the status of the materials of aristocratic culture (the culture we have come to call high). The law, for all its apparent elasticity, could not handle such a request overnight.[11] Curiously, the problem lay not with the low order of culture but with the nature of the labor involved, a labor integrally connected to machines. Printing presses were one thing, cameras quite another, and no small stumbling block; they kept the French law from granting the technological authors their rights until 1957, long after the law had been modified to take in architecture and sculpture (1902), a good seventy years behind the law of other industrialized nations.[12] But to account for the technologies, the law could not be modified; it had to be rewritten.

In their hundred-year effort to gain these privileges, those who made photographs, records, and movies were obliged to devise justifications for the value of their materials, their medium, and for their rights to use the title, author. They and their advocates argued with the law; they produced their own voluminous definition of the author.[13] Their definition follows a pattern. Generally it was maintained that a human factor overrode the mechanical process; upon close inspection, a human mark, the trace of a cultural act, could be discerned. Alphonse Lamartine wrote one such apologia: initially he had condemned the photograph as abject, a plagiarism of nature, utterly soulless; after seeing the work of Adam Salomon, he changed his mind and wrote a public retraction. He ex-

11. Or for that matter anyone else. See especially: Greenberg, op. cit.; Walter Benjamin, "The Work of Art in the Age of Mechanical Reproduction," *Illuminations*, ed. Hannah Arendt, trans. Harry Zohn (New York: Schocken, 1969), 217–51; Thomas Crow, "Modernism and Mass Culture in the Visual Arts," in *Modernism and Modernity. The Vancouver Papers*, ed. Benjamin H. D. Buchloh, Serge Guilbaut, and David Solkin (Halifax: Nova Scotia College of Art and Design, 1984), 215–64. On the law's evolution, see *Dalloz*, op. cit. The full texts of the laws in question are given in the *Recueil Sirey*.

12. The late arrival of architecture and sculpture to copyright stems from the fact that these professions were not of academic parentage. The institutions supporting the various cultural professions were at odds with one another in the Ancien Régime and the law of 1793 records those differences. For more on this subject see Pouillet, *Traité théorique et pratique de la propriété littéraire et artistique*. It should also be noted that the entrance of architecture and sculpture into this law in 1902 speaks worlds about the new legitimacy of that work by the end of the nineteenth century: it was part of the national culture, often represented a culture of the state, and consequently merited much more than simple legal protection. The 1902 law is a symptom of the widening authority of the so-called industrial arts.

13. A number of these texts have been anthologized by André Rouillé in his book, *La Photographie en France 1839–1870. Les principaux textes* (Paris: Macula, 1986). For a discussion of the debates during the Paris World's Fair of 1855 over whether photography was art or industry see his article, "La Photographie française à l'Exposition Universelle de 1855," *Le Mouvement social*, no. 131 (April–June 1985), 87–103.

plained that the photograph needed to be seen as the result of the particular photographer's labor. This was typical enough but he went one better: the photographer worked principally with nature, to wit, the sun, Lamartine claimed, and left the machine out of it entirely.[14] Hippolyte Taine made a more pragmatic contribution to the debate: "Photographic work," he wrote, "is property; it belongs to the producer under the same title that gives the engraving to the engraver, and in the two cases, the property should be protected."[15] For all the rhetoric, which culminated in the claims for photography as a fine art, the objective of the photographers was simply to occupy a place in culture; they would have been content with lowlying regions, the wetlands of the field. Listen to the photographer Bulloz in 1890 arguing for his rights:

> All that we are claiming is that a photograph can take on the character of a personal creation. There is no question here of sentiment; photographers are not demanding to be assimilated to the ranks of the master painters; none of them would dream of asking the law to declare them the equal of Baudry or Cabanel.[16]

These terms were neither academic, nor gratuitous: if they succeeded, they could have real social, legal, and market value. This is why the photographers' offensive provoked the fierce debate that is with us still. They can be accused of throwing the definition of the author permanently up in the air.

The positive, defining justifications of the photographers and their kind, not to mention the volume of photographs, records and movies they made, were read, considered, and critiqued. In the response to this invasion, we can locate another, defensive discourse on the author, a relatively negative discourse that worried. It worried over the decline of the author and the old hierarchies of the arts; it disliked the new forms of labor; it wrongly pinned the trouble on the use of the machine, seeing it as a barrier that prevented the imprint of a human being's spirit on a certified, authorial material; it mourned a mirror stage of cultural work in which the self appeared and could reflect; it saw a dark future with no guaranteed Ideal-I. The debate lengthened, still other positions were de-

---

14. Alphonse Lamartine, "Entretien 36. La littérature des sens. La peinture. Léopold Robert," *Cours familier de littérature*, vols. 6–7 (Paris: chez l'auteur, 1858), 411 and 43 respectively.

15. Quoted without reference by A. Bigeon, *La Photographie et le droit* (Paris: Mendel, 1894), 18.

16. J.-E. Bulloz, *La Propriété photographique et la loi française* (Paris: Gauthier-Villars, 1890), 3. See also M. E. Potu, *La Protection des oeuvres photographiques. Extraits de la Revue Trimestrielle de Droit Civil* (Paris: Sirey, 1912) and Léon Vidal, *Absence d'un texte légal réglant les droits d'auteur afférents aux oeuvres des arts mécaniques de reproduction. Diversité d'opinions relatives à cette question. Solution qui semble la plus rationnelle.* (Extrait des Mémoires de l'Académie de Marseilles) (S.l.: s.d.).

veloped and these are the famous ones, the essays of Mallarmé, Benjamin, Foucault, and Barthes.[17] This discourse had little effect upon the disposition of the law, which continued on with its duties, maintained the cultural distinctions such as they already were, and upheld its brute definition of cultural work. But while all this talk was going on, the new technologies had imposed themselves and other, newer technologies, like television, had arrived. This seemed to warrant a revision of the law. The older but not the newest culture by technology was legalized in 1957.

The 1957 law expanded the definition of the author to include those who worked in dance and pantomime, cinema and photography, translation and maps. Industrial design and advertising were denied admission. The field of culture had grown vast however and the text of the law had grown longer too:

> The disposition of the present law protects the rights of authors and covers all work of the mind, whatever the kind, the form of expression, the merit or the destination. The following are considered work of the mind: books, brochures and other literary, artistic, and scientific writing; lectures, speeches, oaths, pleas and other work of this nature; drama and musical theatre; choreography and pantomime when the work is recorded in writing or otherwise; musical compositions with or without words; cinema and work obtained by an analogous process; drawing, painting, architecture, sculpture, engraving, lithography; artistic and documentary photography and work obtained by an analogous process; the applied arts; illustrations, maps; plans, sketches and models related to geography, topography, architecture or the sciences. The authors of translations, adaptations, transformations or arrangements of works of the mind enjoy protection under this law, without prejudice to the rights of the author of the original work. The same follows for those authors of anthologies or collections of diverse work who by the choice and arrangement of the material do the work of intellectual creation.

Titles were protected as well as works and even the name of the author was covered:

> The author enjoys this right with respect to his name, his quality, and his work. This right is attached to his person.[18]

Authorship still covered all levels of culture, high and low, but it had now spread to many media and to the separate signifiers of authorial work, like the title and the name of the author. The author's name alone could

---

17. Mallarmé, Foucault, Barthes, op. cit.; Walter Benjamin, "The Author as Producer," from *Understanding Brecht*, trans. Anna Bostock, introduction by Stanley Mitchell (London; NLB, 1977), 85–103.

18. Loi 11 mars 1957, *Recueil Sirey*, 1957, 124.

signal the body of his work so effectively that even in a detached state, the name was covered with *droits*.

After 1957 authorship was identified by more than a happy combination of a medium and a person: it could designate a rather immaterial position, a reputation and a generalized cluster of forms, stereotypes, trademarks. It was not so clear where one should be looking to find the reflection of the author's self. Authorship had become patently defined now by the reproduction of the work; it had taken on many of the characteristics of overtly commercial, brand name products; in many cases there was no single original. The law tried to cover all possible situations; it made special provision for collaborative work, such as cinema, where there was no single author.

Cinema, in fact, needed special consideration by the law. It bestowed author's rights on directors, and in this way only served the *politique des auteurs* that had been mounted during the 1950s by the *Cahiers du Cinéma*, but it also gave rights to some of the other members of the film crew, notably to the writers and the composers, and it gave control over the finished work to the production company.[19] This denied the contribution made by those who worked on the image itself and it had the effect of submitting all the authors to the will of the producer. It amounted to an authorial control by capital. The law recognized the open exploitation of the cultural field by a culture industry, as Bernard Edelman has brilliantly demonstrated; it furthermore made cultural property, the fantasmic cinema no less, take on some of the characteristics of ordinary, gritty, factory-made work. The modernization of the law in 1957 began to undermine the old, clear distinction between culture and industry.

The law ushered in a new level of *ennui* for those wanting to understand what an author is. It had cut into the mass media, pulling Hollywood film and news photography in and leaving advertising out, making the legal distinction between culture, the culture industry, and industry even more arbitary than before. It made it more difficult to conceive of a single mass culture. The new law's definition of the author did not adequately explain what constitutes creative work or what separates it from the run of the mill. It did not explain the privileged economic dynamic of the cultural field. It did not explain that this field is actually industry's inner sanctum. It did not explain that cultural forms can be industrially produced. It did not help us to make a clear distinction between the cultural subject and the industrial subject. The law however is not supposed to explain itself. That work takes place elsewhere. Explanations were not slow in coming but they were seldom adequate. The author question has kept coming up. Michel Foucault was led to ask it once again in 1969.

19. *Cahiers du Cinéma. Ecrits. La politique des auteurs. Entretiens avec dix cinéastes*, préface de Serge Dancy (Paris: Editions de l'Etoile-Cahiers du Cinéma, 1984). See also *Theories of Authorship*, ed. John Caughie (London: RKP, 1981).

Foucault did not call in the law to supply answers to his essay question, "What is an Author?"; oddly, he did not even mention it. He was more concerned to see what knowledge had made of the author and to understand why most intellectuals were calling the author a dead letter. Foucault therefore undertook to measure the disappearance of the author, though much of what he measured is actually the difference between the old law and the new. The sum of these differences, according to Foucault, amounted to this:

> We can conclude that, unlike a proper name, which moves from the interior of a discourse to the real person outside who produced it, the name of the author remains at the contour of texts—separating one from the other, defining their form, and characterizing their mode of existence. It points to the existence of certain groups of discourse and refers to the status of this discourse within a society and culture. The author's name is not a function of a man's civil status, nor is it fictional; it is situated in the breach, among the discontinuities, which gives rise to new groups of discourse and their singular mode of existence. Consequently, we can say that in our culture, the name of an author is a variable that accompanies only certain texts to the exclusion of others: a private letter may have signatory, but it does not have an author; a contract can have an underwriter but not an author; and, similarly, an anonymous poster attached to a wall may have a writer, but he cannot be an author. In this sense, the function of an author is to characterize the existence, circulation, and operation of certain discourses within a society.[20]

Foucault's essay turns on some of the law's new points, notably the name of the author and its separate existence, its ability to designate what Foucault calls an author-function. But when he separated the authors from the writers, he was not technically correct: one remained an author so long as one did not abandon one's rights; certain kinds of employment, underwriting and some kinds of journalism, for example, involved such an abdication. And when Foucault described the circulation and operation of discourses, he neglected to explain that this takes place within a market economy even though this economic condition, we have seen, defined the author in the first place. But the economy is Foucault's blind spot. His author had to exist in a disembodied, non-reflecting, dispersed state, in knowledge, not in the world. This led him to posit an author disconnected from the procedures of everyday life, something which experience tells us is simply not true. Authors function, whether the state of knowledge recognizes their existence or not.

Barthes had written a similarly elegiac essay, "The Death of the Author," in 1967. But the occasion for Barthes's essay was unusual. It was

20. Foucault, op. cit., 123–24.

written for an American magazine, *Aspen,* nos. 5 + 6, edited by Brian O'Doherty and dedicated to Stéphane Mallarmé.[21] *Aspen* 5 + 6 was something of a Franco-American cultural effort: Alain Robbe-Grillet, Marcel Duchamp, Michel Butor, Susan Sontag, George Kubler, John Cage, Morton Feldman, Merce Cunningham, Robert Rauschenberg, Tony Smith, Robert Morris, Sol Lewitt, Mel Bochner, and Dan Graham were among the contributors. (There was also work by Hans Richter, Lazzlo Moholy-Nagy, Richard Huelsenbeck, and Samuel Beckett.) Yet for all the great authorial names, the magazine moved toward a denial of old-style authorship. In many ways it chipped away at the traditional separation that had been legislated between the high culture and industry. If anything, it behaved like low culture, where the kind of omission posited by Mallarmé and the kind of subordination to the mechanics of the statement described by Foucault were unremarkable and commonplace.

*Aspen* 5 + 6 is kept in a white box. Barthes's essay is boxed in, one of twenty-eight pieces, nothing more than a pamphlet stuck between movies, records, diagrams, cardboard cut-outs, and advertisements. The box encapsulates the spreading field of modern culture in a way that is quite advanced. For example, Marcel Duchamp was asked to record his essay on the creative act at 33 RPM; his voice is unmistakeably his own, his breathing perceptible:

> What I have in mind is that art may be bad, good or indifferent, but, whatever adjective is used, we must call it art, and bad art is still art in the same way as a bad emotion is still an emotion.
>
> Therefore, when I refer to "art coefficient," it will be understood that I refer not only to great art, but I am trying to describe the subjective mechanism which produces art in a raw state—*à l'état brut*—bad, good or indifferent.[22]

There is nothing mysterious here; Duchamp signed his name, lent his voice, and subordinated his idea to some French common sense. It is the working definition of art as a quantity not a quality, the zero-degree of the law.

Duchamp's text keeps motley company, much of it technologically based. Brian O'Doherty's *Structural Play #3* (Fig. 3) uses a reduced, vir-

21. The English translation of Barthes's essay was made by Richard Howard. Jérôme Serri has organized an exhibition and catalogue which collects Barthes's work on the image, though the *Aspen* box is missing from the group. Pavillon des Arts, Paris, *Roland Barthes. Le Texte et l'image* (1986). The box should be understood in the context of Brian O'Doherty's other work, an idea of which can be gotten from the exhibition of his drawings, National Museum of American Art, *Patrick Ireland. Drawings 1965–1985,* essay by Lucy Lippard (1986).

22. "The Creative Act" was written in 1957 as a talk for a meeting of the American Federation of the Arts in Houston. The text has been reprinted in *Salt Seller: the writings of Marcel Duchamp (Marchand du Sel),* ed. Michel Sanouillet and Elmer Peterson (New York: Oxford, 1973), 138–40.

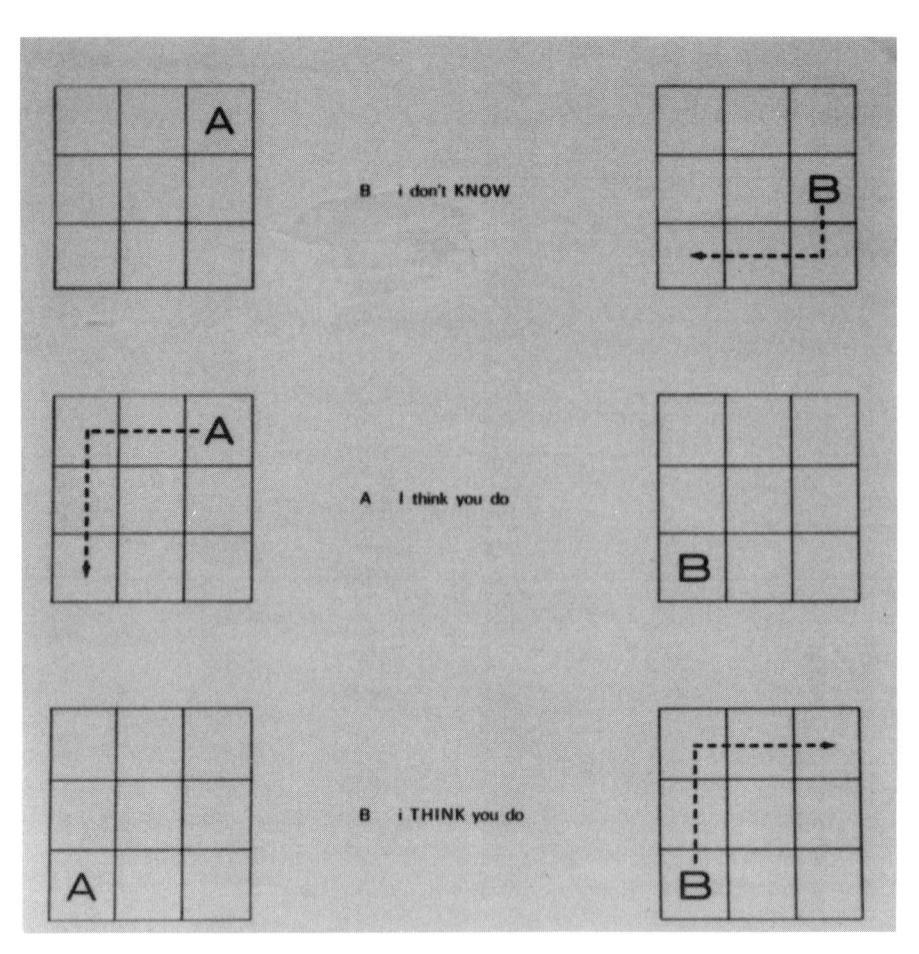

*Figure 3.* detail from *Structural Play #3*, by Brian O'Doherty, *Aspen*, 5+6 (fall/winter 1967).

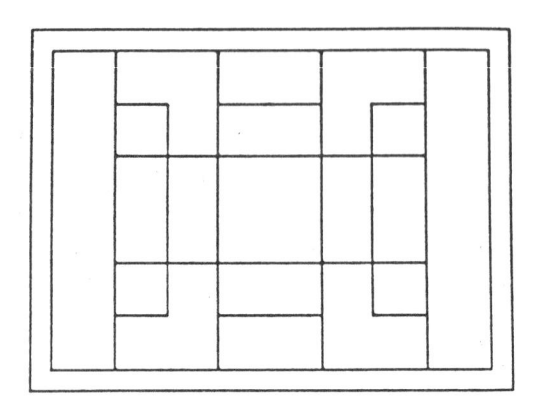

*Figure 4.* detail from *The Maze*, by Tony Smith, *Aspen*, 5+6 (fall/winter 1967).

tually technical drawing to lay out cultural sense: A and B are moved impersonally around a grid; they dialogue in the diagram. The same standardized geometry goes to make Tony Smith's *Maze* (Fig. 4), one man's mark now inseparable from another's. The box's sheaf or advertisements collects a Bolex brochure for home movie equipment together with subscription blanks for *Artforum* and *Aspen*. It is in this context that the subjectivity of the author is siphoned off: Dan Graham writes a "Poem, March 1966" which proposes a scheme, literally a word count, to be set into final form by the editor of the given magazine. The *Maze* exists as a diagram, a photograph, and a group of black cardboard pieces, more like a kit ready to be assembled than an aesthetic thing-in-itself. Sol Lewitt introduced his "Serial Project #1, 1966," by describing the work of the serial artist:

> The aim of the artist would not be to instruct the viewer but to give him information. Whether the viewer understands this information is incidental to the artist; he cannot foresee the understanding of all his viewers. He would follow his predetermined premise to its conclusion avoiding subjectivity. Chance, taste, or unconsciously remembered forms would play no part in the outcome. The serial artist does not attempt to produce a beautiful or mysterious object but functions merely as a clerk cataloguing the results of his premise.

With its technical drawings, advertisements, and author-producers, its technological look that refers to a technologically oriented social order, not some sign of modernist purity, with its desire for scientific objectivity and its recognition of the real conditions for cultural production, the box breaks a host of taboos. It does not confine itself to the cultural field; furthermore, it puts the new means and the economic realities of art side by side. It exposes modern form as a complex of machinery, marketing, impersonality, rationality, power, and scientific truth; it takes these materials over and tries to work with them; it beautifies and on occasion mimics the practices of the noncultural zones. It asserts its own position as a cultural product tentatively engaged with a larger, uncultured but technologically sophisticated world. The box shows how authors, including modernists, can do critical work. In that respect it is a model box. Barthes, for his part, was out of step. Faced with these particular new cultural conditions, he backed off, away from any new science of the text or language game. He would only advance the idea of an authorless literature; for him, assimilation to the forms of industry or kitsch was unthinkable; impersonality meant death.

The law had helped to generate and to consolidate all of these positions and more, though it did not alone produce them and it could not control them. The classic texts on the author split away from the law. They try to disregard its terms, to escape. They remain oriented toward the high culture artist and traditional, self-reflecting art; they tend to assume a desire for upward mobility; they are full of nostalgia for the days when spirit and material were obviously married; they repress the commerce. In part this stems from the fact that the series of agreements between culture and industry has seemed to prohibit any real analysis by legitimate culture of its relations to the industrial complex: culture is to leave industry alone. Culture is to be theorized in the abstract, detached from the working definition that the law provides. This is one of the keys to its ideality. When the ideal could no longer be maintained, the discourse on the author, forever repressed, turned morbid.

The dead ends of the texts do not tell all. There were authors who could at once see and manipulate the law that governed their work though, since these authors tend to exhibit their ties to the economy, we are prone to dismiss them as commercial connivers, the rag and bone men of the field. Yet we find them among the downwardly mobile low culture suppliers and among the entrepreneurial modernists. What remains of their practice usually takes the form of objects not texts. Yet in the bits that survive we can read something more about the author. The bits have been scattered across the cultural field; they can be photographs from the wetlands or ready-mades from the heights.

Already in the nineteenth century there were photographers who worked illegally as authors, hoping to force better definitions of the author out of the courts.[23] When, in the 1860s, the first cases in which the *droits d'auteur* of photographers were proposed, contested, and tried, the courts came up with a loophole in the law which gave the subsequent courts the right to decide on a case by case basis what kind of production was in question, whether the particular photograph was art or industry, whether the photographer was an author working with a medium or an ordinary citizen working a machine.

When the courts did apply the 1793 law to the photograph, they did so with the rationale that photographs were drawings of a kind.[24] But the court was unable to divide art from industrial photography as drawing had been divided because all photographs appeared to them to function according to the same code of representation. All photographs appeared to reproduce external appearance, like the authorial drawing, and not, like the technical drawing, to measure internal structures of things. Photography could not therefore be covered, as the technical drawing was, by patent law. Nor, because of the role of the machine was it clearly copy-

---

23. Elizabeth Anne McCauley is preparing a book-length study of the commercial studio during the Second Empire. Until its publication, one can only refer to her article, "Of Entrepreneurs, Opportunists, and Fallen Women: Commercial Photography in Paris, 1848–1870," *New Mexico Studies in the Fine Arts*. v. 9 (1984), 16–27. See also Jean Sagne's book, *L'Atelier du photographe 1840–1940* (Paris: Presses de la Renaissance, 1984).

24. Potu, op. cit., 737 and 764. A. Bigeon, *La Photographie et le droit* (Paris: Mendel, 1894), 12–21.

rightable. The photograph fell between the cracks in the existing law into a no man's land; technically it could be considered neither culture nor industry. It was impossible to claim rights to a photograph without an argument. So the court looked for a reflection of the author's personality or personal skill; with enough of one or the other, the photograph could be considered as a protected drawing. Using this logic, by 1900 most of the important court decisions gave the photographer his *droits d'auteur.* They were still not automatic, it must be said, since the law itself had not been revised, but the photographer might have *droits:* to call oneself an *auteur* meant that one was actively laying claim to them.[25] The title could designate a photographic practice like pictorialism with all the cultural ambitions of painting; it could just as well be used as a cover to gain economic privilege for more technical pictures that served the material needs of production.

Atget called himself an author or, more precisely, an *auteur-éditeur,* from at least 1902 on (his career as a photographer began in earnest about 1897 and continued until his death in 1927).[26] As a title it is neither common nor descriptive. One can understand by it that the *auteur* half is meant to refer to the *droits* to which he felt entitled, and more immediately to the point, which he expected to be observed by those who bought his photographs. Atget was ready to publish these photographs, hence the *éditeur* half, though this functioned more as a sign of his professional desire than anything else. His work rarely saw print; and his dreams of publishing remained dreams. *Auteur-éditeur* was a practical epithet.

At the same time that he claimed the authorial privilege for himself, Atget used one of the lowest of all photographic forms available to him, a form that was for all intents and purposes industrial, the photographic document. When asked, he referred to his work as *documents,* for the sake of a sales pitch, he might call them *documents artistiques.*[27] Atget did not inflate the value of his photographs; the word document brought them down; it identified them as study sheets holding useful information (the proverbial facts) in pictorial form. There were technical conventions

25. Two court cases that did not allow the photographer to work as an author are worth citing. Viot vs. Laurent fils, Nancy, 14 March 1903, D. P. 2.296 and Tricaud vs. Raoult, Toulouse, 17 July 1911, D. P. 2.161.

26. Atget wrote a business letter to the South Kensington Board of Education in November 1902 to which he attached his business card calling himself "Auteur-Editeur." My thesis, *Atget's Seven Albums, in practice* (Ph.D., Yale, 1983) takes up this question in detail. The books of John Szarkowski and Maria Morris Hambourg, *The Work of Atget,* vv. 1–4 (New York: MOMA, 1981–1985) provide a good survey of the pictures.

27. Atget's use of the terms *document* and *document artistique* can be seen in his business letters which have been collected in Appendix 1 of my thesis. For a contemporary definition of the term, see A. Reyner, *Camera Obscura,* quoted in *Ve Congrès international de photographie. Bruxelles 1910. Compte rendu, procès-verbaux, rapports, notes et documents,* published under the direction of Ch. Puttemans, L.-P. Clerc et E. Wallon (Brussels: Bruylant, 1912), 72.

for showing the facts in pictures; the document is really the photographic equivalent of the technical drawing.

Throughout his career Atget produced several different kinds of documents simultaneously. His clients were also several: architects, decorators, the trades of the building industry, set designers, painters, illustrators, antiquarians, and the topography files of the major Parisian libraries.[28] Each had their own specific uses for documents; they bought Atget's in order to satisfy their professional, not their aesthetic needs. In fact Atget's photographs functioned rather like technical drawings did in the manufacturing process: they were a step, a preliminary diagram that would help produce another commodity and nothing more. It would be possible to use these photographs as evidence for an argument that photography was rightfully subject to patent, not copyright law because the picture was not self-sufficient but was bound by a relation to a product.[29] Sometimes Atget's photographs would contribute to the reproduction of a Louis style, sometimes to a caricature of *la vie parisienne*, sometimes to a historical article on *Vieux Paris*. In all of these cases, the document was consumed, absorbed into the labor process, and contained, so to speak, in the client's own product, which might or might not be a cultural good. Atget took pictures of Paris that were destined to work: they made the spectacle labor.

The technical passages in the document were standard, full of identifiable technical signs. *Au Tambour* contains the same technical signs, for example as *A l'Homme armé* (Fig. 5). There are the signs for architects and metalworkers, who looked carefully at the way the building facade and its grillwork fit: the forms of the picture that look like an architectural drawing.[30] There are also other technical signs for the eye of the antiquarians, who cared more for the old metal sign, wanted therefore to see the sign as a specimen for their histories. These two different kinds of technical signs produced functions for such photographs; they constituted its use value and gave it the ability to enter the market as a commodity. By their impersonality they somewhat trouble the status of the photograph. At most, accompanied by a lawyer, one could claim that they belong with the lowest forms of culture.

The construction of the technical sign in the photograph was not formulaic. Most of Atget's photographs display more than one technical

28. See Chapter 1 of my thesis for a full discussion of this point.
29. See Pouillet, *Traité théorique et pratique de la propriété littéraire et artistique*, 127ff. for a discussion of the difference between a photograph and a *dessin de fabrique*, see also Bigeon, *La Photographie et le droit*, 3. See the Toulouse decision (1911) regarding the industrial character of the photographs in question.
30. Two of the paper albums collected in the Atget Archive of the Museum of Modern Art in New York group some of the sign pictures under a *fer forgé* rubric to make a selection of documents useful to metalworkers. They are titled, "Album No. 1 Vieux Paris et Environs Grilles, Lanternes Enseignes" [with one line crossing out the word "Enseignes"] and "Album No. 2 Enseignes et Vieilles Boutiques du Vieux Paris."

Figure 5. *A l'homme armé*, photograph by Eugène Atget, 1900. Collection of the Caisse Nationale des Monuments et des Sites, Paris.

A L'HOMME ARME

sign and more than one function; the functions doubled up with a single image and produced a functional ambiguity that allowed the document to play between markets. It is easy enough to factor out the functions and easy enough to imagine hypothetical viewers seeing what they wanted, dispensing with the extraneous, not strictly technical elements in the image and noting a certain superfluity at the periphery of their professional vision, some excess. Atget's practice was predicated on the play of the functions and their possible combinations; it smells of commerce. He adjusted his practice over time to let certain functions dominate and then recede, giving more room to others. In 1908, for example, he took a group of his old sign pictures and made photographs of his photographs to produce the appropriate detail of the sign alone, stripped of its excesses, though a little watery now at the edges (Fig. 6). This operation did not however produce a new stage in Atget's subsequent pictures of signs. That same year at *Au Tambour* the multiple functions are let loose in his usual way: the technical signs bump against each other; plenty of intermediate space is left open. Into one such space, the pane, Atget worked his shadow.

The pane was not crucial to any of the technical signs. It ought to have been kept neutral in order to preserve the pictorial integrity of the facade but what transpired on or behind this pane of glass was immaterial to the professional viewer.[31] By working his shadow into the free space between the technical signs, Atget dampened the perfection of his document without undermining its different usefulnesses. He was knowingly making a grade B document. This enabled him to insert himself among the signs, to make his authorial presence if not his personality felt, and to show his true position as an *auteur:* he did not identify himself with the technical signs of the image; the document is fetishized in the intermediate spaces that bind the signs together and hold the functional ambiguity in place. It is in the binding and manipulation of the signs that Atget emerges as an author.[32]

As if this were not sufficient, the shadow fetish takes another tack. It appears in a pane that is half mirror, half not, in the place where one can see through the looking glass. There we find one body in the process of changing magically into another; the photographer's head is swallowed up and replaced by an apparition. The pieces of the image in the pane do connect up into a two-part human form; they too are bound and manipulated images. They construct another photographer, not exactly Atget, in the pane. This has the effect of making *that* man appear to take the

---

31. In point of fact, reflections of windows were not considered good form and photographers' manuals warned against including them. See Georges Brunel, *Encyclopédie de l'amateur photographe* no. 2 (Paris: 1897), 93.

32. There was some disagreement over whether or not it was possible to insert the author's personality into a photograph. See Bigeon, op. cit., 38–39 and C. Puyo, "La Photographie pictoriale," *Ve Congrès international de la photographie,* 443.

*Figure 6. A l'homme armé*, photograph by Eugène Atget, 1908. Collection of the Bibliothèque Nationale, Paris.

picture. It is a bit like signing Rose Sélavy's name to a French window (Fig. 7).

Yet Atget's work had no pretension to avant-gardism; his materials were those of any documentary photographer; his combinations are made with the same technical signs used by his peers. For him, authorship involved this impersonality; the law's desire for personality was not to be taken too seriously. He was cheating when he called himself an author; he had neither the right nor the right kind of work to back up the claim in court. But for Atget, the law existed to be exploited for his own gain and since he never had to defend himself in court, the ploy worked. Atget bent the law to traffic between the cultural and the industrial zones; he hustled his work back and forth across the border, playing to any market he could. We can see from his success that the copyright law was not actually able to keep culture pure. By the same token, industry could mistake the low cultural object for an ordinary commodity. Cultural distinction could not guarantee an ideal existence.

Duchamp's distinction was to compromise the very idea of authorship. His *Fresh Widow* took a scale model made by a nameless carpenter, the kind of model one would submit to the patent office, if one had gone so far as to reinvent the French window. And yet there is nothing novel about this design, the requirement for obtaining a patent; nor is it highly original, the keyword for copyright. There is no place for self-reflection in the black leather panes. But at each step, Duchamp's self was effaced; the window was signed finally by a fiction, Rose Sélavy.[33] There is not a single, culturally certified material in evidence; add to this the play on the model and there is no reason whatsoever to consider this a cultural object; the window is lawless. And yet, unlike Atget, Duchamp writ his misdeed large, claiming "COPYRIGHT" (in English) on the sill of his work.

Duchamp used the legal term as a signal: the noncultural object could be appropriated; culture could stomach the alien. The window has already gone down in the history of modern art; it is catalogued as sculpture. But Duchamp did not use copyright to mediate the distinction between culture and industry; he showed that the two can become hopelessly confused and arbitrarily separated. Duchamp gave the author question the cruelest answer. Authorial distinction was artificial. If not in principle, in practice culture would live with the greatest of compromises.

Duchamp negociated no truce between culture and industry; instead he took the law into his own hands, and discovered a surprising, apalling flexibility. It so happens that this was a premonition of things to come. Of late the cultural field has been seen as one of the few remaining zones for new industrial development; its ability to take the industrial object is no

33. There is much more to be said about the nonaesthetic in the *Fresh Widow*. See my "Ready-made Originals: the Duchamp Model," *October*, no. 37 (fall 1986).

*Figure 7. Fresh Widow*, miniature French window by Marcel Duchamp, 1920. Collection of the Museum of Modern Art, New York.

longer questioned; investments quicken; industry has decided that it does want authors in its ranks. The cultural field together with its economy is in the process of extensive renovation. In recognition of the new state of affairs, the principle of the law has been revised so that the privileged entrepreneur can now become an author. The terms of the old dialectical pact between culture and industry have been jettisoned. Culture's economic distinction is being refined.

In 1982 the French legislature had to concern itself with yet another negociation between the zones of culture and industry, the trouble at the border caused this time by the appearance of new technological materials and a new stage in industrial production, late capitalism. On the surface of it, the new copyright law, passed in July 1985, looks to be an amendment of the old: rights are extended to some neglected groups, the performers, including circus performers and puppeteers, and the typographic designers, and to two new media, to what is in France called the audiovisual (in America video) and to computer software.[34] Certain clarifications in the drawing up of contracts have made it possible to acquire a kind of copyright for advertising. But the extension of rights is a cosmetic change compared to the rest. The culture set forth by the law is regulated by a group of lengthy sections on contracts that set up the administrative procedures for cultural business; in those sections it is apparent that certain parcels of the cultural field are to be opened up to wholesale industrial exploitation. Which is to say that within the law itself, the old integrity of the zones, culture and industry, has been compromised; culture has been quickly, easily, incomprehensibly invaded. As Bernard Edelman complained during a colloquium on the new law:

> ... The status of the author has been profoundly shaken. In effect we no longer have a single author but a multitude of authors, of which each represents their own economic interests. This multiplication of status will carry with it a multiplicity of interpretations, once again, according to the special interests—the advertising industry, the cinema, television, the recording industry, the computer business. . . . I pity the judges who will find themselves in the presence of such a melting pot and will have to sharpen interpretations that are at once heterogeneous and coherent! If you will, I find that this law will get us lost on the way to unlikely horizons. . . .[35]

The French definition of the author has gone vague for a reason.

The Ministry of Culture, which under Jack Lang was responsible for

---

34. Loi 3 juillet 1985. A useful copy of the law, which prints it alongside the 1957 one in adjacent columns, may be found in *Droit d'auteur et droits voisins. La loi du 3 juillet 1985. Colloque de l'IRPI sous le haut patronage de M. Jack Lang (Paris, 21 et 22 novembre 1985)* (Paris: Libraires techniques, 1986), Annexe ll.

35. Ibid., 168.

shepherding the new law through the legislature, saw the industrialization of culture as part of a deliberate modernization of France moving toward the time when culture would go peacefully, hand in hand, with both state and capital. A new official culture has emerged and a ministerial communiqué offered up a sketch of it:

> Guardian of the cultural patrimony, promoter of recognized, traditional culture (opera, museum, classical music, dance, theatre), the Ministry of Culture suddenly saw itself taken by the emergence of the new movements (song, rock, jazz, but also advertising, fashion, design) in the new technologies (computer, cable) and assumed a strategic role in the renewal of French industry. At this point, the Ministry of Culture becomes a sort of "Ministry of the Culture Industry" in which its politics becomes integrated into the global strategy of the French government.[36]

These are the conditions generally recognized as the postmodern ones for culture. But they are subject to interpretation. Fredric Jameson in an article published the same summer as the communiqué, the summer of 1984, dramatically reversed the usual reading of the scenario, where industry steps in and authors die.[37] Where others saw the industrialization of culture, Jameson saw the acculturation of industry, an aesthetic production blasting out into commodity production generally and seeming to know no bounds. Culture, rather than submit to invasion, escapes.

It turns up at the Beaubourg. For much the same, euphoric, Jamesonian sense of culture was put forward in the summer of 1985 by Jean-François Lyotard and Thierry Chaput in their great exhibition, *Les Immatériaux*, or, *The Immaterials*, sponsored by the Centre pour la Création Industrielle of the Centre national d'art et de culture Georges Pompidou. The new technologies provide the raw materials of the postmodern condition: owing to their newness, no governing model for culture is available, only slippery categories and an absence of borders; even the human body is shown to break down (artificially induced genders and layers of skin grafts were part of the proof). The different confrontations between the human being and the new technologies were laid out over a labyrinth of rooms, niches, and hallways, each dedicated to the exploration of a certain subject, like the simulated smell, the angel, the second skin, the hurried eater, the invisible man, the inverted reference, the words that

---

36. Dominique Wallon, "Culture et industries culturelles," communication présentée à la réunion de clôture des Rencontres franco-québecoises, juin 1984, document reprographié, Ministère de la Culture. Cited in Bernard Miège, Patrick Pajon, Jean-Michel Salaün, *L'industrialisation de l'audiovisuel. Des programmes pour les nouveaux médias* (Paris: Aubier, 1986), 23.

37. Fredric Jameson, "Postmodernism, of the Cultural Logic of Late Capitalism," *New Left Review*, no. 146 (July–August 1984): 53–92. See also Clive Dilnot, "What is the Post-Modern?", *Art History*, v. 9 (June 1986): 245 63.

are objects, living speech. "All copies," the room full of xeroxes, let the visitor make photocopy objects on the spot in order to demonstrate the range in the copy, the inexactness, the unrecognizable patches where the photocopy verges on X ray. The catalogue illustration summarizes the possibilities by a single example, a slab of Swiss cheese, looking for all the world like its own negative or a cloud full of stones (Fig. 8).

The role of the individual author in this dematerializing complex was never too clear, though Lyotard, like Jameson, heroically delared the collapse into vagueness to be a sign of liberty. Body, mind, and object were let loose into a tumultuous libidinal economy with a past and a present. In the old, modern days, parents had genders and authors spoke using the name of the father. Postmodernity offers another sexual order (significantly Lyotard's version of Genesis is devoid of sin) and endless potential for discourse (the myth of total communication).[38] Insofar as there was a parental economy of the modern, it was the market economy but here Lyotard tumbled backward into the old clichés, notably the one where an economy limits the classic concept of freedom: painting done in collaboration with the market economy is understood simply as prostitution.[39] The bustling, not-so libidinal economy behind postmodernism could not be articulated without dampening the freedom hypothesis. The law was not invoked.

The law was in the process of being written while the exhibition was being prepared; it was not perhaps the best time to make an appeal. But its presence was felt. As part of the exhibition, twenty-six French intellectuals were installed in front of word processors and asked to supply a data base with the material for keywords, like author. An artificially induced, rather laconic, debate was transacted by microchip and published as so many fragmentary passages in the part of the catalogue called *Epreuves d'écriture*, or *Writing Samples*. In the meditations on the word author, the juridical definition actually makes several entrances, though it is more an abstract point of reference than a real help. It is simply one definition among many, neither authority nor butler; it exits as quickly as it entered. Jacques Derrida, in his contribution to the definition of the author put it well:

> Up until what point are we the authors of our texts on the author? We have submitted ourselves to the necessity of a concept and to a rule for the game, to a list of words as well and of other authors, whereby the author in the end remains fairly indeterminate, disappearing. Is there an author in this common enterprise? Who? Where? The so-called disappearance of the author still passes perhaps by the experience of a certain sociotechnical factor (the word processor, an anonymous central tele-

---

38. Jean-François Lyotard, "Maternité," *Les Immatériaux. Inventaire* (Paris: CCI, 1985).
39. Lyotard, "négoce peint," op. cit.

## toutes les copies

Tout peut être photocopié. Mais la ressemblance de la copie avec l'original dépend de l'angle d'exposition et de sa durée. Le méconnaissable peut avoir lieu. Des faces inconnues révèlent le monstrueux dans le familier. Avantage de l'empreinte sur le prétendu original, de la technique perverse sur la perception droite, de l'inconscient sur la «réalité».

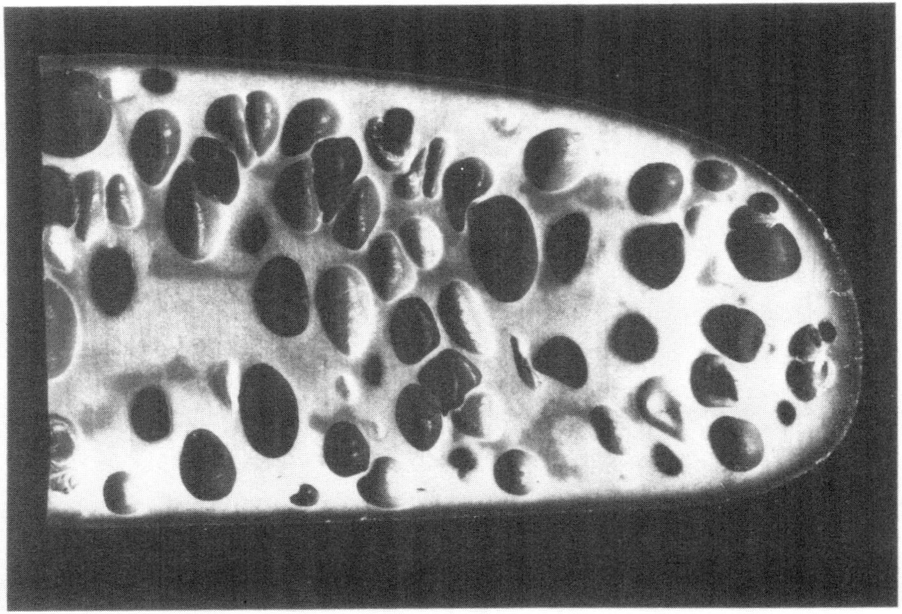

| matériau | toutes les copies |
|---|---|
| matrice | |
| matière | trace de trace |
| matière | |
| maternelle | tous les auteurs |

Boîte transparente exposant des objets sélectionnés, contenant un photocopieur. Un aromatique fournit des photocopies de ces objets à la demande des visiteurs ou selon son propre choix. Simultanément un télécopieur relié à l'Atelier des Enfants du Centre Georges Pompidou fait parvenir d'autres compositions. Les photocopies sont affichées, exposées, encadrées constituées en archives de cette expérience.

Liliane Terrier, photocopie d'un morceau d'emmenthal, 1984.

*Figure 8. All Copies*, text by Jean-Francois Lyotard, photocopy by Liliane Terrier, lay-out by Jean-Louis Boissier. *Les Immatériaux*, Centre National Georges Pompidou, Paris, 1985.

phone system, etc.) which reflects now what has been happening in the "cultural world" for a long time, forever. Unless, through the immaterials' machine, losing tone and hand, in renouncing for all time our old mirrors, we did not again seek a supplementary authority, an oh so symbolic authority, it is true, so that neither the image nor any other living thing any longer came back to us. But let us not forget, all is still signed, no one has the right to touch the text of another, our copyright is well protected just like in the good old days of modernity (seventeenth to twentieth centuries).[40]

The law was present, yes, but as an irony.

The new copyright law is capable of much more. Its terms remind us that a cultural distinction still exists, complicated by its business dealings, but distinct nonetheless, and legally binding. Furthermore it puts postmodern culture of the new technologies into some kind of order, and articulates its limits and taboos. The law reveals the constraints that have been placed on cultural liberty. It cuts out culture from industry in specific ways that can be defined, that are material, and that lack euphoria. The law shows clearly that the cultural field has been invaded by industrial interests, but that the markets have not merged. Culture remains apart, resting on its contracts.

The contractual obligations of authors vary but they give structure to the amorphous postmodern. The rules governing contracts prescribe different rules for different venues. The author of a novel, for example, can make claims that the author of a screenplay or the author of a computer game cannot. When it comes to the actual negociation of contracts, authors' rights are and have in actual practice long been variable, subject to the contractor, the firm, the special interests as Edelman calls them, which is to say, in the case of the culture being made with the new technologies, industrial interests. Now it should be noted that in practice copyright was always subject to invasion by other interests: artists had to permit museums, for example, to charge reproduction fees for works in their collection and by the turn of the century abuses of artists' copyright were so flagrant that a special law had to be passed declaring that authors did not automatically abandon their reproduction rights when the work was sold.[41] But the new law recognizes the potential of bigger, telescoping markets that can be exploited by a number of means, satellite transmission, cabling, cassettes, disks; so it becomes necessary, more profitable for all concerned, to define the author contractually as part of a collective effort. This shuffling of the contracts makes for a noisy, contorted, rather too discriminating law which has been much discussed,

40. Jacques Derrida, "Auteur 139," in *Les Immatériaux. Epreuves d'ecriture* (Paris: Centre national Georges Pompidou, 1985), 19.
41. Loi 9 Avril 1910. For more on this point, see Edouard Cooper, *L'art et la loi* (Paris: Achille, 1903).

one deputy, Alain Richard, admitting that, especially when it came to the software legislation, there was "hair on the soup."⁴²

One might say that too many cooks have spoiled the copyright law; certainly the simple mediation it used to perform is a thing of the past. The software sections are so full of exceptions that they begin to resemble patent rather than the traditional, unilaterally generous copyright. The author of the computer program written while in the service of an employer has no rights whatsoever over the work; the employer becomes the author, though in the case of software the rights are only good for twenty-five years after the copyright has been filed. It so happens that this part of the law was written to conform to recent developments in international law, notably in the United States, and yet the law wavers elsewhere too. The author's rights for the performer do not get passed on after death to the heirs. Those who work within the context of an audiovisual production can expect the producer to divy up the rights money according to the conventions of the profession. This entails larger cuts for well-known actors and writers, lesser gains for the other authors on the team. The law is still not clear about the rights of those who actually make the image for the piece. Authorial distinction now varies with the terms of the deal. If one reads the new law through to the contracts, culture can no longer be mapped as the same flat land.

The mediating function of the new law, because of its very complexity, opens up inequalities, uneven developments, gaps, and, with them, new critical distances. They shed light on vagueness. The cultural object can be seen as the sum of so many interests and so much labor, a sum that busily pedals about the marketplace in search of reception. The cultural object is more often than not the work of a team of authors; it exhibits the tensions and the struggles of the collaboration. Texts, images, stars, directors, and producers all have different degrees of power, different investments in the piece, different roles to play that will register in the work itself. By dissecting the authorial parts of a work, it is possible to cut into the illusion of seamlessness, so powerful in the rhetoric around the new technologies and to propose roles for the individual subject.⁴³ It is possible to plot a politics of cultural labor and possible to imagine a collective of authors, individuals who do not lose themselves when working with others. All of which assumes the existence of authors who have left their mirrors for more responsible positions. It also assumes the continuing necessity of a cultural politics.

---

42. The admission was made during the conference, *Droit d'auteur et droits voisins. La loi du 3 juillet 1985*, 176.

43. See Marc Guillaume, "Téléspectres", *Traverses*, no. 26 - Rhétoriques de la technologie (October 1982), 18–28.

# Contributors

EDWARD BALL is a writer living in New York City.

MAURICE BLANCHOT has most recently published a book about Michel Foucault.

PIERRE BOURDIEU is Professor at the Collège de France, director of studies at the Ecole des hautes études en sciences sociales and of the journal *Actes de la recherche en sciences sociales.* Among his many books to have appeared in English translation, the most recent is *Distinction: a Social Critique of the Judgment of Taste.*

TOM CONLEY, Chairman of the Department of French and Italian at the University of Minnesota, has taught courses touching on the notion of the *quotidien* at the Graduate Center of CUNY.

JOAN DEJEAN is Professor of French at Princeton University. She is the author of *Literary Fortifications: Rousseau, Laclos and Sade,* and is currently writing a book on Sappho's presence in French literature.

SUSAN HANSON is Assistant Professor of French at Hamilton College. She is presently completing a manuscript on the novels of Nathalie Sarraute entitled *The Politics of Suspicion: Lessons and Strategies.* Her translation of Blanchot's *L'Entretien infini* will be published by the University of Minnesota Press.

ALICE YAEGER KAPLAN is Associate Professor of French at Duke University. She is the author of *Reproductions of Banality: Fascism, Literature, and French Intellectual Life.*

EREC KOCH is a graduate student in the French Department at Yale University. He is currently completing a dissertation entitled "Order and Disorder in Pascal."

HENRI LEFEBVRE is the author of over forty books, among them *Introduction à la critique de la vie quotidienne.*

CHRISTINE LEVICH is a graduate student in the French Department at Yale University and is working on Christine de Pisan.

MOLLY NESBIT is Assistant Professor of Art History at Barnard College, Columbia University. Her book *Atget's Seven Albums* will be published by Yale University Press.

LINDA ORR is Associate Professor of French at Duke University. She is the author of *Jules Michelet: Nature, History and Language* and is at present working on the period of the German Occupation of France.

ADRIAN RIFKIN teaches in the Department of Fine Art at Portsmouth Polytechnic. He is currently coediting a collection of texts in translation by Rancière, Cottereau, Faure, Dalotel and Freiermuth.

KRISTIN ROSS is Associate Professor of Literature at the University of California at Santa Cruz. She is completing a book about Rimbaud and the political language of the 1870s.

WOLFGANG SCHIVELBUSCH divides his time between Berlin and New York. He is the author of a history of stimulants and spices, and of *The Railway Journey: Trains and Travel in the 19th Century.*

GREGORY L. ULMER, Professor of English at the University of Florida, is completing a book entitled: *Teletheory: Academic Writing in the Age of Television.* He is the author of *Applied Grammatology.*

The following issues are available through **Yale University Press,** Customer Service Department, 92A Yale Station, New Haven, CT 06520.

\* 63 The Pedagogical Imperative:
Teaching as a Literary Genre
(1982) $12.95
64 Montaigne: Essays in Reading
(1983) $12.95
65 The Language of Difference:
Writing in QUEBEC(ois)
(1983) $12.95
66 The Anxiety of Anticipation
(1984) $12.95

67 Concepts of Closure
(1984) $12.95
68 Sartre after Sartre
(1985) $12.95
69 The Lesson of Paul de Man
(1985) $12.95
70 Images of Power:
Medieval History/Discourse/
Literature
(1986) $12.95

71 Men/Women of Letters:
Correspondence
(1986) $12.95
72 Simone de Beauvoir:
Witness to a Century
(1987) $12.95
73 Forthcoming Issue
(1987) $12.95

Special subscription rates are available on a calendar year basis (2 issues per year):

Individual subscriptions   $22.00
Institutional subscriptions   $25.90

---

**ORDER FORM**    **Yale University Press,** 92A Yale Station, New Haven, CT 06520

Please enter my subscription for the calendar year
☐ **1986** (Nos. 70 and 71)          ☐ **1987** (Nos. 72 and 73)

I would like to purchase the following individual issues:

_____

_____

For individual issues, please add postage and handling:
Single issue, United States   $1.50
Each additional issue   $.50
Connecticut residents please add sales tax of 7½%.

Single issue, foreign countries   $2.00
Each additional issue   $1.00

Payment of $ _____ is enclosed (including sales tax if applicable).

Mastercard no. _____

4-digit bank no. _____ Expiration date _____

VISA no. _____ Expiration date _____

Signature _____

SHIP TO: _____

_____

_____

---

See the next page for ordering issues 1–59 and 61–62. **Yale French Studies** is also available through Xerox University Microfilms, 300 North Zeeb Road, Ann Arbor, MI 48106.

\***The Pedalogical Imperative,** edited by Barbara Johnson, is now available once more.

The following issues are still available through the **Yale French Studies** Office, 2504A Yale Station, New Haven, CT 06520.

| | | |
|---|---|---|
| 19/20 Contemporary Art $3.50 | 43 The Child's Part $5.00 | 57 Locus: Space, Landscape, Decor $6.00 |
| 23 Humor $3.50 | 44 Paul Valéry $5.00 | |
| 33 Shakespeare $3.50 | 45 Language as Action $5.00 | 58 In Memory of Jacques Ehrmann $6.00 |
| 35 Sade $3.50 | 46 From Stage to Street $3.50 | |
| 38 The Classical Line $3.50 | 47 Image & Symbol in the Renaissance $3.50 | 59 Rethinking History $6.00 |
| 39 Literature and Revolution $3.50 | | 61 Toward a Theory of Description $6.00 |
| 40 Literature and Society: 18th Century $3.50 | 49 Science, Language, & the Perspective Mind $3.50 | 62 Feminist Readings: French Texts/ American Contexts $6.00 |
| 41 Game, Play, Literature $5.00 | 50 Intoxication and Literature $3.50 | |
| 42 Zola $5.00 | 53 African Literature $3.50 | |
| | 54 Mallarmé $5.00 | |

**Add for postage & handling**

Single issue, United States  $1.00                Single issue, foreign countries  $1.50
Each additional issue  $.50                           Each additional issue  $.75

--------------------------------------------------------------------

**YALE FRENCH STUDIES,** 2504A Yale Station, New Haven, Connecticut 06520

A check made payable to YFS is enclosed. Please send me the following issue(s):

Issue no.                    Title                                                              Price

_____          _____          _____

_____          _____          _____

_____          _____          _____

                                                            Postage & handling     _____

                                                                            Total     _____

Name _____

Number/Street _____

City _____ State _____ Zip _____

The following issues are now available through Kraus Reprint Company, Route 100, Millwood, N.Y. 10546.

| | | |
|---|---|---|
| 1 Critical Bibliography of Existentialism | 11 Eros, Variations... | 25 Albert Camus |
| | 12 God & the Writer | 26 The Myth of Napoleon |
| 2 Modern Poets | 13 Romanticism Revisited | 27 Women Writers |
| 3 Criticism & Creation | 14 Motley: Today's French Theater | 28 Rousseau |
| 4 Literature & Ideas | 15 Social & Political France | 29 The New Dramatists |
| 5 The Modern Theatre | 16 Foray through Existentialism | 30 Sartre |
| 6 France and World Literature | 17 The Art of the Cinema | 31 Surrealism |
| 7 André Gide | 18 Passion & the Intellect, or Malraux | 32 Paris in Literature |
| 8 What's Novel in the Novel | | 34 Proust |
| 9 Symbolism | 21 Poetry Since the Liberation | 48 French Freud |
| 10 French-American Literature Relationships | 22 French Education | 51 Approaches to Medieval Romance |
| | 24 Midnight Novelists | 52 Graphesis |

36 37 Stucturalism has been reprinted by Doubleday as an Anchor Book.
55/56 Literature and Psychoanalysis has been reprinted by Johns Hopkins University Press, and can be ordered through Customer Service, Johns Hopkins University Press, Baltimore, MD 21218.

## Special Offer

Each New Individual Subscriber to **Style** will receive a FREE COPY of a number from volumes 17, 18, or 19 by subscribing to either volume 20 (1986) or 21 (1987) before December 31, 1987.

### Style

Editor: Harold F. Mosher, Jr.
Publisher: Northern Illinois University

A quarterly journal publishing articles, reviews, and bibliographies on stylistics and on the theory and practice of new approaches to literature, especially those dealing closely with texts.

### Titles of Issues and Essays—Vol. 20, 21

**Volume 20 (1986)**
**20th Anniversary Volume**

■ **Number 1:** *Conventions*—Irene Fairley, "The Reader's Need for Conventions"; Marianna Torgovnick, "*Pale Fire* as a Fable for Critics"; Monika Fludernik, "The Dialogic Imagination of Joyce"; Christopher Brown, "The Rhetoric of Closure in *What Maisie Knew*"; Ruth Ronen, "Poetical Coherence in Literary Prose"; Timothy Pace, "George Eliot and Displaced Religious Confession"; Ann Dobyns, "Style and Character in the *New Arcadia*"; reviews

■ **Number 2:** *Medieval Semiotics*—Jonathan Evans, "Episodes in Analysis of Medieval Narrative"; Allen Frantzen and Charles Venegoni, "An Archeology of Anglo-Saxon Studies"; Martin Irvine, "Anglo-Saxon Literary Theory"; Ruth Hamilton, "Repeating Narrative and Anachrony in *Cleanness*"; Britton J. Harwood, "Signs and/as Origin: The *Nun's Priest's Tale*"; Matilda Bruckner, "Jaufré Rudel and Lyric Reception"; Peter Haidu, "The Semiotization of Death"; Donald Maddox, "The Semiosis of Assimilatio in Medieval Models of Time"

■ **Number 3:** *Narrative Poetics*—Michael Riffaterre, "On the Diegetic Functions of the Descriptive"; Meir Sternberg, "Dialogue as Monologue"; Marie-Laure Ryan, "Embedded Narratives and Tellability"; Susan Sniader Lanser, "Toward a Feminist Narratology"; Anne Waldron Neumann, "Characterization and Comment in *Pride and Prejudice*"; Evelyn Cobley, "Description in Realist Discourse: The War Novel"; David Richter, "Bakhtin in Life and in Art"; Reviews by Wallace Martin, Marie-Laure Ryan, Susan Léger, and David Pickering

■ **Number 4:** *Annotated Bibliography for 1985*

**Volume 21 (1987)**

■ **Number 1:** *Rhythm and Rhetoric*—Essays on Rhythm and Meaning, Metricality in John Webster, The Iterative, Rhetorical Context, Henry James's Later Style, Keats's Letters, and others; plus reviews.

■ **Number 2:** *Deconstruction*—Essays on Reading Post-Modernism, Deconstruction and Theology, A Daughter's Da in *Bleak House*, Metaphor in Joyce, and others; plus reviews

■ **Number 3:** *New Metrics*—Guest Editor: Marina Tarlinskaja. Scheduled essays by Marina Tarlinskaja, James Bailey, Beth Bjorklund, M. L. Gasparov, Bruce Hayes, Daniel Laferriere, Ian Lilly, Geoffrey Russom.

■ **Number 4:** *Annotated Bibliography for 1986*

### Titles of Issues for Choice of a Free Copy

**Volume 17**
■ Number 1: General Issue
■ Number 2: *Narratology*
■ Numbers 3 & 4: Annotated Bibliographies for 1981 and on Scientific Language

**Volume 18**
■ Number 1: *Poetics*
■ Number 2: *Recent Theory*
■ Number 3: *Psychopoetics*
  Guest Editor: Mieke Bal
■ Number 4: Annotated Bibliographies, 1982-83

**Volume 19**
■ Number 1: *The Modern Novel*
■ Number 2: *Orality and Rhythm*
■ Number 3: *Readers and Authors*
■ Number 4: Annotated Bibliography for 1984

Here is what *TLS* has to say about *Style:*
"*a testimony to the continuing interest intelligent people have in literature*"
(August 8, 1986)

---

**Please Enter My Subscription to *Style***

☐ Volume 20    ☐ Volume 21
and send me a free copy of a back number.
My choice in order of preference is:
#1 Volume _____ Number _____
#2 Volume _____ Number _____
#3 Volume _____ Number _____
(*The supply of some numbers is limited.*)
My check for $18, covering one new individual subscription of four numbers and postage and handling for my free copy of a back number, is enclosed. (*Student rate: $11*) Add $4 to these rates for postage outside the U.S.

Please make checks payable to **Style** and send to:
The Associate Editor for Business Affairs, *Style*, Department of English, Northern Illinois University, DeKalb, Illinois 60115-2863.

_____
Name (New Individual Subscriber)

_____
Address

_____
City           State           Zip Code

UNIVERSITY OF CALIFORNIA PRESS

# representations

"Now widely regarded as one of the hottest new journals around."
—*The New York Times*

*Representations* 16

"An extraordinary journal. I can't think of another one published in this country which I find as enjoyable and as continually stimulating."
—*Susan Sontag*

$6 at bookstores or by subscription for $20 per year
Journals Department, 2120 Berkeley Way, Berkeley, CA 94720

## The Superstitious Mind
*French Peasants and the Supernatural in the Nineteenth Century*
Judith Devlin

An intriguing examination of popular religion, traditional medicine, witchcraft, apparitions, demonology, and magic in nineteenth-century rural France. Devlin demonstrates that many of the impulses and mental processes now considered superstitious constituted a wholly reasonable response to the pressures of a harsh and impoverished life. **"Fascinating... Breaks new ground."** —Eugen Weber, *TLS* 12 illus. $30.00

## Hubertine Auclert, The French Suffragette
Steven C. Hause

This book—the first full biography of Hubertine Auclert in any language—is "**a lively and interesting account** of the life of the foremost French suffragist." (Joan Scott) Basing his work on Auclert's voluminous writings and on her personal papers, Steven C. Hause paints a vivid picture of a woman with an unhappy personal life and a politician determined to win the political rights of French women and convert France into a republic of social justice. 13 illus. $28.50

*Now available in paperback*
## Confessions of a Concierge
*Madame Lucie's History of Twentieth-Century France*
Bonnie G. Smith

"A sidewalk-level view of eighty years of French history: it is **sometimes familiar, sometimes surprising, and always interesting.**" —Phoebe-Lou Adams, *Atlantic Monthly* $7.95

Yale University Press
Dept. 574
92A Yale Station
New Haven, CT 06520